Judging
MERIT

Judging
MERIT

Warren Thorngate

Robyn M. Dawes

Margaret Foddy

Psychology Press
Taylor & Francis Group

New York   Hove

Psychology Press
Taylor & Francis Group
270 Madison Avenue
New York, NY 10016

Psychology Press
Taylor & Francis Group
27 Church Road
Hove, East Sussex BN3 2FA

© 2009 by Taylor & Francis Group, LLC
Psychology Press is an imprint of Taylor & Francis Group, an Informa business

Printed in the United States of America on acid-free paper
10 9 8 7 6 5 4 3 2 1

International Standard Book Number-13: 978-0-8058-5835-8 (Hardcover)

Visit the Taylor & Francis Web site at
http://www.taylorandfrancis.com

and the Psychology Press Web site at
http://www.psypress.com

Contents

Preface and Acknowledgments

Life in society, as Jon Elster (1992) notes, tends to be controlled by three forces. One is economics. One is politics. The third is local justice. It is a term Elster uses for the congeries of judgments affecting our fate that come from panels, committees, boards, and individuals who examine our claims and requests for resources—trophies to transplants, green cards to Nobel prizes, grades to parole—and decide whether to grant our wishes or not.

Contemporary society is rife with local justice. Consider, for example, one of its manifestations: the application form. Rare is the week without completing one. There are forms to fill out for credit cards, parking spaces, jobs, promotions, health benefits, tax relief, library cards, rebates, court dates, and life mates. We submit them, usually to some faceless agent, wait, and eventually receive a judgment or decision. When the judgment or decision is favorable, we collect our prize and feel relief or joy. When it is unfavorable, we feel disappointment, perhaps curse "the system" for its unfairness, and likely complete another form another day.

What goes on between submitting an application form and learning of the outcome? Or between producing any other record of performance such as a job interview, piano recital, art portfolio, or film audition and the awarding of a contract or prize? In all cases, one or more people, called *judges* or *adjudicators*, sit down, examine the forms or performances submitted, and make judgments about something called *merit*. Decisions about outcomes are then made according to the merit judged. People who are judged to have sufficient merit are given at least some of the resources they request. The rest are not.

The book in your hands is about merit and how it is judged. We have written the book from our perspectives as research psychologists who have spent long careers studying biases and errors of human judgment and decision making. Biases and errors are detectable in discrepancies between what is true and what is judged or decided. Judging someone to be guilty when innocent—or innocent when guilty—is an error, perhaps reflecting one or more biases. When a building collapses during construction, errors of engineers' judgments and contractors' decisions are evidenced in the rubble. There is in such cases, at least in theory, some objective truth against which a judgment or decision can be measured.

Not so for judgments of merit. As we discuss in chapter 1, people and things do not possess merit in the way they possess height or weight or handedness. Merit is a subjective reaction of the judge—it lies somewhere among countless neuron paths just behind the eye of the beholder—not an objective property of the person or thing being judged. This subjective fact can lead philosophers to argue that errors of merit judgment cannot occur. If merit is subjective, then ultimately all merit is a matter of taste, for which there is no accounting.

Even so, people often agree on criteria of merit, just as they agree on the meaning of words and the direction that the hands of clocks should rotate. The criteria vary from one situation to the next. Criteria for judging the merit of applications to medical school, for example, are not the same as criteria of merit for judging trophies in dog shows. Even so, within any given situation, criteria can be mutually accepted or rejected by all who judge and who are judged. Deviations from the judgments produced by using these criteria properly can then, in principle, be measured, discussed, and rectified. This is what we attempt below.

Being psychologists, we are trained to examine how judgments of merit are made in order to seek clues about why judgments of merit often go wrong. Many flaws of products can be detected by flaws in processes, leading us to hope that fixing the latter will fix the former. The first seven chapters of this book begin by addressing some of the personal and interpersonal flaws of many processes by which merit is judged. They end by suggesting how the processes might be improved, constrained, or augmented to reduce the chances that people without merit will be rewarded or people with merit will be ignored. Not surprisingly, we have discovered no panacea. There is, to our knowledge, no single method of judging merit that will eliminate errors, banish biases, and lead us all to the promised land of infallible merit judgments. Saint Peter may know such a method, but we won't know how it works until Judgment Day.

The first seven chapters address sources or error and bias in judging merit, and the last two address likely consequences of these biases and errors. Here we rely on computer simulations and speculative reasoning to understand trade-offs between various strategies for limiting the bad effects of merit judgments. We show, for example, how the gains in validity and fairness of merit judgments derived from following prescriptions of the first seven chapters can often be wiped out as the number of people seeking merit judgments increases. And we offer a few suggestions for avoiding such consequences.

Judgments of merit are most often found in two types of situations: tests and contests. As we discuss in chapter 1, tests are situations in which all applicants who pass some minimum standard are given what they applied for—think of tests for citizenship and a driver's license. Contests are situations in which the supply of what is desired is limited and given only to a subset of applicants whose merit is judged to be greater than that of others—think of contests for president, Olympic medals, building contracts, and Academy Awards. As we study tests and contests of merit, we are struck by their variety. They can be as small and informal as a test to determine whether a child deserves dessert after dinner (vegetable eating was a common criterion in days past). They can be as large, formal, and complex as a contest to determine which city merits the Olympic Games, who receives Rhodes Scholarships, or who deserves the title of world's best pianist.

Analyzing the merit judgments of these diverse tests and contests is no easy task. Each test and contest has its idiosyncrasies, so it is difficult—make that impossible—in one book to provide detailed analyses and prescriptions for them all. The same difficulty faces medicine. There are thousands of diseases, most of them requiring specific medications or surgeries for proper treatment. A general prescription—"Drink plenty of liquids and get lots of rest"—does not go far toward curing the lot, though it may be less harmful than some alternatives—"Drink nothing and stop sleeping."

One step in utility above platitudes are prescriptions based on analyses of tests and contests that share features with other tests and contests. For better or worse, most of our analyses and prescriptions come from tests and contests in academia, particularly contests for research grants. Most of these contests are big and bureaucratic, so prescriptions derived from analyzing them are probably not too useful for a small bookstore owner interviewing walk-in applicants for a part-time job as clerk or for a retired accountant trying to decide which 3 of 15 charities to support after judging the merit of their brochures. But there are many other contests that do share the big and bureaucratic features of those we analyze. Included are national competitions for university admission or scholarships, jobs in large corporations, government contracts for building construction, polling or advertising, even competitions for fame on reality or idol TV shows. We hope that some of the analyses and prescriptions we generate here will be useful for these and similar situations requiring merit judgments.

Margaret Foddy kindly but tenaciously negotiated this book and led us through the first phases of its development. Tragically, Margaret suffered major health problems before the book manuscript was completed, leaving her unable to work on revisions since then. We revised her double standards chapter as best we could, but the merit of the chapter belongs to her. Robyn and I know she would thank her husband, Pat O'Malley, for his patience and support. We would also like to thank Pat for giving us the title of our book.

After 38 years of teaching, this is my first and perhaps last book as a senior author, so I have a career's worth of gratitude to express in writing. Please bear with me. I thank my late parents, Mitchell and Edith Thorngate, and my sister, Linda Canzoneri. I thank my mentors, Duncan and Lois Courvoisier, Charles McClintock, David Messick, Robert Knox, Tom Storm, William Petrusic, Michael Humphreys, Ivan and Miriam London. I thank my colleagues Lloyd Strickland, Reza Zamani, and Johanna Filp. I thank my students Miho Hotta, Halla Thorsteinsdottir, Fatemeh Bagherian, Liu Jing, Wang Zhigang, Mahin Tavakoli, Claudia Rocca, and Francesca Ruscito. Above all, I thank my partner of 25 years, Barbara Carroll. From these dear people I have learned three lessons. Science is art with numbers. Ideas are more interesting than data. People are more important than ideas. The best of what I write comes from them.

Books require reviewers and publishers. We have had great ones. Thanks to David Messick for his read of the manuscript and his excellent suggestions for improving it. Thanks to Paul Dukes and Lee Transue for their patience and good sense in steering this book to port.

Warren Thorngate
February 2008

Author Bios

Warren Thorngate is a professor of psychology at Carleton University in Ottawa, Canada. The author of about 100 articles on human judgment, decision making, statistics, and social psychology, he is a past president of the International Society for Theoretical Psychology, former newsletter editor for the Society for Judgment and Decision Making, associate editor of three academic journals, and a cofounder of Opera Lyra Ottawa. Dr. Thorngate also pursues teaching and research interests in the Third World, lecturing in universities throughout Latin America, Russia, Poland, and Iran. He has served as a visiting professor at the University of California (Berkeley), La Trobe University (Melbourne), Carnegie Mellon University, Iran's Institute for Cognitive Science Studies, and the University of Tehran. Professor Thorngate recently cofounded (with Dr. Fatemeh Bagherian) the Center for Social Psychology Research at Tehran's Shahid Beheshti University and serves as its scientific director.

Robyn M. Dawes is the Charles J. Queenan, Jr., University Professor of Psychology at Carnegie Mellon University. The author of over 120 articles published in refereed journals, he is known for two books: *Rational Choice in an Uncertain World* (Harcourt, Brace & Jovanovich, 1988), recipient of the APA William James Book Award, and *House of Cards, Psychology and Psychotherapy Built on Myth* (first published by Free Press, 1994). He has also recently published a book entitled *Everyday Irrationality: How Pseudo-Scientists, Lunatics, and the Rest of Us Systematically Fail to Think Rationally* (Westview Press, 2001). Professor Dawes has been elected a fellow of several scientific organizations (most recently, the American Statistical Association) and in 2002 was inducted into the American Academy of Arts and Sciences.

Margaret Foddy is professor of psychology, sociology, and anthropology at Carleton University in Ottawa, Canada. After receiving her Ph.D. in Canada, she spent 25 years in Australia, teaching and doing research at Latrobe University in Melbourne. She was founding president of the Society of Australasian Social Psychologists. Dr. Foddy's research ranges from the study of status in small groups, overcoming evaluative biases in personnel evaluation, to work on group-based trust in social dilemmas. She was lead editor of the book *Resolving Social Dilemmas* (Psychology Press, 1999) and has published several journal articles and book chapters on these topics.

1

Introduction

Jenny Brown, 62, is enjoying dubious celebrity in Britain for her performance in a cake competition. Her "Victoria Sponge" placed second in a Bake-Off, despite the fact that she was the only entry. Judges put her at second because her cake showed rack marks. Brown says she's not offended at coming in second to no one. After all, she bested one of the contest's organizers, whose fruit scones also competed against no one a few years ago, but came in third. ("Being an Also-Ran Can Be Lonely," 2007. p. 50)

*P*erhaps in heaven all God's children can have whatever they want. On earth, things desired have a pernicious tendency to be in short supply. Good land, food, water, housing, and energy never seem as abundant as the demand for them. University degrees, interesting jobs, competent mechanics, punctual doctors, movie roles, gold medals, corner offices, parking spaces, research grants, publications, beauty, admirers, fame, status, attention, and time all seem to be more coveted than possessed. These and thousands of other desiderata not only define the goals of most human activity but prompt a fundamental question about the distribution of scarce resources: Who should get them and who should not?

Civilizations have devised dozens of ways to answer this distributional question. One of the oldest means of distributing a scarce resource is aggression and its cousins: threat and intimidation. Whether fights between families or tribes, games between soccer teams, or wars among enemies, "To the victor belong the spoils" (William Learned March, 1831). Land, food, virginity, slaves, versions of the truth, and treasures of all kinds have been absconded for millennia by violent ploys. They still are. Street variations include mugging, swarming, extortion, and kidnapping. Home variations include screaming matches, physical violence, and restraining orders. Corporate variations range from hostile takeovers to lockouts to bullying the board.

Probably as old as aggression, another common and equally ignoble means of distributing scarce resources is theft (cf. Commandment Eight of God's Ten, Robin Hood). Variations include breaking and entering, stealing, swindling, fleecing, cheating, cooking the books, picking pockets, or robbery (theft with a pinch

1

of threat or violence). The variations all serve the end of (re)distributing limited resources through deception or stealth.

Limited resources can also be distributed according to power, status, or privilege. Royalty tend to receive more than an equal share of goodies, gifts, and media attention, as do pop stars, movie stars, and politicians. More employees straighten their desks and manners for visits by CEOs than for visits by cleaning staff. Auctions accrue more money for autographs of professional athletes than for autographs of assistant professors. Surgeons tend to get better restaurant tables and higher credit limits than the rest of us. Politicians are more likely to be given free tickets to hockey playoffs than are street people. Only executives have access to executive washrooms. And in the world of unions, seniority rules.

Close to privilege are good connections—known also as favoritism, cronyism, nepotism, double standards, pork barreling, taking care of one's own, networking, and, in Farsi, *parti bazi*. Family, friends, and members of other in-groups tend to distribute more goodies to one another than to members of out-groups; we tend to scratch each other's backs more than the backs of *them*. Perhaps the tendency has some sociobiological advantage for propagating gene or friendship pools. Those who accept such in-group bias often seek to exploit it through arranged marriages, private school enrollments, country club memberships, groupie affiliations, or bribes. Out-group members who reject the in-group bias often try to overthrow or otherwise displace in-group members. When successful, out-group members usually become the new in-group and transfer in-group biases to themselves.

Scarce resources can also, of course, be distributed in a market. From dusty bazaars to Internet investment sites, market rules prescribe that people with something valuable to trade should get as much of a scarce resource as can be obtained by trading. As a result, rich people, who by definition have more to trade, tend to get more scarce resources than do poor people. This explains why rich people live in nicer homes than do poor people and drive more and newer cars, go on more holidays, have better health services, and tend to live longer if not happier lives. If the poor people owned a scarce resource, they might become rich by trading it, but such ownership is rare. As Karl Marx repeatedly noted, supplies of scarce resources have a plutocratically perverse tendency to concentrate among the rich—a result that Lenin argued could be limited by state-controlled distribution. Alas, if capitalism seems good at developing resources but not at distributing them, communism seems good at distributing resources but not at developing them. Tensions between the political right and left seem driven in large part by attempts to revolve this paradox.

Not too distant from the market is another venerable means of distributing scarce resources: luck. Sometimes it is called gambling, betting, entering a lottery, or flipping a coin. Sometimes it is called fishing or farming. In all such transactions, the distribution of a scarce resource is explicitly left to the whims of nature or chance. In principle, this leaves no possibility of aggression, theft, privilege, connections, or current wealth influencing the outcome. In fact, opportunities for chances to choose new owners of a limited resource usually require an ante of some kind; bets are bought, not given away. Rich people can ante more often than poor people, stay in the game longer, and thus increase their chances of luck favoring their kind (Thorngate & Hotta, 1995).

The chronicle of social, economic, and political experiments also documents assorted attempts to distribute or redistribute scarce resources according to principles of equality (everyone gets an equal chance or share) or need (each gets what each requires). Though normally associated with left-wing political principles, these attempts are manifested every day in the mechanical insensitivity of traffic signals to status, wealth, or time constraints, in the regimented uniformity of economy-class airline meals, in the status indifference of first-come-first-served cues and paid-up insurance claims, and in school programs that distribute A+ grades to everyone needing a pick-me-up of self-esteem, or that divert teaching time to the developmentally challenged, leaving the unchallenged, well, unchallenged. They are also manifested in a wide assortment of taxes, including progressive income taxes that require those who have more income than they need to subsidize those who have less.

Then there is merit. With a pedigree traceable to the *Analects* of Confucius (ca. 300 B.C.) and to the concept of Judgment Day, the principle of merit simply states that *resources should be distributed according to ability or accomplishment* rather than according to the other criteria mentioned above. Endorsed by such historical figures as Thomas Jefferson (2nd Inaugural speech, 1805), Napoleon (*La carriere ouverte aux talents*), and used effectively by Genghis Khan, the principle of merit has been growing in popularity at least since it began to be used for awarding wreaths in Ancient Greece's Olympic Games. The merit principle has been an ideal of democratic elections—voters judging the merit of candidates or proposed legislation—for a few thousand years. It is known to all of us who sweated to learn whether our grade point average, SAT, GRE, MCAT, or reference letters were sufficient to continue our education. The principle has infested large corporations and government bureaucracies, stimulating the submission of vast numbers of résumés, curriculum vitaes, portfolios, and similar indicants of accomplishment, past and future. It has sparked fistfuls of dubious measures of productivity for allocating promotions or layoffs. The merit principle has been adopted in the distribution of scholarships, research grants, journal space, commercial contracts, business loans, film funding, summer camps, pet ownership, parole, and gun licenses. In many countries it is the primary principle for deciding who is allowed to legally immigrate or is given a passport or denied a visa. As evidenced by the proliferation of application forms in almost every area of life, the merit principle is arguably the fastest growing rule for distributing limited resources in modern organizations and societies.

One of the most important reasons for the rising popularity of the merit principle is likely an assumption that the principle is more just or fair than the alternatives. Most people resent losing their job to make way for the boss's boyfriend or cousin. Most talented people rejected from university do not appreciate parents bribing the university with a cash donation in exchange for acceptance of their mediocre children. Most people are upset when their wealth is diminished by aggression or theft or when drug dealers win lotteries. In comparison to these means of distributing scarce resources, judging merit seems quite civilized. Many people may not receive the resources they believe they merit. But if the procedures for making judgments of their merit were seen as fair, then losers could at least console themselves by noting that everyone received fair consideration and that justice was done (Lind & Tyler, 1988; Tyler, 1994, 1996).

Are procedures for judging merit always fair? Almost certainly not. Indeed, anecdotal evidence indicates that unfair procedures are as common as the February flu. Even compensating for sour grapes and wild conjectures of those deprived of the rewards they believe they deserve, there is cause for concern. Almost everyone who has served as a member of more than one adjudication committee has stories of questionable, if not blatantly prejudicial, practices. Consider a sample of the kinds of red-flag statements that sometimes emerge from adjudication committees:

> Yes, this candidate looks better on paper than my cousin. But have you heard the rumor she sells cocaine to children? I don't know if it is true, but why take the chance? I have never heard such a rumor about my cousin. Let's hire him.

> John has six publications, all in good journals. Mary has eight publications in good journals and twelve publications in so-so journals. Clearly John is the superior scholar. (see Hayes, 1983)

> Alice had three promotions in three years, but she got married last month, and I'm a bit concerned about her future commitment. What if she gets pregnant and takes off for a year? Benita is single and new. After I read her résumé, it occurred to me that the company might benefit from a fresh face. Let's hire Benita.

> Yes, Melvin's painting is technically superior. But it just seems to lack a certain je ne sais quoi. My eyes are telling me, "Beautiful!" but my gut is telling me, "Derivative." Why give a prize for that?

> I don't know anything about good science, but I know what I like.

> Yes, Professor Cuesta teaches and does research in the area we advertised. But Professor Luna does wonderful work in my area, and has frequently referenced me. Think of the synergy. Clearly, we should hire Luna.

> Well, I strongly disagree with you. So let's make a deal. I will allow you to hire this one, if you agree to hire my favorite.

> Does this committee have a policy about the criteria we should use to make judgments, or should we just form a holistic gestalt about each applicant?

> Let's put every application that anyone questions for any reason into a pile called Mixed Reviews and debate them if we have time and money left before we leave.

> Martha is my mother's neighbor, and I know she does wonderful work. She would be delighted to get this promotion, and so would her husband, who needs the money for his eye surgery.

[Note: If you do not cringe at the statements above or do not recognize the biases they suggest, read on! This book may help.]

Privacy laws and research ethics being what they are, we will probably never know how often such statements are made in camera or how often other forms of biases and bungles sully deliberations of merit. Still, the large and growing popularity of the merit principle suggests that it would be useful to examine the nature of merit, how it is judged or misjudged, the consequences of such judgments, and what if anything might be done to improve the judgment process. These are the goals of our book.

WHAT IS MERIT?

Many things we judge have objective standards that allow us to assess the accuracy or validity of our judgments. We can check the accuracy of our judgments of people's height, weight, or writing speed with rulers, scales, and stopwatches. Similarly, we can check the accuracy or validity of tomorrow's weather or stock market forecasts by waiting a day. Alas, we cannot do the same for merit. There is no "merit meter" we can wave over the heads of applicants to determine how much they deserve, how much they may claim, of a scarce resource. Like judgments of beauty or political expertise (see Tetlock, 2005), judgments of merit are subjective. Although it is sometimes assessed by examining physical records, merit itself has no physical referent.

One interesting consequence of the subjective nature of merit is that thousands of different merit criteria have evolved, almost as many criteria as there are tests and contests in which merit is assessed. Consider, for example, the 300+ different sports competitions in modern Summer Olympics. Each competition has a set of rules about how races will be run and winners will be chosen, and among the rules are merit criteria. Who merits a medal? One competition awards medals according to how long it takes competitors to run 100 meters. Another competition gives the same medals according to how long it takes to run 200 meters. Still another gives the same medals according to how long it takes to swim 200 meters on your back. One more gives the medals for jumping over a bar unaided; another for jumping over a bar with the aid of a pole. Others give the medals for hanging from rings, for doing flips, for walking fast or shooting arrows. Or consider the *Guinness Book of World Records*. It now lists over 40,000 world records, from the highest city to the fastest pumpkin carving, each distinguished by different merit criteria. Indeed, there is even a world record for the number of Guinness World Records held by a single person:

> The individual who holds the most Guinness World Records is Mr Ashrita Furman. He holds the records for, among others, long-distance pogo-stick jumping, most glasses balanced on the chin, most hop-scotch games in 24 hours and fastest time to pogo-stick up the CN Tower. ("Guinness World Records," FAQ 9, n.d.)

Merit criteria vary not only among different kinds of contests or competitions but also within the same kind. This can be seen in the variations of application forms for the same kind of award. Some university application forms, for example, ask who in the applicant's family graduated from the university; other university application forms do not. Presumably, the difference occurs because pedigree is important for judging the merit of applicants at some universities but not at others. Do you merit a tourist visa to Australia? It seems to depend, in part, on whether or not you agree to the terms of the online application form ("Australia Migration," n.d.), which include the following: "Information or materials which are offensive, pornographic, unsuitable for minors' access or otherwise of a criminal or violent nature may be accessible through this site either as a result of hacking or material placed on linked websites. The Department makes no representations as to the suitability of the information accessible for viewing by minors or any other person." Do you merit a tourist visa to Iran? In contrast to Australia, it seems to depend, in part, on supplying the name of your father (but not your mother; "Iranian Consulate in Ottawa," n.d.).

Merit criteria can even vary among judges assessing the merit of the same set of applicants in the same competition. Job interviewers, for example, frequently disagree on the criteria for judging job applicants. Should the interviewers consider the reputation of the applicant's university? Should they consider number of jobs held in the past 5 years and, if so, is more merrier? Should they consider the strength of the applicant's handshake? Or the sincerity of the applicant's smile? Even if they agree on which criteria should be used to assess merit, judges might disagree on the weights assigned to these criteria (Is a smile more or less important than a handshake?). Or they might disagree on the rules of combining criteria (Should all applicants with "dead fish" handshakes be eliminated while those with fierce grips be judged on university grades and those with moderate grips be judges on previous jobs in past 5 years?) Or they might disagree on the value assigned to one or more criteria (Was that smile sincere or insincere? Was the handshake fierce or moderate?). Judges might even disagree on whether it is good or bad to disagree. Some might argue that disagreements reflect a healthy variety of perspectives and that, if one applicant is judged meritorious from several different perspectives, the judges can be more confident in their judgments.

In view of such variety in defining merit and assessing it, we might be tempted to despair. A clear definition of merit seems impossible. There are so many ways for judges to disagree, and there is no objective way to determine whose definition should prevail. Even so, despair seems premature. In almost all assessments of merit, a few criteria seem more sensible, credible, relevant, or preferable than others. We believe, for example, that most patients prefer to judge the merit of surgeons by the success rate of their surgery rather than by their astrological sign or golf score. Similarly, we think that most scientists prefer to assess the relative merit of two scientific theories by conducting controlled experiments rather than by inviting the competing theorists to participate in a fishing contest or a mud wrestling match. If people cannot eliminate by objective standards all but one of thousands of possible criteria for judging merit, they can still almost always reach consensus about all but a few.

Of course, what can be done is not always what is done, and what is done is not always done well. Voters often fail to reach consensus about the most suitable criteria for judging political candidates despite attempts of political strategists to influence their criteria selection. Perhaps this is because opposing strategists try to set the campaign agenda to favor their own candidates and cancel each other out. Perhaps it is because voters are not required to reach consensus and see no reason to do so. Similarly, decisions of the court are sometimes overturned on appeal, occasionally because there is no consensus among judges about which laws or precedents should prevail. Even when concerted efforts are made to reach consensus about fair criteria, many fail. Canadian history is littered with failed attempts to agree on criteria for distributing federal tax money to provinces, for judging the merit of immigration applicants, and for settling aboriginal land claims. And judging from the variety of newspaper headlines around the world, there is still no editorial consensus on what constitutes news.

A consensus about criteria of merit, if reached, may still be subject to criticism. Once upon a time, employers shared a tacit consensus that old people, ugly people, married women, and members of ethnic or racial minorities did not merit a job—or at least a good job. It has taken considerable criticism for the consensus to be reformed—a work still in progress. Today there appears to be a consensus that students should receive high grades and praise for all work attempted, in part because of criticism about stuffy old criteria, such as scholarship, cogency, and expression, once used to assess such work. Criticism of the new consensus is mounting (e.g., see Kahne, 1996; Mansfield, 2001; Schneider, 2000) and, we trust, will eventually lead to reform.

Finally, consensual criteria, even if defensible, may sometimes not be useful, either because no information is available for judging on these criteria or because the available information cannot distinguish the applicants. There is, for example, high consensus among judges, applicants, and observers of thousands of competitions that liars and cheaters do not merit what they are lying or cheating to obtain. Unfortunately, it is often difficult to detect lying or cheating and, if undetected, their importance for judging merit cannot be manifest, nor can criteria, however important, that show no variation among applicants. Most engineers agree that it is highly important to have an engineering degree in order to merit an engineering job. But if all applicants have an engineering degree, then no distinction on this important criterion can be made and other, perhaps lesser, criteria (remember those handshakes!) must be used to detect a difference.

In sum, distributing scarce resources according to merit is no slam dunk. Variations in the definition of merit and the criteria for judging it, difficulties of reaching consensus on fair criteria, criticisms of criteria employed, and lack of variation among applicants can present daunting challenges to fair use of the merit principle. But consider the alternatives. If scarce resources are not allocated according to merit, other means must be found. Sometimes a good case can be made for some of the alternatives; it is probably more efficient and arguably more fair, for example, to require those wanting a parking space downtown to rent one from a meter rather than to apply to a curbside committee for a space according to the merit of their trip. On the other hand, if the merit principle is not used to allocate resources, some of the alternatives are frightening. If triage, though flawed, cannot be used to decide who will see emergency ward doctors first, then we might resort to threats, privilege, or bribes. If we cannot decide who merits land or responsibility, then we might resort to aggression or intimidation. Judging merit is often troublesome. But the principle of merit is sufficiently desirable that it seems worthwhile to try perfecting it before resorting to less desirable alternatives—which is why we are writing this book.

Our task is to examine how judgments of merit are made and why they often go wrong and to explore ways that the judgments might be improved. But if merit has no objective definition, how can we discuss whether judgments of merit are right or wrong or consider how to improve them? We think a defensible answer lies in assessments of the fairness of merit judgments and their consequences.

Judgments of merit can be said to be good if applicants and observers, as well as judges, assess them as fair; the higher proportion of people who assess them as fair, the better the judgments. The technical term for their agreement is *consensual validation*.

As with judging merit, there is more than one criterion for assessing the fairness of merit judgments. As a result, most judgments of merit widely deemed to be fair have at least five properties. First, fair judgments of merit use criteria and procedures deemed valid by a high proportion of applicants and observers. Judges should therefore avoid criteria or procedures, such as taking bribes, deemed to be invalid. Second, fair judgments are consistent. Judges using the same information should make the same judgments, and the same judges should make the same judgments over time. Third, fair judgments are efficient. Judges should not require applicants to invest vast amounts of time and effort to apply, nor should judges take a day short of forever to make their judgments. Fourth, fair judgments produce equitable outcomes. Judges should reward people whom applicants and observers consider worthy and not reward people whom observers consider unworthy. Finally, fair judgments are transparent. Judgments of merit, like justice, should not only be done but be seen to be done; secrecy should be limited and accountability should be evident (Lerner & Tetlock, 1999, 2003).

JUDGING MERIT IN TESTS AND CONTESTS

Judgments of merit are a means to an end, and the end is the distribution of resources. The link between the means and the end can be of two kinds. The first kind is called a *test*. The second is called a *contest*. Tests occur whenever judges or their organizers give requested resources to everyone who passes a minimum standard. Examples include tests for entrance into the next school grade, tests for welfare eligibility, tests for insurance payments, tests for driver's licenses, and tests for prison sentences. In all such cases, contestants expect the resource to expand or contract according to how many pass or fail the test of merit. Judges, like their courtroom colleagues, need not concern themselves with comparing applicants, only with assessing whether or not each applicant meets their minimum, consensually validated standard.

In contrast to tests, contests occur whenever the resource to be allocated is fixed and is allocated according to comparisons among applicants or their applications until the resource runs dry. Most contests have only one first prize or only a limited number of prizes; such limits are maintained regardless of whether the contest has 10 or 10,000 applicants. Companies rarely increase the number of jobs available according to how many qualified applicants come forward. Sports organizations rarely duplicate trophies in case several athletes do well. Film companies do not triple-cast a lead role just because three good people pass an audition. Judges give the limited rewards to the applicants they believe are better than the rest, even though many losing applicants might meet some minimum standards.

Many young people are raised to believe that life progresses as a series of tests and that they will get what they want by passing these tests. For many North American children, their belief is justified. Almost all parents, for example, reward their children when the children meet some minimum requirement ("Eat your vegetables, then you get your dessert."), not when they do better than others ("There is one dessert. Whoever eats the most vegetables will get it."). Advancement from grade 1 to grade 2 depends on meeting a minimum standard of learning; few schools set an upper limit on the number of grade 1 students allowed to enter grade 2. This is likely why young people must make an often painful adjustment to an adult world where a large proportion of resources are not allocated by tests but by contests. Medical schools do not expand their classes to suit the number of their applicants. Airlines do not buy more planes to accommodate all would-be pilots.

Because tests require judges to assess merit according to some agreed-upon standard, and contests require judges to make comparative judgments, we might argue that they are different kettles of fish. But few contests lead judges to compare applicants directly, simply because it is too time consuming. A judge who wishes to compare, say, 20 applicants two at a time (a so-called paired comparison task), must think about $20 \times 19/2 = 190$ pairs; 30 applicants would require $30 \times 29/2 = 435$ pairs. So judges in most contests make their assessments one applicant at a time, as do judges of tests. Contest judges then compare their assessments of each applicant—normally a mechanical process. Test judges usually make binary (yes/no, merit/no merit) judgments as they go. Contest judges usually make more nuanced judgments ("extremely meritorious, very meritorious, meritorious, questionable, dog food") as they go and then reward applicants with the most positive nuances. Otherwise, the tasks of judges in tests and contests tend to be equivalent, and the processes judges use to accomplish their task can be assumed to be equivalent.

We have chosen to illustrate judgments of merit more often with examples of contests (we also call them *competitions*) than with examples of tests. We offer two reasons. Contests appear to be more common than tests, especially in the adult world. And contests are more controversial, especially when a large number of applicants who meet some minimum requirement for passing a test do not receive a reward they believe they deserve. *Distributive justice* is said to occur when people believe they get what they deserve—usually assessed by passing a test (Frohlich, 2007). *Procedural justice* is said to occur when the means by which judges make their assessments are believed to be considerate, unbiased, and fair (Lind & Tyler, 1988). It is tempting to assume that procedural justice breeds distributive justice—good means lead to good ends (see Tyler, 1994, 1996). As we shall see in chapters 5, 6, and 7, this assumption is frequently wrong.

CHAPTERS TO COME

Our task is to determine how to make judgments of merit fairer by making them more valid, consistent, efficient, equitable, and transparent. To do so, we discuss why judgments of merit are often invalid, inconsistent, inefficient, inequitable, and opaque and then suggest how to reduce these consequences by manipulating their causes. It is a formidable task because judgments of merit are rarely straightforward. To address the task, we have divided the remainder of the book into three sections. The first section examines the psychology of judgment and decision-making applied to judgments of merit. Chapter 2 considers different ways of conceptualizing merit judgments and biases and then discusses three common ways of *increasing* the chances of bias in order to argue why these three should be avoided. Chapter 3 shows some of the ways the literature on diagnostic and predictive judgments can be used to improve judgments of merit. Chapter 4 considers how judgments of merit are influenced by double standards—judging one group of applicants by different standards than another group.

The second section of our book examines procedural and social influences on judgments of merit, especially in the conduct of large and formal contests or competitions. Chapter 5 discusses how procedural rules of merit competitions—rules applied before, during, and after merit judgments are made—can influence the fairness of competition outcomes. Chapter 6 examines how different solutions of some common logistic problems of running tests or contests can affect how committees make judgments of merit. And chapter 7 examines how the characteristics of judges and their social interactions can influence group judgments of merit made by committee.

Our final section of the book considers how structural and evolutionary factors shape and constrain the outcomes of merit-based competitions. Chapter 8 considers how the size of a contest can affect its outcome, vitiating the best attempts to reduce judgment errors and creating new difficulties for competitors. Chapter 9 considers how the results of one merit competition can influence subsequent competitions and how applicants and judges coevolve their respective roles. We examine possible links between the evolution of competitions and the rise of revolutions, as well as the fascinating dialectical processes that govern the evolution of competitions for attention.

We did not want this book to be a rigorous and exhaustive scholarly review. We wanted instead to offer logically sound arguments for improving the quality of merit judgments and the fairness of tests and contests in which these judgments are made. Each chapter to follow begins with a discussion of research and theory that addresses the causes of cracks and limits in the adjudication process. Each chapter ends with some practical implications—suggestions for improving the quality of merit judgments or preserving fairness of tests and contests where merit is assessed. We have attempted to minimize technical details in our chapters, hoping to make the chapters more readable to those unfamiliar with or uninterested in these details. Still, it was not possible to justify some of our prescriptions and proscriptions without some technical discussion. If you are a nontechnical but trusting soul, we invite you to trust our judgment, skim the technicalities, and save yourself for our recommendations.

Competitions of merit bring together five different constituencies. First are the donors—people or organizations possessing the limited resource that others desire. Included are philanthropists, employers, government agencies, university admissions offices, voters, and suppliers of prizes of all kinds. Second are the competition organizers—brave souls who must organize and conduct the tests and contests that lead to the distribution of the limited resource in question. Third are the judges—those who must evaluate the merit of performances, applications, promises, or whatever else is used to assess merit. Fourth are the competitors, contestants, or applicants seeking the limited resource. And fifth are people who watch—audience members seeking entertainment in viewing what competitors do and how judges judge what they do. In many small competitions the constituents of these five groups overlap. If, for example, Bob and Martha Baker were seeking a new cashier for their local bakery, they would likely be the donors (of the salary), the organizers (of the job competition), and the judges (of the applicants). In larger competitions, they rarely overlap; indeed, they often form distinct subcultures and sometimes develop unhealthy disrespect for each other.

Our book provides little of use for those who want to squeeze more entertainment from merit-based competitions to satisfy the desires of an audience; we can do no better than to refer them to books on entertainment advertising and promotion or suggest they watch how TV game shows are constructed. We wrote the book primarily for competition donors, organizers, and judges wishing to improve the fairness and efficiency of the adjudication process. Yet we think the book will also be of interest to competitors. While it is often true that not everyone who competes for a coveted resource merits it, it is equally often true that some who do not merit the resource receive it and that some who do merit the resource do not receive it. Giving a coveted resource to those of lesser merit sullies the competition and sours the competitors, especially those with greater merit who did not receive the prize. In large contests there can be dozens to thousands of people with merit to burn who do not get what they deserve or desire. These are often people whose skills are squandered or whose talent is ignored. Civilizations decline in direct relation to the squandering of their talent. So it is worthwhile to consider how merit-based competitions can preserve and nurture as much talent as possible and to learn the limits of what is possible.

We provide no magic solution for ensuring that all people of merit always get what they deserve or desire; on the contrary, we show why such a solution is out of reach. We do, however, provide some understanding of why (to paraphrase Mick Jagger) even meritorious people don't always get what they want. We also show how competition organizers can reduce the chances of bias and error. Because not all competitions are well run or fair, knowledge of how to distinguish the good ones from the bad can be useful for helping prospective competitors judge which competitions merit their entry and which competitions do not. Fools rush in, but wise competitors look before they leap.

2

Merit and Bias

C onsider an evaluation of a very simple type of merit. In American baseball, the pitcher throws a *strike* whenever the ball goes over home plate between the knees and the lower (armpit) shoulders of the batter. Otherwise the pitcher has thrown a *ball*. If the batter swings at the ball, no matter where it is, and misses it, that is also a strike. Let's consider the case where the batter does not swing at the ball. The umpire stands behind home plate and determines whether the pitch has been a strike.

There is an apocryphal story about three umpires, a story that illustrates three approaches to whether the pitch is a strike or a ball.

The first umpire states: "I calls them like they is"—implying that there is an external criterion (summarized above) for determining what is a strike, and that this umpire is able to appreciate as a matter of direct judgment whether that criterion has been met.

The second umpire states: "I calls them like I sees them"—implying that while the external criterion exists, determining whether it has been met is a matter of human perception and judgment.

The third umpire states: "They ain't nothing 'til I calls them"—implying that the final criterion of what is a ball or strike is a social one, depending on what the umpire says.

But now (and we're modifying the story its original form) the first umpire can say to the third: "If that is true, why do you bother to look?"

The three umpire stories illustrate characteristics of merit and how it is judged. For the first umpire, merit is considered to be part of a performance of the individual whose merit is judged. It is the pitcher who throws a ball or a strike, and it is the umpire who makes the judgment. The judgment, moreover, involves an implicit belief in "naïve realism"; that is, belief that the ball is *really* over the plate and at the proper height—or not. The umpire, whether or not he believes that there is some judgment involved in determining that, refers to an outside criterion.

In the case of calling a ball or a strike, the belief that the criterion has been met also involves human perception and judgment. There could be "electric eyes" adjusted for each batter's height and other electric eyes emanating from the plate, to see whether the ball has gone over it. But the standard baseball game does not include such electronic devices and hence requires human judgment—just as assigning a number to the performance does, as in the evaluation of the gymnast or ice skater. About the only evaluation of merit that does not include the human judge is a score on a standardized test, but even here someone at some point has determined that the number of items answered in a particular direction (e.g., "correctly") should be used to evaluate the merit involved.

Even though a final judgment is determined by a human or humans (as in a panel of judges), the judgment need not be arbitrary. The furor in recent years over the judgment of a Canadian versus a Russian pair of figure skaters illustrates that we do not accept the statement of the third umpire as the sole criterion of work. Such controversies illustrate the implicit belief that the judgment of merit is really about something "out there"—once again "in" the performance to be evaluated.

We can trace the history of Western philosophy from Plato to Locke to postmodernism in much the same way that we trace the beliefs of the three umpires. Plato believed in absolute qualities—which were meant to reflect the "pure forms" in his heaven, and while we may be "in the cave" and hence not able to appreciate these qualities as well as if we could observe them directly in heaven, it is these qualities that we attempt to judge. Locke and the other British empiricists emphasized the role of the human in making such judgments; our perceptions and judgments are all-important in determining whether the quality exists, and the importance of mind in assessing the world went to the extreme in the philosophy of Bishop Berkeley, who maintained that the world only existed because "the mind of God" appreciated (or perhaps constructed) it. But if we do not believe in a Berkeley-type god, then the human mind becomes all-important, and if we decide that it is the *only* important thing in the universe, then we are led to the type of arbitrary judgment espoused by the third umpire. For example, the "emotivist" theory of ethics holds that ethical statements are similar to cheering at a football game—"It's ethical if I approve it, and I urge you to approve it." The philosophy termed *postmodernism* takes this argument to its extreme, claiming that all judgments are relative, usually with a political implication. If, for example, I judge that a certain path is the way to reach the peak of the mountain, then what I am merely doing is urging other people to follow it. (But does not the peak exist independent of paths?)

Having noted these characteristics of judgments of merit, we will refrain from an attempt at an overall definition. Instead, what we will do is show how judgments of merit differ from other, related judgments. We begin by distinguishing a judgment of merit from a simple preference. Here, we are following the philosophy of Chaplin, John, and Goldberg (1988), when they attempt to distinguish between a personality state versus a personality trait.

First, judgments of merit involve some principle or at least have some reference to principles or to characteristics that are supposed to be applicable to all judgments of a particular performance (e.g., the pitcher's performance, the performance of the ice skaters). Preferences, in contrast, can be specific. "I happen to like steak tartare, and that's that."

Second, *de gustibus non disputandum est* ("there is no disputing matters of taste"—said the old woman as she kissed the cow). But judgments of merit can be disputed, in particular by other people who are considered expert judges. Does that present a vicious (i.e., solipsistic) circle? No, because there are criteria not just for judging whether a particular performance or behavior involves merit but also for determining whether someone can be considered an expert. For example, gymnastics and ice skating judges are trained by others and, most important, these judges are trained to attend to publicly agreed-upon criteria for the judgment. While the judgment may be ultimately "subjective," it is based on what philosophers of science sometimes term *intersubjective agreement*. (At the trivial extreme, we must all read a gauge the same way.)

This final criterion about expertise involves an implication about how we determine the reliability of a judgment of merit. Consider a bathroom scale. Is it reliable? The answer to this question is whether it produces the same number on multiple occasions (so close together that we have not gained or lost weight in the meantime) and whether the people looking at the scale agree on this number. That does not mean that the scale is valid. It may, for example, consistently yield a number that is three pounds greater or three pounds less than the number that would be obtained from a more accurate measurement device.

In determining whether a preference is reliable, we simply measure its intrapersonal consistency; does the person have the same preference on multiple occasions? In contrast, the reliability of a judgment of merit must be assessed by the consistency across judges (even at the trivial extreme of scoring a standardized test in the same way). That does, of course, get us back to the "circle," because we are not interested in the consistency in the numbers produced by judges whom we do not regard as experts.

A final criterion that differentiates a judgment of merit from a simple preference is that we think that merit judgments must be unbiased. There is no such requirement for a judgment of preference. For example, it would be absurd to state that I have a "biased preference." I just know what I like. ("I don't know anything about modern art, but I know what I like to look at.")

Specifically, we are worried about three types of bias. In their pure form, the first two of these three types may be emotionally based. I might specifically prefer the ice skating performance of my own child, and I am aware of that bias. That is why people often absent themselves from making an evaluation of the performance of people to whom they are close; that is why—for example—the American Psychiatric Association and the American Psychological Association prohibit sexual contact between therapist and client, because such contact may lead the therapist to lose objectivity. The same criticism may be made of professors who have affairs with students whom they must grade. (When one of us, RMD, was a member of the ethics committee of the American Psychological Association, he maintained that having an affair with a client or student would make the therapist or teacher even more devoted to helping than would indifference. No one laughed.) It is in recognition of such specific biases that we often take precautions to avoid them. For example, if a husband and wife are in the same academic department, neither is expected to have input in the evaluation of the other's research or teaching.

(For a number of years—in fact, until 1954 when the University of Oregon specifically got rid of its antinepotism rules—spouses were not even allowed to be in the same academic department, again because there might be a necessity to evaluate each other, and that would involve a clear "conflict of interest.") That university—followed by others—believed that such rules were inevitably biased against women, which they were; for example, when a husband and wife moved to a major public university in the 1960s, the husband was given an appointment in the psychology department, whereas the wife, who was every bit as much a "psychologist"—and an eminent one—as the husband, was give an appointment in the social work department, thereby denigrating both her and the social work department.)

That sort of emotional bias is one of which we may be aware. Most of us are aware of the fact that we may overvalue the performance of our spouse or children, and if we did not, we might have a more serious problem than "bias." There are other emotionally based biases of which people may not be aware. For example, we often find ourselves immediately liking or disliking someone on first meeting. Is it that our "intuitions" about what other people are like are so valid that we should trust these impressions? Or is it that the person simply reminds us of somebody whom we particularly liked or disliked in the past, even though we may be unaware of the characteristics that trigger the associations?

We need to worry about such emotional biases of which we may not be aware. A lot of recent work on implicit racism has indicated that, for example, we might be racist in our judgments while believing ourselves to be totally objective or even especially lacking in racism. What happens is that judgments are affected by the simple presentation of a Black or White face along with the required judgmental response. The same technique has found many of us to be implicitly biased against women or older people (even though we ourselves might be considered "older"!). These biases are difficult to overcome, because we are often unaware of them. But even if we become aware of them, how do we compensate?

Then there is a set of biases that might be partly emotional and partly cognitive. In the chapter in this book about funding decisions (chapter 6), we run into the problem that judgments of merit are often based on whether the researcher seeking funds does research that is either like the evaluator's or may lead to the conclusion that the evaluator's work has been invalid. Naturally, researchers want their research to be supported and influential, so that it may appear that they are emotionally biased if they favor research like theirs or research meant to support—rather than reject—their ideas. But it is also true that these evaluators are most knowledgeable about their own research and the research closely related to it. Could a positive evaluation then not be at least partly a function of knowledge as well as wish? Again, the problem is that both these factors may be implicit rather than consciously recognized, and there is no way of even differentiating between them, let alone correcting for them.

Finally, there are biases that we can consider purely cognitive. Consider, for example, a famous study by Nisbett and Wilson (1977) in which young women at the University of Michigan were asked to say which dresses they liked (and a very few actually received one of the dresses they chose). The researchers arranged the dresses in different orders, and, consistent with the left–right reading orientation in our culture, the participants tended to scan them from left to right. The dresses at the rightmost position, or close to it, tended to be chosen, even though these were different dresses in different orders. Why?

One very plausible hypothesis is that each dress must have some positive characteristic not shared by others (specifically not shared by the previous one scrutinized) or it would not be on the market. (Except for extraordinary "compensating factors," a product that is worse than others on all dimensions important to consumers will have poor sales and disappear.) Thus, as the participants scan the set of dresses, they would note some valuable characteristic of each that they have not observed previously. The study deserves replication in Israel, where reading is from right to left.

But is that the only explanation? No, because there is an extensive literature on what are termed *primacy* and *recency* effects in both memory and judgment. When stimuli are presented in different orders, those presented toward the beginning of a set and toward the end are best remembered and often the best liked. The bias is strong enough that the simple order in which people or proposals are evaluated may have a strong effect on the final judgments of merit. Clearly that is a "bias," because none of us would endorse as a general principle that the order in which we make our judgments should affect them—particularly not when we are attempting to judge "merit," which is thought to be primarily a characteristic of the thing judged, not of the judge. Bruine de Bruin (2005) epitomizes the phenomenon quite neatly in a paper entitled "Save the Last Dance for Me."

Now let us consider a hypothetical situation in which we have successfully eliminated all the forms of biases. What do we have left? Only random error. In this case, we can use the mathematics of standard psychometric test theory to make certain inferences. This theory is based on a very simple hypothesis, which is that any individual's observed score on a test consists of a true score component (T) plus an error component (E) where the error is uncorrelated with the true score. (If it were correlated, we would have a bias rather than a random fluctuation.) But this very simple model has some pretty powerful implications. For example, when we average a number of observations of the same performance, our average is a better estimate of the true score than is a single observation. (This result becomes quite critical when we consider committee evaluation versus individual evaluation of merit.) The reason is very simple. Although errors do not compensate for each other (again they are random), the average error decreases with sample size, whereas the true score is unaffected. Thus, we often trust committee evaluations of merit more than individual evaluations, even when each individual evaluation is unbiased.[1] Alas, when committee members influence each other's judgments, the trust is often unfounded (see chapter 6).

In our context of evaluating merit, the model applies whether we regard the true score as simply a function of the thing (or performance) evaluated or as a joint function of that and the unbiased judgment of the evaluator. In fact, it is possible to reformulate standard psychometric test theory by defining the true score as the expectation of observed scores. And the larger the sample of observed scores, the better their average approximates their expectation.

PRACTICAL IMPLICATIONS

Our overview of the many forms of potential bias in evaluating merit, above, leads us to conclude that if and only if we can eliminate all of these, we can adopt a standard "mental test theory" model that a judgment consists of a true score plus a random error. To the degree reality approximates that model, we can make several inferences, for example, about the value of having multiple judges rather than single judges (see chapter 6).

What we wish to do now is to elaborate some correctable bad habits leading to avoidable biases and present research evidence about the nature of these biases. Each section below will contain advice about "how not to do it," together with the research rationale underlying this advice. (The late, eminent statistician John W. Tukey refers to such advice as *badmandments*, but—unfortunately or not—this term has not received widespread use—unlike, for example, *stonewalling* or *satisficing*—so we do not use it here.)

BAD HABIT A

- Do not take notes, rely on your memory for making a final evaluation, which you will of course make only after you have observed all the evidence.

There are two lines of research that indicate why you should not adopt this memory-based reliance. The first involves the nature of retrospective memory and how it is biased to make sense of what happened earlier by systematically distorting recall. The second line of research involves the superiority of "online" judgments to retrospective ones.

RMD once served on a social science research council committee on cognition and survey research. As part of the service, he organized a workshop on retrospective memory, held in Palo Alto, California, at the Center for Advanced Study in Behavioral Science in 1986. There were many people at the workshop who presented their own research about the "sense making" property of retrospective memory, which is important to survey research for the simple reason that most questions involve such retrospection. ("How often have you been unemployed?" "When was the last time you were in a hospital?" And so on.) A majority of those presentations concerned retrospection about periods ranging from weeks to many years; the report of the conference can be found in a chapter by Pearson, Ross, and Dawes (1992) in the book *Questions About Questions: Inquiries Into the Cognitive Bases of Surveys*, edited by Judith Tanur. Here, we will discuss only evidence about how short-term retrospection can generate bias, i.e., about retrospective biases that distort what happened in the last few minutes or hours, because such time periods are those associated with evaluating merit.

The prototypical example can be found in the doctoral dissertation of Patricia Hines from the University of Oregon's Psychology Department (Hines, 1974). As the subtitle of her dissertation suggests—"The Effects of Behavior Tracking and Expected Deviance on Teachers' Impressions of a Child"—Hines was primarily concerned with how expectations can influence perception and judgment. It turned out, however, that she found more evidence for the effect of retrospective belief than for the effect of expectations while the impressions were being formed.

Undergraduates from the University of Oregon observed two videotaped interactions between a child and a teacher, each lasting about two minutes. The first was a standard tape shown to all participants. In the second tape—the one that forms the basis of the dissertation—the child behaved somewhat badly. It is not clear whether this child should or could be labeled "disturbed," because the degree to which the behavior is inappropriate is ambiguous. Prior to observing the second tape, half the participants (Group A) were told "the child (James) was recruited by a psychological clinic in order to study what is normal or typical in child behavior." The other participants (Group B) were told "the child (Chad) is one of a group of children who were referred to a psychological clinic for the treatment of home behavior problems." Thus, the participants were given an expectancy that the child would either behave normally or behave in an aberrant manner. The actual videotape shown was, however, identical in the two conditions.

After observing the interaction, but prior to filling out any ratings about their impression of the interaction, half of the participants in Group A were told, "I'm very sorry to have to tell you this, but we just showed you the videotape of the wrong child. Don't worry—we won't make you watch another videotape. We will just ask you to rate the child whom you saw. You actually saw Chad, one of a group of children who were referred to a psychological clinic for the treatment of home behavior problems." Similarly, half the participants in Group B were told, "I'm very sorry to have to tell you this, but we just showed you the videotape of the wrong child. Don't worry—we won't make you watch another videotape. We will just ask you to rate the child whom you saw. You actually saw James, who was recruited by a psychological clinic in order to study what is normal or typical in child behavior."

All participants were then asked to rate how the child interacted on an "impression scale" that clearly had a favorable versus unfavorable dimension. The results were striking (see Hines, 1974, figure 2, p. 63). The initial expectancy while watching the interaction had a strong effect on the favorability rating; participants who were not told of a "wrong video" rated Chad less favorably than James. But for participants told about the wrong video and given a second expectancy, the second expectancy (again, given after the interaction was finished and the child was no longer observed) had a much stronger effect. The child who was thought to be a clinic child at the time of the rating was judged much less favorably than the child who was thought to be chosen to see how normal children behave. Consistent with her entire approach to the project, Hines labels this retrospective belief a *final expectancy*, but it is possible to question whether the term *expectancy* is appropriate at all.

What was happening was that the participants were thinking back to the two-minute interaction and presumably picking up cues consistent with what they believed at the time of this retrospection or perhaps interpreting behaviors consistent with their retrospective beliefs. (It is not possible to distinguish these two explanations in the Hines study, but for the purposes of this book, this distinction is not important.)

How can there be such a strong effect? After all, these participants had an expectation when they were observing the interaction, and the hypothesis that this expectation would bias their judgment is fairly direct and noncontroversial. What happened, however, was that the judgment was also biased—and more so—by what they believed at the time they were making it, even though there was nothing left to observe. That result appears to be counterintuitive, but it should not be.

What happens when we retrospectively try to make a judgment? We are in the "here and now" attempting to make a judgment about what happened in the "there and then." We are not at the point of observing the information on which our judgment is based; rather, we must select and evaluate this information right now. While the phenomenological appearance of memory is that of reliving our actual experience—particularly for those of us whose memory is primarily visual and autobiographical (where words are important only if we recall that somebody said something)—careful studies of memory since the work of Bartlett published in 1932 in his classic book *Remembering* demonstrate that the actual process of remembering is a reconstructive one. Naturally this reconstruction can occur only at the time we are attempting to recall what happened, what we have read, etc. Particularly in recent times, given the claims that it is possible to recover repressed memories (usually of horrible experiences), researchers have become sensitive to the possibility of false memory. Here, what we must be sensitive to is the strong possibility that memory is influenced by belief at the time of recall.

It follows that relying on memory without taking notes is a poor procedure. In every single example discussed by Pearson, Ross, and Dawes (1992), distortions of memory occur that are consistent with beliefs at the time of recall. The Hines (1974) dissertation demonstrates that this bias can occur even in very brief intervals, and it is precisely in such intervals that we tend to be evaluating merit—whether of a performance, or of a person, or of a proposal.

We have mentioned previously that there is a recency bias in judgment, and here is an important mechanism for such a bias. What we observe last will be important in forming our overall impression, and that in turn will bias what we recalled earlier. We are aware that many people, including some very smart ones, claim to be absolutely immune to such effects ("I recall things exactly as they happened"), but even some of these people will state that they know that their recall is unbiased because they have talked about what they recall to friends or written about it. It is precisely such recounting that leads to leveling and sharpening (underemphasizing and overemphasizing) of the actual experience, sometimes even to the point that people inadvertently create a conflict between the experience itself and how they have described it to others. For example, Schooler and Engstler-Schooler (1990) demonstrate that asking witnesses to a crime to describe the culprit is a poor procedure, because when asked to pick out the culprit from a lineup, people often pick the suspect who most closely matches their description, as opposed to the actual culprit—at least in "staged" crimes.

In fact, police lineup procedures themselves are very suspect because, when given the alternative, witnesses will select the one most like the real culprit in their memory and then convince themselves—often with the help of a police observer who wants them to be confident that they really did see this person commit the crime. Given, for example, a lineup of six people, the witness believes that one of them must be the true culprit, which leads to the judgment based on similarity rather than recall. A far superior procedure is to present suspects one at a time, without telling the witness how many will be presented—and hence leaving the witness the freedom to say "no" for all the people presented (see Wells, 2005).

We note in passing that many judges do not allow jurors to take notes during criminal trials. The result of the consequent reliance on retrospective memory will enhance confidence in the verdict but not necessarily accuracy.

BAD HABIT B

- If you think the whole is greater than the sum, ignore the parts.

Determining who wins a competition, which grant proposals are funded, or whether someone is promoted is usually based on a final, overall evaluation. Thus, especially if one has not taken notes, one should make this evaluation immediately— and worry about the details later. Research has shown, however, that such holistic evaluations are generally inferior to evaluations based on the components that lead to them, leading to prescriptions to "divide and conquer ..." your own biases (see chapter 3). For example, evaluation of a research proposal may be based on the proposer's description of what is to be done and an evaluation of the "track record" of the proposer in previously publishing important scientific work. For example, the quality of a dive may be based on the style of the takeoff from the board or platform, the acrobatics while in the air, and the degree to which entry into the water is achieved at a right angle with the minimal splash. A holistic evaluation of a research proposal is one in which judges attempt to integrate information about two or more features of the proposal—features such as the innovativeness of the research idea and the researcher's past record of accomplishment—"in their heads" or intuitively to achieve an overall evaluation. Diving judges try to make holistic evaluations by assessing the merit of all aspects of a dive as a configuration in their heads to arrive at one numerical score meant to integrate all aspects of the dive.

The problem with most holistic judgments is that they are not just based on retrospective memory but that they often denigrate or enhance one or another aspect of the behavior as part of a "halo effect"—which (usually unconsciously) tends to provide a consistency between the components that is greater than is justified by the components themselves. In contrast, "disaggregated"—as opposed to holistic—judgments are more prone to evaluating the components in an unbiased manner, even if their evaluation serves simply as a preliminary to making the holistic judgment.

There is a great deal of evidence about the superiority of disaggregated as opposed to holistic judgments; this superiority has been demonstrated in contexts ranging from predicting the longevity of people with a fatal liver disease to the chances that bank loans will be repaid, to the frequency with which psychiatric patients will behave violently, to the chances of success in a Ph.D. program, or to the chances of staying out of jail on parole. In these examples, some of the components in the disaggregated judgment are evaluated in an obvious manner (e.g., undergraduate grade-point average) but some involve perceptual expertise of the judge (e.g., characteristics of a liver biopsy).

What has been found is that a statistical (or "mechanical") evaluation of the component is more predictive of a related physical or social outcome (e.g., death or success) than are holistic judgments of people socially regarded as experts in their relevant fields. For example, a statistical weighting of number of convictions, age of first arrest, and number of prison violations is far superior to predicting whether someone will fail on parole than is the overall impression, intuition, or holistic judgment of a parole interviewer, even though this interviewer has access to the three components. That does not mean that the degree of predictability is the same across all contexts; for example, it is very hard to predict whether someone will remain out of jail on parole, whereas it is much easier to predict a business bankruptcy or whether a loan will be repaid. The point is that when the clinical/intuitive prediction is compared to the statistical one, the latter usually wins, hands down. The problem, apparently, resides in the inability of the human judge to combine information in an optimal way or even in a manner approaching optimal. Even those cases where the human judge believes that her judgment is entirely intuitive and not related to any mechanical weighting procedure, the weighting procedures outperform the intuitive judgment.

The late Paul E. Meehl was the first to point out this superiority in a famous book evaluating "clinical" versus "statistical" prediction (Meehl, 1954). He compared the two types of prediction, intuitive/holistic and statistical/mechanical, based on exactly the same information. Later, Sawyer (1966) was able to include studies where clinicians had more information than was used in the model; for example, standard background variables plus whatever could be garnered by a clinical interview—and still the statistical amalgamation was superior. (Sawyer suggested that if the judgment of the clinician were to be used, it should be entered simply as a variable in the statistical prediction equation.)

Roughly 30 years after the publication of his classic book, Paul Meehl (1986) was able to conclude:

> There is no controversy in social science which shows such a large body of qualitatively diverse studies coming out so uniformly in the same direction as this one. When you are pushing 90 investigations [now closer to 150], predicting everything from the outcomes of football games to the diagnosis of liver disease and when you can hardly come up with a half dozen studies showing even a weak tendency in favor of the clinician, it is time to draw a practical conclusion. (pp. 372-373).

The initial publication of Meehl's book and subsequent developments were greeted with much skepticism and objection. Apparently, people felt that intuitive, holistic expert judgment had to be valid, and certainly more valid than a dry, mechanical statistical model. Only one of these objections need concern us here: the objection that we often do not know the details of an optimal statistical model meant to predict something, so developing this model would take a great deal of effort, and, even were it developed, it would be relevant only to a particular context for making a particular prediction (hence, we must fall back on holistic, clinical judgment).

Dawes and Corrigan (1974), however, published a paper about linear models in general, pointing out that if they formed the basis of a statistical prediction rule, the precise value of the coefficients were not particularly important, provided they were in the right direction (see also, Thorngate, 1980. Optimizing prediction is often a matter of a "flat maximum," in which models close to the very best make predictions close to the very best prediction.) Thus, it is possible to have confidence in the superiority of simple additive prediction rules even when the weights in the predictions are not known precisely. Such weights constitute a weighted average of the predictor variables. As Dawes and Corrigan put it, "The whole point is to know what variables to look at and then to know how to add" (p. 105).

The robustness of the linear weighting schemes has one very clear implication for the current problem of evaluating merit. If we have an external criterion defining merit, we should use an optimal prediction scheme and ignore the holistic intuition of our judges. If, as is more usual, we do not have a precise external criterion, we can still use a weighting system, because we know that whatever the actual optimal model might be for predicting merit, the outcome of a reasonable weighting scheme will provide us with something close to what we want. We can establish this closeness by using interjudge agreement as a substitute for an external criterion, in this case comparing the agreement of weighted, disaggregated judgments of one judge with those of other judges—as opposed to the agreement of judges making holistic judgments with these other judges. Thus, even though the holistic judgments may be based on a set of components used in the disaggregated judgments (where these components are weighted), the reliability of the weighting systems may be superior—again because people are not as good as they believe themselves to be at combining various bits and pieces of information. For example, Arkes, Shaffer, and Dawes (2006) find that even when judges are asked to make both component judgments and holistic judgments, the holistic judgments correlate more strongly with those of other judges when the component judgments are made first in a context of evaluating scientific merit. One problem with making holistic judgments first is that judges may distort their component judgments in order to be consistent with their prior overall judgments.

For the weighted average (linear) models that are optimal or near optimal to do well, one very important condition must be met, technically termed *conditional monotonicity*. This means that independent of all the other variables, each variable considered singly must predict in a particular direction. For example, independent of the number of past convictions and the age of first arrest, the number of prison violations must predict failure on parole. Independent of how well the diver takes off from the diving board or platform or how well the diver enters the water, the quality of the acrobatics in the air must predict merit in a positive direction. Independent of the creativity of the proposed research, the better the track record of the researcher, the better the proposal. Note that this condition does not imply that the relationship is a strictly additive one; it need not be, because conditionally monotone relationships (always rising or always falling) can often be well approximated by additive relationships.

This condition does not even imply that there can be no interaction effect between the variables. What is prohibited by the condition is what is termed a *crossed interaction* between the variables—that is, an interaction where the direction of one variable and not just its magnitude is different depending on the value of the other variables, not just the magnitude of the effect.

It is easy to hypothesize such crossed interactions or even to define the variables in the way that the cross must exist, but it is much more difficult to find them in the types of contexts studied by psychologists and other social scientists. First, consider the possibility of redefining variables. It can be pointed out that when the price of a stock is going up, sales are positive for the company, but when the price of stock is going down, sales are negative. Framed in this manner, the relationship constitutes an almost prototypical crossed interaction. But we can reframe this result by talking simply about profit and loss; in fact, profits versus losses appears to constitute a very simple variable compatible with our thinking about how well a company is doing. The stilted definition in terms of the crossed interaction disappears.

Moreover, interaction need not imply crossed interaction. For example, some of my colleagues (Cohen & Willis, 1985) find that whether stress leads to physical symptoms (of colds, not cancer) is affected by whether people have what is generally termed *social support*. People who are well supported by others appear to be much more immune to stress than are those who are isolated; at least, the people with the social support are less apt to develop serious symptoms, whether during a season for developing colds or having cold viruses squirted up their noses (in a controlled experimental study). Why is this interaction monotonic? Because there is no crossover, in that people with low social support are more apt to develop symptoms when they are not stressed (or, to put it another way, that in the absence of stress, social support predicts having symptoms rather than avoiding them). This relationship between stress, exposure, and social support is fairly typical of the type of interaction found in psychology and other social sciences. As another example (see Dawes, 1969), prisoners who are both alcoholic and placed in a stressful situation consume twice as much (nonalcoholic) liquid in the waiting room prior to talking to a psychologist than do prisoners who are not alcoholic or not placed under stress. (Again, nonalcoholics do not drink a great deal when not under stress, which would have to occur if the interaction were truly a crossed one.)

We maintain, in the context of judging merit, that the conditional monotonicity assumption noted above is almost always viable. Each component of the behavior, person, or proposal to be evaluated should necessarily have a clear directional relationship with the final judgment, or the whole concept of "merit" would become ambiguous. (How could, for example, entry into the water that is vertical without creating a splash be meritorious in the context of poor acrobatics but not in the context of good acrobatics?)

Of course, for all these principles about conditional monotonicity to apply, each proponent must be consistently oriented in a way that is positively or negatively oriented toward overall merit. A few variables must be transformed in order to satisfy this criterion. For example, if we want somebody to be "moderately aggressive" in a particular job or other social role, we can orient a component to be largest when it approaches the desired level of moderation. Or, conversely, we can simply define extremity as negative.

Perhaps the most striking example can be found in the evaluation of some judges whom former president Richard Nixon nominated for the Supreme Court and who were subsequently turned down by the Senate. To the complaint that they were "mediocre," Senator Hruska of Nebraska claimed that "us mediocre people as well deserve representation on the Supreme Court." Hence, we could define a variable in this case—to reflect this good senator's judgment—as "degree of mediocrity." Note that in both of these examples, aggression and mediocrity, there is an ideal point, or at least region, that is defined as somewhere toward the middle of a dimension that has a clear direction. In surveying characteristics that have evaluative connotations, we consistently find that more is better, more is worse, or a moderate amount is best; rarely do we find that the extremes are desirable (as in hot or iced tea or coffee), and almost never do we find that there are a number of dips and peaks that relate the evaluation of a dimension to the dimension itself. Thus, redefining dimensions in terms of desirability—where necessary—is not very difficult.

BAD HABIT C

- Be inconsistent.

Strive for consistency. We, of course, recommend consistency with other judges as a criterion for assessing possible validity. Here, however, we are discussing consistency within a judge—for example, consistency between component judgments and an overall judgment or consistency by emphasizing components that appear to be consistent with each other.

If a judge is convinced of the superiority of the "divide-and-conquer" strategy of judging merit by first assessing components of merit and then adding up individual assessments rather than making holistic judgments, and if the judge consequently forms any holistic judgment automatically on the basis of combining components, then, of course, there has to be a consistency between component judgments and a holistic judgment. That is not a bias. A bias can occur, however, when the process is conducted "backwards," i.e., where a holistic judgment is formed first (perhaps explicitly but often implicitly) and then the components are evaluated or weighted in a way to be consistent with this holistic judgment. Example: Holistically speaking, my cousin seems best suited for this job, so I will heavily weigh her strengths and ignore her weaknesses but weigh the strengths and weakness of other applicants equally. That defeats the whole purpose of the component evaluation rule, although we suspect that when people realize that the end result of the evaluation will be a single judgment (e.g., number denoting the performance of the concert pianist or the funding priority of a research proposal), there will be some type of what we deem to be inappropriate feedback "in the wrong direction," from the overall judgment to component judgments. In fact, one of the striking features of Arkes et al.'s (2006) study evaluating scientific merit is that the "mechanical" combination of component judgments led to greater interjudge reliability than did holistic judgments despite the fact that when evaluating components, the judges were aware that they would also make an overall judgment.

In this chapter, we have emphasized that many different weighting schemes, provided that components are weighted in the correct direction, can be considered.

The resulting weighted judgments are, of course, meant to apply to all the instances under consideration. Using different weighting functions for different applicants—especially choosing these functions post hoc to be consistent with an overall judgment—defeats the purpose of a component analysis completely and sets the stage for double standards. Nevertheless, in discussion groups or committees, judges may inconsistently propose different weights in order to be consistent with the outcome they desire; that is, "truth" based on holistic evaluation.

Another method for achieving consistency is to emphasize those components that are consistent with each other. In fact, doing so appears to increase confidence in the evaluation made. Here, we can do no better than to quote from a very famous paper by Amos Tversky and Daniel Kahneman (1974):

> The internal consistency of a pattern of inputs is a major determinant of one's confidence in predictions based on these inputs. For example, people express more confidence in predicting the final grade-point average of a student whose first-year record consists entirely of B's than in predicting the grade-point average of a student whose first-year record includes many A's and C's. Highly consistent patterns are most often observed when the input variables are highly redundant or correlated. Hence, people tend to have great confidence in predictions based on redundant input variables. However, an elementary result in the statistics of correlation asserts that, given input variables of stated validity, a prediction based on several such inputs can achieve higher accuracy when they are independent of each other than when they are redundant or correlated. Thus, redundancy among inputs decreases accuracy even as it increases confidence, and people are often confident in predictions that are quite likely to be off the mark. (p. 1126)

In summary, as we examine how to make bad judgments of merit, it becomes clear how to make good ones. Avoid the three "I"s: informal, intuitive, and inconsistent. Instead, decide what components or features of applications are important for judging merit, and judge each application by these features only. Make your judgment of each feature separately. Write down your separate judgments. Then add them up, weighing them in the same way for each application. The prescription is mechanical, likely more time consuming and less exciting than flying by the seat of your gut feelings. But it will produce noticeably fairer and better judgments of merit.

NOTE

1. For uncorrelated numbers, as we assume the error numbers to be, the variance of their sum is the sum of their variances. Assuming that n have the same variance, then the variance of their sum is n times that variance. But, the variance of a constant times a variable is equal to the square of that constant times the variance of the variable. When we average, we are multiplying the sum by the quantity $(1/n)$, which means that even though the variance of the sum is n times the individual variance, the variance of the average is $(1/n)^2$ times n times that original variance, or the original variance divided by n.

3

Lessons from Clinical Research

*T*here are two characteristics of judging merit that are the same as those found in predicting important human outcomes. The judgment of merit is difficult, just as it is difficult to predict such important human outcomes as staying out of jail on parole or succeeding in medical school. The judgment of merit is also multifaceted, just as many characteristics of humans must be considered simultaneously to predict what will happen to them or what they will do.

It turns out that there is a substantial research literature about how best to predict important human outcomes. We turn to this literature now to yield some principles—or at least suggestions—about how best to access merit. Before proceeding, however, we will point out that the multifaceted nature of predicting important human outcomes exists in the multitude and complexity of the variables used to make the prediction, not in the outcomes themselves. People on parole are either sent back to jail or they are not. People entering medical school either succeed in obtaining an M.D. or they do not. Many characteristics (i.e., facets) must, however, be considered in attempting to predict these simple outcomes. In a similar manner, the final outcome of a judgment of merit can be quite simple. The piano or figure skating competition yields a winner (or winning team), and often a ranking involving second or third place, or even a set of tied rankings involving "honorable mention." What yields these judgments is often, in contrast, multidimensional and complex. In a similar manner, we must (or at least we do) consider past grades, scores on aptitude tests, and statements in letters of recommendation to make the judgment about who will do well in medical school when we decide whom to admit. (Alas, one of us [RMD] knows of a male doctor who also considered gender and marital status on the grounds that unmarried women are "immature," married ones are "not sufficiently interested in medicine," and divorced ones are "neurotic"—considerations he apparently made with little or no awareness of what he was basing them on.)

Before proceeding, we want to make the strong argument that these important human outcomes, while simple, are profound ones. RMD was once asked to justify in court why the research about how to predict them was relevant to the "really deep judgments" made on a purely intuitive basis by the clinical psychology experts on the "opposing" side. But what is more profoundly important in some-one's life than staying out of jail or ending up back in it? Or succeeding or failing at a chosen profession? Or even (in one example to be discussed in some length) living versus dying?

To anticipate the conclusion of this chapter, we mention three findings that the reader might find a bit jarring. The first is that despite the complexity of the variables leading to the predictions, they are best made on a simple statistical basis rather than an intuitive one. Intuition may be used to decide on the identity of the important pre-dictive variables, or even how to code their nature, but the human mind is not good at making an intuitive integration of multiple—often incomparable—predictors. The second is that the integration of the information on the basis of statistical predic-tion rules (SPRs) is often very simple, involving no complex interactions or configural transformations of the relevant input variables. The third is that rather than attempt-ing to attend to and integrate—even on the basis of an SPR—as much information judged relevant as possible, it is often best to restrict the number of the variables considered and, in particular, to be able to determine which of the variables that may at first appear to be relevant are not and to systematically ignore them. Gender, for example, may be an important variable to ignore when determining who is a good musician for a symphony, and that the way of systematically ignoring gender is to have auditions behind a screen or curtain (see Osborne, 1994).

Psychologists have been interested in predicting important human outcomes for many years. For example, in the Second World War, Bloom and Brundage (1947) wished to predict who would do well in military schools that attempted to prepare recruits for their specialty training. Similarly, again in the wartime context, psy-chologists attempted to predict who would "get his wings" in pilot training school, and the prediction was so successful that even a member of the U.S.S.R. Academy of Sciences admitted to RMD during a scientific exchange in 1979 that the U.S.S.R. had copied our system for selecting pilots—despite its ideological commitment to the idea that environment, and not aptitude, was responsible for all individual differences, and hence that selection for training would be irrelevant. Finally, of course, being themselves primarily employed in educational, business, or military environments, psychologists have long had an interest in predicting which students in these environments would succeed or fail. (Traditionally it was possible for stu-dents to fail as well as to succeed, although there was a brief period a few years ago in the self-esteem era that prohibited failure in some institutions; many students who did poorly in these could tell how their teachers really evaluated them only after discovering that they could not obtain good jobs after graduation.)

As noted in chapter 2, the late psychologist Paul Meehl published a stunning book in 1954 summarizing what is known about these predictions. The book was entitled *Clinical Versus Statistical Prediction: A Theoretical Analysis and a Review of the Evidence* and summarized about 20 studies involving the predictions of important human outcomes in which the prediction was made by two methods. In one, an experienced clinical psychologist or personnel officer made an intuitive prediction—for example, of who would stay out of jail on parole, who would do well in an academic institution, or even who would respond favorably versus unfavor-ably to electric-shock therapy for depression. The other prediction was made by simply amalgamating the predictor variables in an optimal statistical manner. The comparison of these two modes of prediction was "pure," in the sense that both were based on exactly the same input information; that is, even though psychologists in general would interview subjects in addition to looking at test scores or ratings from letters of recommendation, they were presented only with the numbers that were used in the statistical prediction. In no case was the intuitive prediction reliably superior, though there were a few virtual ties. The "horse race" between clinical versus statistical predictions has since been run many times over (e.g., Dawes, Faust, & Meehl, 1989), culminating in exactly the same conclusion 40 years later (Grove & Meehl, 1994)—only this time based on about 140 studies rather than about 20.

Meehl's book was not met with universal enthusiasm. He seemed to be concluding that expert, experienced clinical psychologists were no better than simple little systems involving the addition of numbers in predicting important human outcomes, because that was what he was finding; moreover, the "reduction" of important human characteristics to "mere numbers" was considered to be both a substantive and ethical offense to not only the expertise of the clinical psychologists but to the people themselves who were studied. Surely, *something* had to be wrong with the book and its conclusions. There were two major objections.

First, clinical psychologists typically do not make judgments on the basis of the same types of numbers or categories that are used in SPRs. Thus, in order to achieve a "pure" competition between clinician vs. actuarial model, Meehl may have unfairly constrained the clinicians to do something that clinicians cannot generally do, which is to be expert at integrating numbers and category information. Instead, what clinicians usually do is have some sort of personal contact with the people they are judging—for example, in a "clinical interview"—and surely such contact might provide valid information for the clinical predictions. To judge the predictive power of clinicians, it is necessary to allow them to predict in a manner that they can do well!

A second main objection is that, while these SPRs were carefully accessed from the amount of "shrinkage, when in prediction accuracy applied to a sample of people other than those from which they were constructed, the actual construction of such a rule is a difficult process. Moreover, we might expect to find different rules for different situations—at least slightly different rules for slightly different situations. Would not clinical predictors be justified in "falling back" on their intuitions until such rules are developed for the specific situations they encounter? In fact, one expert statistician (Nathan King, personal communication, September 18, 1982) proposed that judgment initially be made on the basis of clinical intuition, but then after a certain number of people are observed—that number depending upon the clarity of the outcome and the number of variables predicting it—prediction should be "switched" to the use of the optimal SPR. It turned out that neither of these objections were valid.

First, in 1966, Sawyer was able to find studies in which the information available to the clinicians subsumed that available to the SPR; the most popular type of studies was where the clinician had all of the information used in the SPR plus whatever could be gleaned in a clinical review. Even then, however, the predictions of the SPRs were superior. Moreover, as indicated in the previous chapter, Sawyer provided information that the way in which this extra "wholly clinical" information should be integrated with the information used by the SPR should itself be part of an SPR. That is, rather than looking at the prediction rule as some sort of "floor" from which the clinician could improve the prediction, the floor turned out to be a ceiling, where any included judgment of a clinician must be included as a new variable in an expanded SPR.

The objection about having to develop an optimal model was countered by work of Dawes and Corrigan in 1974. They noted that most of the models studied were linear ones—i.e., those that involved a "weighted average" of the predictor variables (suitably standardized and comparable, usually using standard scores). Consequently, Dawes and Corrigan asked what would happen if weights other than optimal ones were used in these linear models. To answer that question, they constructed what they termed *random linear models*, which consisted of weights that were in the proper direction but otherwise chosen according to random samplings from a normal or a uniform distribution. These weights were then applied to standard scores. (The rationale for assuming direction was that in most predictive situations people would know at least the direction of the predictions; moreover, most have a very simple monotone relationship with the criteria. Others most often have single peaks or single dips—for example, "moderate" assertiveness being valuable in interpersonal relationships—and then could be recoded in terms of difference from the peak, again standardized.) In the contexts that Dawes and Corrigan had available for study, even these random linear models outperformed the predictions of clinical experts. Wainer (1976, 1978) showed that deviations from optimal weighting did not matter much in the predictions when linear models were used. Dawes (1979) developed the term *improper linear model* to characterize these types of models that were not derived from optimization procedures but nevertheless provided outputs close to those that would be obtained from such procedures.

Occasionally there may in fact be interactions in the predictions, but they are not of the type where high-highs and low-lows predict in one direction, whereas high-lows and low-highs predicted in another; for example, it is never the case that people who have low aptitude test scores are better off if they likewise have a poor academic record than if they have a good one, but rather are better off if they have a high aptitude test score combined with a good academic record. The interaction that may result is one where the effect of high-highs or low-lows is amplified by the interaction effect; for example, it may be particularly predictive of future success in academic or professional training program if a good record is combined with high aptitude test scores, more predictive than would be found by looking at the aptitude test scores or the academic record alone. (Ditto for low aptitude and a low record.) That type of interaction is termed a *monotonic* one and, as mentioned in chapter 2, just as these linear models are very good approximations for single variables that have a monotonic relationship to a criterion, they are good approximations in the presence of monotonic interactions. (In fact, the interaction effect is all that is left over after the main effects are removed. In the context of what is termed *crossed interactions*, where high-highs and low-lows are similar, then the interaction effect tends to be predominant. In the context of monotonic interaction effects, however, there is often very little deviation left over to assess the interaction.)

One advantage of the improper model over a proper one is that it is not necessary to have a reasonable sample—or even a sample at all—in order to construct the improper model. Previously, Dawes and Corrigan (1974) had concluded that "the whole trick is to know what variables to look at and then to know how to add," and the improper linear models incorporate this "trick."

It must be emphasized that in many of these contexts prediction is not very good. As pointed out in chapter 2, for example, it is extraordinarily difficult to predict who will or will not meet conditions of parole, particularly because there may be a number of crimes committed by parolees that are not prosecuted, and hence a parolee who has not reformed may in fact be included in the set of successful ones. In one state's jails, the correlation coefficient indicating the success of the models used is about .23 (which, incidentally, is the correlation coefficient between smoking and lung cancer),[1] but the correlation of the judgment of the parole interviewer with whether or not people succeed is much worse (.07.), even when this interviewer had access to the variables coded in the SPR predicting success. When translated into number of victims and number of failures, the difference between .23 versus .07 is profound. In contrast, the prediction of bankruptcy within the next 3 years of business is not that difficult; the single variable consisting of the ratio of assets to liabilities alone does a fairly good job.

Does this research history completely negate the need for any human judgment? No. Consider the statement of Dawes and Corrigan (1974) about what variables to look at. Let us give a very concrete example of their trick. Einhorn (1974, 1975) studied the judgments of the world expert on Hodgkin's disease about the severity of the disease process as judged from biopsies. Einhorn had a rather simple, unpleasant criterion: the number of days that the patients lived after the biopsyies were taken. The study was done in a time when Hodgkin's could not be stopped, and they all died. Of course, the judgment of severity is not identical with a prediction of how long patients will live, but survival length appears to be an excellent indicator of severity.

In addition to the world's expert, two apprentices made judgments on the severity of the disease process. The correlation of these judgments with actual survival time was virtually zero in all cases. At the time, Einhorn himself had Hodgkin's and was under the care of the world's expert; Einhorn was greatly relieved by his doctor's lack of predictive accuracy, because this expert had predicted that Einhorn had about 6 months to live. In fact, he survived for another 22 years.

Does that result mean that longevity was unpredictable? No. Looking at characteristics of the biopsies that the doctors themselves coded, Einhorn was able to construct a fairly simple model of the characteristics of the biopsy to predict longevity; again, after suitable transformation of variables, these models were linear ones. What was happening was that the experts were looking at the correct predictive information, coding it properly, but then losing the valuable information that they themselves had observed when they made overall judgments. It is in the combination of the variables that the SPRs outperform humans, not in the collection of variables. (Statisticians often talk about "selecting models," but they refer to selecting which models to use involving variables that are already coded, not to the selection and coding of the variables themselves. Sophisticated models are available for that type of model selection, but as yet there are no models available for that type of selection and coding accomplished by the doctors that Einhorn studied.)

Why? Because automated pattern recognition is an extraordinarily difficult problem. Even knowing something simple, such as leukocyte count—which did predict longevity in the Hodgkin's patients—it is hard to find that pattern in the confusion of visual input from biopsies.

Now here is something uniquely human in the judgment of merit. There may be variables that we cannot automatically collect and code; for example, the difference between a beautiful versus a dull melody, or an inspired performance versus a pedestrian one may be very difficult to find on the basis of any type of automated system. But let us return to the finding of Sawyer. When there are variables that require some sort of human judgment to code, they should be entered into an SPR, even if it is an "improper" prediction rule.

In fact, it is exactly the power of these improper prediction rules that makes the findings from Meehl (1954) so important in judging merit. The implication of the research is that if we had some terrific criterion for building a rule to judge merit, we should use it. But we don't. Nevertheless, the improper model used in place of this rule can do an excellent job of approximating that rule, even though we do not know the exact nature of the rule. All that must happen is that we know the directional relationship between the variables included in this rule and the criterion of true merit, if we had such a criterion. That is superior to attempting an intuitive integration of all the information. The implication is very clear: divide the multifaceted nature of merit into its components and attempt to combine these according to a simple rule. The rule should be simple. There may be many complex relationships among the components of merit, but even if we could determine them, it is not clear how relevant they would be to the evaluation of merit.

And what happens if we do not follow a simple rule but use our intuition instead? John Locke had the answer to that centuries ago. We tend to think on the basis of associations. Thus, it will be quite possible that we will end up—perhaps without even realizing it—making an association between the conduct or performances we intend to evaluate and some previous example involving great merit or its opposite. This "prototype matching" is better than nothing, but it is not as good as a careful weighting of the components of merit, even though the optimal weights may not be known. Moreover, prototype and stereotype matching is prone to a great many biases; again, for example, because all of the French horn players we know who seem to be outstanding are male, maleness can easily become part of the stereotype. That is neither productive nor fair.

PRACTICAL IMPLICATIONS

It is probably natural for judges to seek the shortest mental path from first impressions to merit judgments. But as we have noted above, taking one step from first impressions to merit judgments is dangerous. Sometimes called *holistic impressions*, gut feelings, or shoot-from-the-hip assessments, one-step procedures go directly from raw perceptions to merit judgments with nothing in between. Such judgments are likely revealed in statements such as, "I just let my eyes drift over the applications until I find one that stands out" or "I trust that my gut will tell me when I have found the winner" or "I can't define what merit is, but I know it when I see it." They are typically made as the result of noticing an uncommon feature of an application that stands out and can be easily assessed and then ignoring more common features that are at least as important. Holistic? Humbug!

Consider, for example, a judge who must decide whether you or another applicant will get a job after university graduation. Suppose you have a slightly higher grade point average than the other person, and you have more relevant work experience. But suppose the other person notes on her résumé that she speaks French, and suppose the judge has a long-dormant interest in learning French to talk to her elderly aunt in Montreal. If there are no guidelines, or only vague guidelines, to follow for making a merit judgment, the judge may very well focus on the unusual language information and ignore or downplay the more job-relevant information ("Her skills seem good enough to do the job, and I love the French connection"), perhaps not even looking at other résumés. ("Why look at more when you've made your decision?") No doubt the other applicant would feel a warm glow for being offered the job. But how would you feel about such a one-step judgment, especially if you spent 3 days preparing your résumé for the job opening but did not bother to note in your résumé that you, too, speak French. Chances are that you, and any other losing applicant, would cry foul if you knew how the judgment was made. Would fairness increase if you challenged the judge about her decision process and she replied, "I looked at the whole package"?

Despite its sensual appeal, there are at least three problems with the one-step judgment procedure. First, it reduces the chances that applicants will know the criteria of judgment and offer information relevant to these criteria, wasting their time in second-guessing the judges and wasting judges' time in assessing irrelevant information. Second, it reduces the chances that a judge can articulate the criteria leading to his judgment and thus reduces the possibility of challenging, justifying, and improving these criteria. Third, it opens large holes for inconsistent or biased judgment.

Thus it is desirable to adopt a two-step procedure. Two-step judgments place a layer of publicly accessible judgment criteria between the raw information that comes from an applicant and the merit judgment that is ultimately made. Figure 3.1 illustrates the difference between the one-step and two-step procedures in a job competition.

Mapping raw information into merit criteria can be, of course, just as subjective, holistic, and prone to error as mapping the information into a merit judgment. Psychometrically preferred criteria are those that have clear and countable referents—for example, judging the merit of applications for car insurance discounts should probably be based on driving records (number of accidents and speeding tickets) rather than reference letters ("My daughter promises to obey the speed limits."). But vague criteria requiring subjective standards—Just how foxy or pretentious is that bottle of merlot?—will probably never disappear. When merit criteria are almost as vague as merit itself, why use them? As Cronbach (1954) showed, the

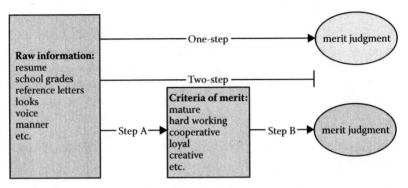

Figure 3.1   Judging merit of a job applicant using a one-step and two-step procedure.

reason can be found in a wonderful statistical principle: systematically combining many small, fallible judgments will increase validity more than relying on a single, fallible judgment. An example: If we asked you each day for 30 days running to guess the next day's high temperature, the average of your 30 little guesses would almost certainly be closer to the real average than would one big guess about the same average you made without the aid of more than a gut feeling.

Criteria of merit have at least one more benefit: When you publicize them to prospective applicants, the applicants can adapt themselves to the information. Some prospective applicants will probably self-select out of the competition because they do not meet eligibility criteria (see chapter 5), thereby decreasing the number of applications that judges must vet—a benefit for judges. Other prospective applicants will likely modify their applications to address the merit criteria, making it easier for judges to discover raw information relevant to each judgment criterion. A simple application form listing questions relevant to the criteria will, for example, guide judges to the information they seek. Most judges become impatient, bored, or testy reading meandering autobiographies of applicants for a job, grant, promotion, and such. Instead, they prefer reading a well-designed application form, allowing them to find information relevant to Criterion X in an applicant's answer to Question X. Structure is good and should be included in merit-based competitions whenever possible.

COLLECTING CRITERIA

Where do criteria of merit come from? How many should you use in a competition? And how can you know which are fair? No doubt donors, organizers, and judges would have suggestions about which criteria should be employed in filtering raw information. So, too, would prospective applicants and audience members. In the interest of fairness, we advise polling as many of these stakeholders as you can for criteria suggestions. Even an informal poll is better than none. With a little luck, a small number (2–5) of criteria will appear on almost everyone's list. These popular criteria would likely be the most important of the lot simply because, by definition, they pass the test of consensual validation. Most, perhaps all, of them should be included on a final list. Do not make the final list too long. Judges start to balk if required to evaluate raw information on more than about 5–7 criteria. So it is prudent to limit your list to this number. This allows you to eliminate criteria that are prejudicial ("Must be tall, good-looking, and blond"), vexatious ("Must swear and spit"), or silly ("Must leap tall buildings in a single bound").

Part of the job of selecting fair criteria is to make them clear. If you have a choice, choose criteria that have an obvious connection to raw information and that have been shown to—or at least seem to—be predictive of merit. Undergraduate grades, for example, are a good predictor of graduate school grades, so an undergraduate grade-point average seems an obvious and useful criterion for selecting who merits graduate school. The sincerity of promises to stay out of trouble after prison does not seem to be a good predictor of recidivism. Sincerity is also quite difficult to define. So, if used at all, the sincerity of promises should probably not be weighted heavily in judging the merit of parole applications.

It is often challenging to find criteria that are popular, clearly defined, and easily measured. Consider, for example, the job of judges who must assess the merit of contemporary art. How can they possibly define clearly, much less agree upon, the criteria that should be used in assessing merit? Perhaps they could reach consensus on a few technical criteria, but these are hardly sufficient to define a work of art. Beyond technique, concepts such as innovation, boldness, profundity, whimsy, juxtaposition, and derivation might pop out of a suggestion box. But linking them to shapes and colors is no easy chore.

What to do? There is always hope that at least a few criteria can be clearly defined and measured. We might make a case, for example, that the amount of time gallery visitors dwell in front of piece of art or the number of prints or postcards sold of each picture at an exhibition are clearly defined and measured indicants of artistic value. But there would no doubt be criticism of these mundane indicants; indeed, many judges may refuse to bend to any clear indicants of merit criteria, arguing that the clearer the indicant, the less its importance.

We offer two retorts. First, what are the alternatives? One indicant might be the number of flamboyant adjectives used to describe a contemporary work of art—a sculpture labeled as "dark, disturbing, difficult, and deep" might out-alliterate a painting that was merely "audacious and fluid." But for those averse to counting, there is little difference between filtering raw impressions through a list of fuzzy adjectives and relying on the one-step adjudication procedure. Which leads to our second retort: If clear criteria cannot be found or accepted, then why have any merit-based competition at all? Without clear and agreeable criteria of artistic merit, a good case can be made for challenging the concept of artistic merit, at least as one capable of allocating prizes fairly. Flip a coin instead, or divide the prize equally among artists, or allow the artists to duke it out amongst themselves.

In sum, organizers are on their way to a fair competition if they load up on clear criteria of merit, easily measured, often requested, and commonly accepted as valid. If such criteria cannot be found, or if the ones employed fall far short of the ideal, organizers can assume that the fairness of their competition would be compromised and problems would follow. Without good criteria, merit-based competitions have no clear advantage over other ways of allocating scarce resources, including lotteries and markets.

Step A

As seen in Figure 3.1, judges who adopt a two-step procedure for judging merit must first translate their impressions of the raw information available from each applicant into the merit criteria. The criteria act as a filter between raw information and the merit judgment, breaking down holistic judgments into manageable parts. A judge using the two-step procedure must find and assess the raw information relevant to each criterion during step A and then combine these assessments into a merit judgments during step B. If the procedure were followed, judges would not ask themselves the one-step, holistic question, "Is this applicant meritorious?" but instead ask, "Is there evidence in the raw information that the applicant is or is not mature? Hard working? Cooperative? Et cetera?"

We recommend that judges use rating scales to assess applications along each criterion. In the example shown in Figure 3.1, a judge might scan the information in each application for evidence of maturity (*not at all mature* 0 1 2 3 4 5 *extremely mature*), work habits (*not at all hard working* 0 1 2 3 4 5 *extremely hard working*), etc. The ratings can then be combined into a merit judgment according to some predetermined rule (see Step B, below). If ratings are impractical, even simple answers—for example: Yes, No, and Don't know—are useful in completing the task of step A. Positive, negative, and neutral judgments on criteria can always be tallied. The total, though not as finely discriminating as ratings, can still do a passable job of distinguishing the meritorious from the slugs (Thorngate, 1980; Thorngate, Wang, & Tavakoli, 2004).

When judges are given the task of evaluating applicants along their merit criteria, there is a natural tendency to make the evaluations one applicant at a time, simply because information about each applicant is usually packaged in its own file or form. Judge Judy, for example, might open the application file of Frank, rate him on criteria X, Y, and Z, then open the file of Paula and rate her on criteria X, Y, and Z, etc. We recommend an alternative: Whenever possible, rate all applicants one criterion at a time. If Judge Judy adopted the alternative, she would rate Frank on criterion X, then rate Paula on criterion X, etc. At the end of the applicant pile, Judge Judy would reshuffle the applications (to avoid position or fatigue effects), then rate each applicant on criterion Y. Once more the pile would be reshuffled and Judy would rate each applicant on criterion Z.

Why is it better to evaluate criterion by criterion rather than applicant by applicant? Focusing attention on only one criterion at a time allows judges to make easier and more consistent comparisons among applicants than does dividing attention among all criteria (Thorngate & Maki, 1974a, 1974b, 1976). Single-criterion comparisons reduce cognitive load. Judges can more easily go back and forth among applicants to compare them on one criterion than to compare them on several.

The task can be facilitated if application forms are structured to isolate information relevant to each criterion in separate questions, boxes, or Web-page form objects. Transfer the information into cells of a spreadsheet—one applicant in each row, one criterion in each column. An example summarizing résumé information related to two criteria for a high technology job is shown in Figure 3.2.

	A	B	C	D	E
1	Applicant	Education	rating	Reference letter	rating
2	A	BEng, Waterloo	5	Creative but lazy	2
3	B	MSc, Toronto	5	Industrious and honest, but difficulty working with others	1
4	C	MSc, Calgary	4	Workaholic	3
5	D	BS, Victoria	3	Excellent worker	5
6	E	BEng, Waterloo	5	technically good, but can't write	4
7	F	AA, Algonquin	2	Excellent employee	5
8	G	PhD, Memorial	5	Superiority complex	1
9					

Figure 3.2   Reorganizing applicant information in a spreadsheet.

Normally, a judge would consider all information for applicant A (row 2 of the spreadsheet in Figure 3.2) and then would consider all information for applicant B (row 3 in Figure 3.2), etc. A judge employing our recommended criterion-by-criterion method would first go down spreadsheet column B as shown in Figure 3.2, rating the education of applicants A–G. Then the judge would go down column D, rating the reference letter highlights for applicants A–G. Focusing on the education column allows a judge to easily assess the applicants' range of education and to concentrate on what he knows about universities and degrees. It also ·encourages the judge to be consistent, visually reminded that applicants A and E both have the same degree from the same institute and should therefore be rated the same. Similar arguments can be made for scanning down the reference letter column.

To be squeaky clean, we also recommend randomizing the order of applicants (rows) in each criterion column and hiding applicant identification (column 1 in Figure 3.2). Judges then could not assume that the same row represented the same person, so halo effects ("I graduated from Waterloo too; we were all creative but lazy, just like applicant A, so I think it is a good reference letter.") could not form. Or consider a variation: Show one judge only one criterion (say, Education in Figure 3.2) and ask the judge to evaluate applicants on it. Show a second judge only one criterion (say, Letter in Figure 3.2) and ask the judge to evaluate applicants on it. Continue this way for as many judges as there are criteria. Keep the judges separated, so they assess independently and cannot be influenced either by each other or by additional information. Then go to step B, below.

Step B

When a judge has dutifully translated each application into ratings on the set of merit criteria (illustrated in columns C and E of Figure 3.2), he can rightly ask, "What now?" The scores on these criteria must somehow be combined into a merit judgment. This is the task of step B. Many judges agonize over step B. They needn't. As discussed previously, simple additive rules do a nice job of combining the information. Additive rules may gloss over nuances of interpretation—downplaying creativity a wee bit for Fred, who scores low on creativity but high on loyalty, or overlooking an average cooperation score for Jane, who scores high on creativity. But what additive rules lack in subtlety, they make up in consistency. Stakeholders can, and probably will, debate how much weight should be given to each merit criterion. But once the weights are negotiated, judges can relax, enter their merit criteria assessments into a formula, and calculate the results.

Just as we believe it is prudent to tell prospective applicants which merit criteria will be used in a competition, we think it is also prudent to tell prospective applicants how the criteria will be weighed and combined. It sounds silly to announce that "This ice dance competition will choose a winner according to technical difficulty and artistic interpretation, but the judges won't tell you how they will combine the scores." It sounds more sensible to replace the second clause with "… these two criteria will be weighed equally and summed for a final merit judgment." The more such information is given, the lower the anxiety of applicants and judges. Anxiety is bad, so anything that lowers it is good.

Judges are sometimes tempted to fiddle with their judgments or fudge the weights after they judge applicants on the merit criteria. The temptation may come from oversight ("Oops! My calculations tell me that the best job applicant isn't a citizen and doesn't have a Green Card"), from social or political pressure ("Oh, oh. The president's daughter didn't even rank among the top six applicants for the job"), or other sources ("Geeze, the best applicant on paper is that arrogant twit, but I didn't want to be politically incorrect by adding humility to my criteria list"). What to do? The temptation to fiddle or fudge would probably be irresistible if the occasions were rare and the deliberations were secret. As Lincoln noted, it is possible to fool all of the people some of the time. On the other hand, if fiddling or fudging solved one problem, the temptation to repeat would likely increase. Yet, as Lincoln also noted, it is not possible to fool all of the people all of the time. Guilt is nature's way of telling a judge not to fiddle with judgments or to fudge the criteria or their weights after the fact. A judge who feels no guilt should be retired.

Though it is not always true, the kind of information that tempts judges to fiddle with their assessments or weights of merit criteria is almost always information relevant to competition eligibility, not to merit. If a scholarship judge ignores an impressive academic transcript after learning that its owner was caught plagiarizing most of his term papers, chances are the judge believes that cheaters are not eligible for the scholarship. If the same judge overlooks poor grades and emphasizes a good reference letter for an applicant who happens to be the president's niece, then chances are the judge believes that president's relatives should be more eligible than others. There are probably some situations in which information unrelated to carefully selected merit criteria should influence merit judgments. If so, competition organizers should consider adding the information to next year's public list of eligibility criteria ("No cheaters. Relatives of administrators will be given first priority"), rather than circulating new, ad hoc rules only to judges.

Spreadsheet programs are handy for calculating merit judgments once the criteria are set, the weights are assigned, and the assessments are in. Suppose a judge, adopting the two-step procedure for the job competition shown in Figure 3.3, rated four applicants—Ali, Betty, Fong, and Dahlia—on maturity, hard work, cooperation, loyalty, and creativity. Suppose the judge, in consultation with other stakeholders, has decided to weigh these five criteria as 10, 30, 20, 15, and 25%, respectively. Figure 3.3 shows how a spreadsheet might be employed to calculate the final merit judgments. The bottom line of Figure 3.3 reveals Fong to have the highest weighted rating (3.95). Thus, we presume Fong should be offered the job. Ali and Dahlia are tied for second place; if Fong declined the offer, then offering the job to Ali or Dahlia would be a toss-up. We should note that if the five criteria were all given equal weights, Fong and Dahlia would be tied for first place, each with an unweighted average of 3.80. In our example, the weights made the difference, but this is not always so.

D20		f_x =SUM(D15:D19)			

spreadsheet example [Compatibility Mode]

	A	B	C	D	E	F
1		Ratings of Applicants				
2	Criterion	Ali	Betty	Fong	Dahlia	
3	mature	3	3	3	5	
4	hard working	3	2	5	3	
5	cooperative	5	4	4	2	
6	loyal	3	5	4	4	
7	creative	4	3	3	5	
8	Criterion	Weights				
9	mature	0.10	0.10	0.10	0.10	
10	hard working	0.30	0.30	0.30	0.30	
11	cooperative	0.20	0.20	0.20	0.20	
12	loyal	0.15	0.15	0.15	0.15	
13	creative	0.25	0.25	0.25	0.25	
14	Criterion	Weighted Ratings				
15	mature	0.30	0.30	0.30	0.50	
16	hard working	0.90	0.60	1.50	0.90	
17	cooperative	1.00	0.80	0.80	0.40	
18	loyal	0.45	0.75	0.60	0.60	
19	creative	1.00	0.75	0.75	1.25	
20	Weighted total =	3.65	3.20	3.95	3.65	
21						

Figure 3.3   Combining assessments in a spreadsheet.

SELECTING AND TRAINING JUDGES

Making translations from raw impressions to merit criteria assessments (step A) is, like politics or opera, an unnatural act, so some training is almost always required. Competition organizers tend to believe that the training occurs naturally in the years before a competition is held. Pick any area of work or leisure that offers competitions; some people involved in it will claim that their experiences give them the skill—perhaps even the right—to make the translations. These people call themselves experts. Competition organizers look for them to use their self-proclaimed expertise as judges.

Most people lacking any experience in a competitive area are ill equipped to judge it. Someone who has never heard Chinese poetry and does not know the language would probably not be a good judge in a Chinese poetry competition. An abstinent judge might raise eyebrows adjudicating a wine tasting competition, especially as she proudly declares a preference for sloshing and spitting wines with the sweetness of soft drinks. Some experience is necessary, if for no other reason than credibility. Applicants rarely appreciate being assessed by novices. This is why scientists protect their right to be judged by peers rather than politicians, and perhaps why the choice of Pope is not put to public vote. It is safe to assume that every stakeholder wants expert judges. They and their credentials increase the status of a competition, signal to applicants and audience members that the donors and organizers take the competition seriously, and reduce the possibility of complaints and challenges. Who are we to question Supreme Court decisions when its members appear so august, and when we assume they are picked for their legal acumen? Why question professional chefs judging British bake-offs?

Yet experts with credentials, as we note in chapter 6, do not guarantee fair merit judgments. Just as great musicians do not necessarily make great music teachers, experts with credentials do not necessarily make good judges in their area of expertise. Experts are as likely to have bad habits and biases as anyone else, and they are as likely to have bad attitudes toward the judgment task. Good judges are made, not born. And to make them good, all judges need training.

We propose that, beyond a modest level of expertise, almost anyone who takes the task of adjudication seriously has the potential to be a good judge. The trick to reaching their potential is learning how to make judgments. Judging is a skill and, like all skills, it improves with practice and feedback. Judges should be taught which merit criteria to assess and how to assess them. Then they should, if possible, be tested in their newly learned skills. Without objective measures of judgment accuracy, it is not possible to determine the accuracy of merit judgments. But it is possible to determine whether judges meet two necessary conditions of judgment expertise. Shanteau and colleagues (for example, see Shanteau, Weiss, Thomas, & Pounds, 2002; Weiss & Shanteau, 2003) have demonstrated that expert judges (a) make finer distinctions than do novices and (b) are more consistent than novices. Prospective judges should thus be able to reach minimum level on a test of these two skills.

Here is one way to devise such a test. Assume that Tara, who runs a pet grooming business, wishes to be a judge of a dog show competition. (See the American

Kennel Club official Web site for its judgment rules: http://www.akc.org/events/conformation/beginners.cfm.) The competition organizers tell her that three criteria of merit should be assessed: (a) obedience, (b) grooming, and (c) poise. Tara is then shown videos of 20 dogs from last year's competition. She watches each video three times, in a random order; after viewing, she rates the dog just viewed on the three criteria using a scale from 0 (*unsatisfactory*) to 5 (superb).

We expect expert judges to make distinctions. If Tara rated every dog the same—say, 4 on obedience, 5 on grooming, and 2 on poise—then either all the 20 dogs were clones trained by twins or Tara is no expert. We also expect expert judges to be consistent. Suppose Tara gave dog A ratings of 4, 1, and 5 when she first viewed the animal, gave the same dog 5, 3, and 1 on second viewing, and gave it 2, 5, and 2 on third viewing. Suppose Tara was equally inconsistent in rating all other 19 dogs. We should then conclude that Tara does not meet the second condition of expertise. Failing either the necessary condition of discrimination or the necessary condition of consistency, the dog show organizers should not allow Tara to judge their contest.

Can Tara be taught to make judgments like an expert? Perhaps. It might help her to watch or talk to judges who previously passed the discrimination and consistency tests in order to learn how they did it. It might also help her to receive feedback on her ratings that tells her the range of her judgments and their consistency from one viewing to the next. If such training attempts fail to improve her marks on subsequent discrimination and consistency tests, it might help to invite Tara to enter one of her dogs in the show and leave the judging to others.

Of course, even discriminating and consistent judges may not be good ones. Discriminating judges might be discriminatory, and consistent judges might be consistently biased. It is thus advisable for competition organizers to ask judges or observers to keep good records of all applications, judgments, and reasons for judgments given during the competition—much as courts do. A post-competition analysis of the records might prove useful in spotting abnormal judgment practices. Even if it does not, the act of keeping records is likely to keep the judges more aware of their duties and task.

NOTE

1. Approximately one in eight smokers eventually develop lung cancer; compare to one in 200 nonsmokers.

4

Standards and Double Standards

*I*n the previous chapters we discussed ways of rating and comparing (e.g., ranking) individuals based on assessments of merit. Standards can result whenever we introduce boundaries to these rankings or ratings. For example, we may decide whether or not a child merits advancement to the third grade depending on whether that child's performance in second grade surpasses a boundary required for advancement. Or we may decide that three people in a piano concerto competition may play well enough (i.e., above a cut-score of enthusiasm on the part of the judges) to be included as finalists.

As indicated in the two examples just mentioned, judgments of whether or not somebody surpasses a standard can be either absolute or relative. A simple example of an absolute standard is one for deciding in which football squad a boy in the high school one of us (RMD) attended should try out for. Anyone who weighed less than 140 pounds was assigned to the "pups" football squad, while anyone over that weight was eligible to play either for the varsity or the junior varsity (more than eligible; in fact, required). Even if someone weighing less than 140 pounds was considered to be a superb football player by the coaches, the school officials believed that such a person should not be scrimmaging with the rest of us.

The three finalists in the piano competition example provide a relative standard. Sometimes, in contrast, standards result from a combination of relative and absolute judgments; for example, the judgment that a grade school student has successfully mastered second-grade material and therefore surpassed a standard for entering third grade might have a bit of relative judgment involved whenever a whole cohort of second graders do very poorly (i.e., the standard might be lowered from the original boundary).

Another important aspect of standards (i.e., of the boundaries) is explication. Standards can range from explicit to implicit, with many gradations between the extremes. The 140-pound football player standard noted above is quite explicit. Implicit standards frequently occur in artistic judgments; for example, "I was especially impressed by the touch of Candidate A when she played the Chopin Interlude." They can also be revealed in reactions to job interviews such as "Candidate B's presentation lacked a certain je ne sais quoi, but Candidate F's answers showed lots of leadership potential." Implicit standards can be a breeding ground for controversy about what boundary was surpassed or not and about who surpassed it, but they do have the advantage in litigious times that they are difficult to second guess and hence rarely result in lawsuits.

How do we choose boundaries that allow us to believe that a standard has been met or missed? Many factors are involved, and the final determination is often a matter of social consensus, pragmatism, and politics. What, for example, should a passing score on a written driver's test be? There are, as far as we know, no published data showing the relationship between driver's written test scores and driving accidents or infractions, but we can speculate that the correlation is rather low. Still, it seems politically incorrect to pass everyone with a score of 10% or more or to fail everyone who scores below 100%. A 90% cutoff score might appear tough but cause few protests if the test were easy ("A red, octagonal sign with four white letters means (a) close your eyes, (b) no parking, (c) honk your horn, or (d) stop?).

Or consider school trustees who must set standards for promotion to the next grade. If scores on standardized knowledge tests decline from year to year but the passing score remains the same, trustees can expect that more students would repeat their previous year. The resulting logistic demands on a school bloated by a cohort of failures and the political fallout from outraged parents would likely be severe. So an old standard of "50% or above to be promoted to grade 7!" might give way to a finagle such as, "An augmented score [add the difference between last year's average and this year's average] of 50% or above is required for promotion to grade 7."

The opposite can also occur. Standards may rise from one year to the next if a greater number of applicants pass last year's minimum standards but the rewards for passing do not keep pace. Grade inflation is a prime example. In years past, only a very tiny proportion of applicants for medical school received a grade average of 90% or above; now, it seems, half the applicants do. Alas, the number of openings in medical schools has not kept pace, so minimum requirements to be considered for medical school have increased. In the lexicon of high jump competitions and beyond, this is known as *raising the bar* (see chapter 8 for a detailed discussion of the phenomenon).

DOUBLE STANDARDS

The raising or lowering of standards not only occurs from one cohort or year, test or contest, to another. It often occurs from one group to another in the same test or contest as well. The result is called a *double standard*: one standard judges apply to some but not all people in a test or contest and a second standard the judges apply to everyone else (see Foschi, 2000). Often one of the two standards is more lenient than the other, allowing a greater proportion of people judged by the lenient standard to pass the test or win the contest and a smaller proportion of people judged by the stricter standard to pass or win.

Double standards are usually associated with favoritism, prejudice, and discrimination, and for good reason: the two standards are often applied to different social groups, preventing a disfavored group from receiving rewards otherwise deserved while promoting a favored group to receive rewards often undeserved. Race, age, and sex discrimination in hiring are prime examples, as are old boy's networks leading a judge's friends or relatives or members of the judge's social groups to be assessed more leniently and thereby to receive more favors than do strangers. So too are "glass ceilings" that retard or prevent women from promotions once hired. Double standards often require members of disfavored groups to provide more evidence of ability, skill, or other forms of merit than those in favored groups (we recall Edith Wharton's quip when hearing that women must be twice as good as men to succeed in a man's world, "That's not hard!"). Likewise, members of disfavored groups are often forgiven fewer poor performances. There is ample evidence, for example, that women earn less money than do similarly qualified men; though there's been some trend to narrow the income difference, it has proved difficult to eliminate.

Still, double standards are not always bad. Many sports, for example, adopt different standards for judging different groups of athletes. Peewee hockey leagues give trophies to teams that would not win the National Hockey League's Stanley Cup. Many men's Olympic events are segregated from women's events, and many women's gold medals are won with performances below the medals of the men's competition. Affirmative action, employment equity, and visible minority hiring programs are frequently promoted despite claims that they accept lower qualifications from minorities than from majorities.

To illustrate a possible virtue of double standards, consider a proposal for adopting them when people discovered that regular aptitude testing of mental ability was excluding a disproportionate number of minority group members from jobs and academic training. The problem arose from two sources: (a) members of minority groups generally performed worse than did members of the majority group on tests devised to predict performance; (b) minority group members generally had poorer performance as well. Had a single standard of aptitude been applied to both majority and minority group members, then the lower test scores and the poorer performances of minority group members could be used to perpetuate their exclusion.

What to do? One or us (RMD) remembers a proposal, suggested by someone in the 1970s (who shall remain nameless), to create a double standard but to make the standard for minority group members *more* stringent than for majority group members. The proposer argued statistically: because we knew that a higher proportion of minority versus majority group members perform poorly (called a *base rate* in Bayesian statistical inference), we should therefore require more evidence of good performance from members of the minority group. Thus, the proposer maintained that there should be two predictors of success: (a) performance on aptitude tests, which would be positively weighted; and (b) minority group status, which would be negatively weighted. The proposal did not engender much enthusiasm, even though the person making it was generally recognized as one of the world's foremost statisticians who specialized in "psychometric" prediction.

Other people proposed a double standard by which minority group members were evaluated more leniently—a form of affirmative action, devised to help level the playing field between majority and minority group members. But the proposal prompted a difficult question: How should such a double standard be set? An explicit standard, such as "racial norming" once proposed by a U.S. National Research Council Committee (see Hartigan & Wigdor, 1989) immediately drew criticism. Such norming refers to comparing each applicant to others in their same group (usually a minority one) rather than to the total pool of applicants. An immediate result is that the same proportion of people in the favored and disfavored groups will surpass any given standard. This "quota" system was strongly opposed by many educators, and was later judged to be illegal by the U.S. Supreme Court, which criticized the rule because members of one group (e.g., minority group members) can be differentially favored by a double standard if and only if members of the complementary group (majority group members) are disfavored (Dawes, 1994).

While it would nice to claim that an affirmative action program does not involve such "reverse discrimination," the claim would be open to criticism if the standards used to assess merit in the program were sufficiently explicit to reveal which people are given a more lenient standard and which are given a stricter one. Explicit standards also allow us to determine what happens to predictive validity of merit judgments when the double standard is applied. Some managers may worry, for example, that admitting more people who meet lenient standards of employment would reduce the average quality of the labor pool. But the reduction is frequently not as large as a naïve judgment might believe it to be (Dawes & Eagle, 1975).

Why? Dawes and Eagle (1976) examined a situation in which a test predicting job performance had an $r = +0.50$ correlation with actual performance but in which members of a disfavored minority group (10% of the applicants) on average scored one standard deviation below members of the favored majority group (90% of the applicants). Half the applicants were chosen for the position. If there were a single standard, 53% of the majority applicants would surpass it, but only 20% of the minority applicants would. When a single standard deviation was added to the scores of the minority group members (as in racial norming just described), 50% of the members of each group would be chosen, and the correlation between predicted and actual performance would go down—but not far. The "validity coefficient" would be reduced from +050 to +044, and the only changes in who is selected would be among those close to the borderline. Moreover, this perfect equality could be achieved by unfairly excluding only 3% of the majority members. Given that many majority members (males anyway) have historically been willing to sacrifice life and limb in war for the good of their group, Dawes and Eagle suggested that the sacrifice of one job prospect might be acceptable.

Despite the merits of Dawes and Eagle's results, there remains widespread distrust of affirmative action and reverse discrimination. Explicating the criteria for deciding who is judged by which standard can increase the consistency and transparency of merit judgments. But explication also brings the double standard into sharp focus and, when publicized, often ignites accusations of reverse bias or other forms of unfairness.

What are judges to do? One of the most common responses is to soften the focus of a double standard with vagaries and euphemisms. Rather than stating explicit criteria for employing different standards (example: "Christian males must score 70 or above on our employment test to be considered for a job; Moslem females need score only 55"), judges are likely to state something more fuzzy and euphemistic ("We encourage women and members of visible minorities to apply"). This allows judges to choose their standard off the record, behind closed doors, and to invoke confidentiality rules to avoid public scrutiny.

Euphemisms can sometimes provide effective rhetorical solutions to political problems, but they likely undermine the ideals of transparency and consistency that contribute to perceptions of the fairness of merit-based decisions. It is especially likely when the judges themselves must rely on fuzzy euphemisms and, lacking explicit rules, turn to implicit criteria for getting the job done. Such reliance sets the stage for eschewing the preferred two-step judgment procedure discussed in chapter 3 and for embracing the three bad habits of judgment discussed in chapter 2. We believe that it is preferable to debate the merits and tenure of affirmative action and to negotiate explicit criteria than it is to retreat into a rhetorical mist.

Double standards can be particularly problematic when they are implicit and determined on the basis of intuition. One of us (RMD) recalls, for example, that a dean of a large and prestigious medical school once asked a colleague to try to figure out why there were so few women admitted to that school, suggesting that this colleague use the same type of procedure that had proved successful in reaching medical decisions in other areas. The colleague did a statistical analysis and found a possible source of the problem. An older male doctor had decided to devote a lot of his professional effort to interviewing applicants, and somehow the females were less favorably evaluated than the males. This doctor was not specifically opposed to females but evaluated such characteristics as "emotional maturity," "seriousness of interest in medicine," and "neuroticism." A statistical analysis indicated that females (unlike males) were judged to be immature if they were not married, to be not sufficiently interested in medicine if they were, and neurotic if they were divorced.

These judgments provided a double standard that the medical school wished to avoid. Again, this is an example of where the favored group (males) benefit from a double standard. That is a major problem with double standards when one group has higher status than another.

While debates continue about the propriety of reversing double standards to compensate for past injustices created by previous double standards, most people still believe that it is unethical to perpetuate double standards that discriminate against disadvantaged groups. Can anything short of affirmative action be done to reduce or eliminate discriminatory double standards? We can find a partial answer by considering in more detail why double standards evolve and how they work; then we can consider how the causes of double standards might be tweaked or controlled to reduce their occurrence.

GROUPS AND DOUBLE STANDARDS

"It's not what you know, it's who you know ..." So begins a famous adage often invoked under suspicion of a double standard. As we noted above, double standards are normally associated with two (or more) groups: one favored and one not. Groups, in turn, are often defined by relationships, including social relationships—who you know. Mother, father, sister, brother, etc., define a group called *family*. Frank, Mary, Azar, Taylor, Bridget, and what's-her-name might define a group called friends, classmates, team members, neighbors, enemies, or members of a street gang. Even people with no relationships to us are members of a group; they are strangers.

Why is group membership so important in creating double standards? And what might be done to reduce the pernicious effects of group membership on judgments of merit? The beginning of an answer can be found in our brain's extraordinary abilities to filter out vast amounts of information reaching our senses, to draw inferences from tiny fragments of information that remain, and to persist in these inferences in the light of contradictory information. These abilities for filtering, inference, and persistence no doubt helped our ancestors protect themselves from predators and lead themselves to prey. But often they also lead us to ignore what we should consider and to believe what we should doubt.

One of the most commonly used fragments of information for making judgments about people, including judgments of merit, is group membership (see Biernat, 2005). Consider, for example, how often people in North America introduce themselves to each other by stating or asking their occupation early in the conversation—"Hi. I'm Mary Jones. I'm a reporter. What do you do?" Occupations reveal one form of group membership: butcher, baker, drug dealer, etc. So, too, do names (Which of the following is more likely to be in the group called Moslems? (a) Frank Smith, (b) Ali Mohammad Khomeini), physical appearance (wrinkles and white hair = an old folk; dark skin = African), possessions (blue uniform = police officer; big house = upper class), and hundreds of other cues.

Most groups are associated with a set of features or attributes known as a *stereotype*. If Mary Jones tells us she is a reporter, we are likely to infer that she is highly verbal, a good writer, assertive, educated, astute, knowledgeable about current events, and perhaps full of herself and alcohol. Why such inferences? Because most people have a stereotype of reporters as people who are highly verbal, good writers, etc. And many reporters have these characteristics, perhaps the large majority of them. If 92% of reporters are highly verbal, 83% are good writers, 97% are assertive, and so forth, then we might declare the stereotype of reporters has quite high validity. But stereotypes do not have to be true to be believed. If only 43% of reporters are highly verbal, 17% are good writers, 28% are assertive, and so forth, then we would consider this stereotype of reporters to be relatively invalid. Even so, the stereotype may persist, perhaps because those who endorse it might not have the time or motivation to test its validity. When stereotypes are generally valid, they can be useful for forming first impressions or making preliminary inferences—which may, of course, change as more personal and idiosyncratic information about a person is known. When stereotypes are generally false, using them for inferences can lead to many errors, some of which are likely to influence judgments of merit.

Features or attributes of a stereotype not only have varying degrees of validity, they also have varying degrees of emotional reaction. Many attributes contained in a stereotype are rather neutral, arousing little emotion. Valid or not, for example, the stereotypical Canadian is likely to include attributes such as reserved, quiet, earnest, hockey-loving, and plain—hardly a set of attributes to shift emotions into high gear. But many attributes of stereotypes are highly charged with emotion. A stereotypical terrorist is likely to include attributes such as heartless, cruel, sadistic, fanatical, untrustworthy, dirty, and dangerous, whereas a stereotypical movie star is likely to include attributes such as beautiful, talented, interesting, glamorous, and spoiled. Both sets of attributes are all but guaranteed to fire up the amygdyla for heavy emotional duty. These emotional reactions make stereotypes as much a matter of the heart as the head.

Emotional reactions to a stereotype can not only lead us toward positive or negative evaluations of members of a group but can also strongly influence whether or not the validity of a stereotype is ever tested or revised. Especially troublesome are invalid stereotypes, leading us to infer that a member of some group has one or more negative attributes such as untrustworthy, dishonest, unreliable, crazy, boring, or dangerous. They are troublesome because the emotions associated with the resulting inferences often either stop us from seeking further information or lead us to filter out or discount further information that might correct our invalid inferences.

Suppose, for example, you meet Adam Major at a party. He introduces himself as a student who pays his tuition fees by working as a male prostitute. Though your stereotype of students might have a mix of positive and negative attributes (valid or not), it is likely that your stereotype of male prostitutes has mostly negative ones (valid or not). Would you (a) continue your conversation with Mr. Major to learn more about students or male prostitutes as a test, possibly to correct your stereotypes? (b) infer that Mr. Major is crazy, boring, or dangerous and excuse yourself to freshen your drink? (c) conclude that Mr. Major is untrustworthy, dishonest, or unreliable and cease believing anything he says? Alternative (a) would be the logically respectable thing to do, but (b) and (c) are more psychologically compelling and, we speculate, more common. Alas, (b) and (c) are also the alternatives that would prevent someone from testing their stereotypes and possibly correcting them. In this way, negative stereotypes are perpetuated.

STATUS CHARACTERISTICS AND EXPECTANCY STATES

Among the dozens to hundreds of attributes or features of a group that define the group stereotype, some are related to the status of a group, loosely defined here as the group's prestige, value, relative position, or social worth (see Biernat, 2005). These parts of a stereotype are called *status characteristics* (see, for example, Berger, Cohen, & Zelditch, 1972; Foddy & Smithson, 1989; Foschi & Foddy, 1988). For example, we generally attribute high status characteristics—smart, educated, professional, skilled, rich, and the like—to members of professional groups such as surgeons, pilots, architects, and professors. In contrast, we often attribute low status characteristics such as poor, lazy, uneducated, and irresponsible to members of groups such as pump jockeys, cleaning staff, and street people. A group's status characteristics can, of course, vary among people and across time. The status characteristics of drug dealers and pimps, for example, seems to be higher among drug addicts and prostitutes than among televangelists, while the status characteristics of CEOs seems to rise and fall with economic trends and scandalous news head-lines (see Hodge, Siegel & Rossi, 1964; Treiman, 1977).

Many sociologists and social psychologists believe that the status character-istics attributed to a group lead people one step toward further inferences about the expected behavior of the group's members (see, for example, Berger et al., 1972; Berger & Zelditch, 1985). These inferences are called *expectation states*. As a general rule, higher status characteristics lead to higher expectations of perfor-mance. Doctors, for example, are generally expected to perform medicine better than dishwashers. Harvard graduates (once of high status) are generally expected to be better at what they do than are graduates of No Name College. Different expectation states often result in different judgments of merit. Thus, the credibil-ity of a witness in court—in essence, a judgment of the merit of his testimony—often depends on the pedigree of the witness; when it is one person's word against another's, a member of the clergy is likely to be believed more than a high school dropout, even though both or neither may be true.

Status characteristics may be diffuse or specific. Diffuse status characteristics, including those believed to be related to gender, ethnicity, religious affiliation or age, are associated with a wide range of behaviors (example: "athletic" versus "won-derful tango dancers"), even when there is no evidence for the association. When status characteristics are diffuse, it is often difficult to assemble evidence to cancel their discriminatory effects, in part because contradictory evidence can be labeled as an exception, assimilated into the general rule, and then forgotten. Consider two diffuse status characteristics in a once-popular stereotype of Chinese: "They work hard and keep to themselves." How might an exception be handled? "Sure, Bing Xiao is outgoing and lazy. But she's an exception to the rule. The vast majority of Chinese still are hard working and keep to themselves."

Specific status characteristics often lead to inferences about performances on specific tasks, and they can "pack a punch" in the formation of performance expec-tations and judgments of its merit. Even so, many specific status characteristics have a narrow range of relevance, and judges may be reluctant to generalize beyond the range. If, for example, a woman can solve her boss's computer programming problem much better than anyone else, her boss might accept that she is an excel-lent programmer. But the boss may not change beliefs about her other skills, about the programming skills of women in general, or about men being better at most things, including other problem-solving tasks. Changing such beliefs may require dozens of other instances in which the same woman solves other problems for her boss, in which other women solve other problems for the same boss, or in which men try and fail. But the women may have few opportunities to prove themselves if the boss falls back on men to solve problems first. The result: the woman or her female colleagues may still be judged as less meritorious than their male colleagues for a promotion to, say, programming manager because "Most of our managers are men, so they must be better than women at management." Damned if you do, damned if you don't.

When judgments of merit require inferences of ability or predictions of skill—as they usually do in hiring and promotion decisions—judges seek information they believe relevant to the inferences or predictions. It seems reasonable to expect that more weight be given to relevant than to irrelevant information in judging merit; for example, that a 10-year track record of sales would be more important in judging the merit of applicants for a sales job than would the font of a résumé. Alas, rationality does not always prevail. Research indicates that when both directly and indirectly relevant information is presented to judges, the directly relevant information tends to be weighted more heavily, but the indirect information is also influential (Berger & Zelditch, 1985; Foddy & Smithson, 1999). Still, information that is only indirectly relevant to merit judgments is often presented before the more directly relevant stuff. When it is, the resulting first impressions—despite their dubious validity—may lead judges to discount more relevant information presented later or discourage them from gathering more relevant information.

To illustrate the discounting effect, consider what can happen when male and female job applicants go for a job interview. Suppose that a judge at the interview believes that the strength of character of people can be detected by the strength of their handshake (a belief that is unsupported by any research). Because men tend to have greater upper body strength than do women, a male's handshake is likely to be firmer than a female's handshake. In North America, handshaking has become an opening ritual of business conversations. If the judge shakes a man's hand, it is likely that the shake will pass the judge's character test, and the interview will then proceed to experience and more relevant matters. But if the judge shakes a woman's hand, it is more likely the shake will fail the judge's character test. So why, the judge might reason, waste time asking about experience when character seems to be lacking? With no personal answer to the silent question, the judge might then skip questions about experience in the interview or ignore the woman's answers, remaining ignorant of what could be the more relevant experience of a superior applicant.

A good deal of the indirectly relevant or irrelevant information available to judges of merit is related to group membership and status characteristics. Many women in Islamic countries, for example, are taught that it is improper to shake hands with male strangers. Western male judges who seek handshake firmness information would likely be befuddled by such women; few such judges are likely to compensate for their reaction with a fair hearing and job offer. In countries such as Japan, Iran, and many in Africa, it is considered rude to stare at people of higher status. Many people from such countries thus pay their respects to high status Western judges of merit by focusing their gaze downward to the side while speaking. This behavior, of course, violates the stereotype of honest people as those who can look you directly in the eye but matches the stereotype of dishonest people as "shifty eyed." There is, in fact, no reliable relation between gaze and lying. The same can happen when judges assess merit on the basis of confidence indirectly assessed by impressions of verbal fluency, posture, gesticulation, and such. People in groups with high status characteristics generally have more of these confidence cues than do people in other groups, such as immigrants. As a result, the high status folks are more likely to be hired (Fisek, Berger & Norman, 2005; Foddy & Riches, 2000; Kalkhoff & Barnum, 2000).

Like handshakes and gazes, the links from verbal fluency, posture, and gesticulation to confidence; from confidence to ability; from ability to skill; and from skill to merit are long, tenuous, and of dubious validity. But like handshakes, gazes, and other dubious or indirect information, they often influence merit judgments. To paraphrase W. I. Thomas, "If judges define situations as real, they are real in their consequences" (Merton, 1968a, p. 477). What might we expect the consequence to be? People who are confident are more likely to get what they want from judges who associate confidence with merit and thus will likely gain more confidence. People who are not confident are less likely to get what they want from the same judges and thus will likely lose confidence. A vicious circle is then formed, leaving the people with little confidence even less likely to be judged meritorious. Social scientists know it as a *self-fulfilling prophecy* (see Rosenthal & Jacobson, 1992). It is also known as the *Matthew effect* (Merton, 1968b; see also the section Track Record in chapter 8), from the Bible: "For unto every one that hath shall be given, and he shall have abundance: but from him that hath not shall be taken away even that which he hath" (Matthew XXV:29).

IN-GROUP BIAS

Among the features or attributes that define the stereotype of a group, one has special importance for judgments of merit: whether or not the judge is a member. Groups to which a judge belongs, to which friends belong, or with which there is some other affiliation or social identity are called *in-groups*. All other groups—the ones to which someone has no affiliation—are called *out-groups*. There is an easy way to tell the difference. People use the pronouns *we, our,* and *us* to refer to members of their in-groups; they use the pronouns *they, their,* and *them* to refer to members of out-groups. In-groups are often associated with phrases such as *inner circle, team, pack, old boys, clique,* and *mafia* (now a generic term). Out-groups are often associated with words such as *alien, foreigner, opponent,* and *enemy*. It is important to consider in-groups and out-groups in judging merit because there is a strong tendency for people to attribute more merit to members of their in-groups than to members of out-groups. This in-group bias is known beyond academia simply as *favoritism*. It pulls judges away from claims of neutrality and raises the hackles of anyone who believes in judging others by what they do rather than who they know.

The late social psychologist Henri Tajfel and his colleagues (for example, see Tajfel, 1970, 1981, 1982; Tajfel & Turner, 1986) can be credited with much of the seminal theory and research on in-groups, out-groups, and resulting biases. Their work began with the observation that people have a tendency to identify with others—members of in-groups—who share a common fate, preference, or category membership. This identification leads to predictable effects, including preference for in-group members, dislike of out-group members, and subsequent discrimination against those "not like us."

While designing laboratory research, Tajfel and his colleagues were surprised at how easy it was to create in-groups and out-groups. Volunteer research participants would divide themselves into in-groups and out-groups on the basis of little more than superficial but common interests or preferences. At the extreme, Orbell, van de Kragt, and Dawes (1988) asked each of 14 participants to draw a poker chip at random from a well-shaken bag containing seven blue chips and seven white ones.

The blue chip people were sent to one room, and the white chip people were sent to another. Although the participants clearly understood that they all shared a common identity as psychology experiment participants, those who drew white versus blue chips treated each other differently. When participants were asked to distribute money to others, they were far more apt to give away money to members of their own group. And when participants were able to discuss their decisions within their own group, they often claimed that the people in the other group did not merit money because they could not be trusted (see also Foddy & Dawes, 2007; Foddy, Yamagishi, & Platow, 2007; Yamagishi & Foddy, 2007). A more dramatic example of such grouping and discrimination comes from Jane Elliot's well-known "blue eyes, brown eyes" class exercise dividing secondary school students into in-groups and out-groups according to eye color (see her Web site, Elliot, 2006).

The ease of forming in-groups and out-groups indicates just how powerful and pervasive the phenomenon is. Indeed, it is no great stretch to imagine that the distinction is somehow genetically programmed—analogous to the distinction between conspecifics and other species made throughout the animal world. Double standards arising from in-group favoritism and out-group aversion or indifference were, of course, around long before social scientists studied them. Wars have been justified for millennia by two simple premises and one conclusion: (a) it is us versus them; (b) we are the chosen people so God is on our side; ergo, (c) we merit God's gift of life but they do not. And people have sought to join powerful in-groups or protested them since recorded history. Records of gift-giving (think frankincense and myrrh) can be found in the earliest records, documenting a universal attempt to improve judgments of merit, curry favor, and create good relations among members of privileged in-groups. Even today, hundreds of cultures beyond the West give careful consideration to the family status of prospective spouses when negotiating marriage for sons and daughters simply because the marriage adds the spouse's family to the in-group, thereby affecting the chances of future resources. The pervasiveness of in-groups and out-groups, and the double standards they engender, suggests that they are difficult to eliminate.

FAVORS

Double standards of merit judgments can arise, as we have previously discussed, from using features of stereotypes related to status and expectations or related to overlapping in-group connections between judges and those judged. But these are not the only sources of double standards. At least one more can be identified, one related to the gift-giving example noted above. When someone does a favor for someone else, it is almost always with the expectation that the favor will in some way, sooner or later, be returned. The expectation is called the *norm of reciprocity* (see Cialdini, 1984), and it appears to exist in all cultures.

The norm of reciprocity can be observed in rituals of gift-giving. Gifts are not so much given as exchanged. Most people feel embarrassed if they are given a gift and do not reciprocate; birthdays are often observed to fulfill the obligations that reciprocity implies. Westerners, for example, routinely bring gifts of alcohol or sugar to their dinner hosts in exchange for the meal; Iranians routinely bring flowers or nuts. Sooner or later, Christmas cards stop coming if none are sent in return, and restaurant service usually declines in proportion to the size of the gift of the tip.

Favors, of course, are not only packaged as gifts of things. Most favors are acts or activities—giving someone a ride, visiting someone in the hospital, taking care of someone's cat or plants, or giving someone a job, medal, handout, chance, etc. Often these favors are done in the spirit of altruism, expecting nothing more than words of appreciation or gratitude in return. But even altruism can be strengthened by "priming the pump." Those who seek a favor can exploit the norm of reciprocity by doing a favor first (see Paese & Gilin, 2000). It need not be a large first favor; indeed, it should not be, because a prospective donor of future favors is more likely to accept a small first favor than a large one (J. Freedman & Fraser, 1966). Business lunches, political donations, free samples, and compliments all serve the purpose of priming the pump of future favors returned.

People who play the role of judges of merit are no more or less immune to the pull of favors than anyone else. The role often requires that its players resist obligations to reciprocate favors previously done by those being judged for merit and to resist temptations to do favors for those being judged (often expecting something in return). Alas, not everyone meets the requirements of the role. Indeed, in some cultures, the role of a judge of merit seems to give license to invoke an exchange of favors; bribes are the rule, and people are ascribed as much merit as their money can buy. To a judge's in-groups such as my relatives, my friends, my graduating class, my cohorts, and my tribe is added another, euphemistically described as *my supporters*. The merit principle is thus corroded by favoritism that favors provide, and the free market of corruption eventually prevails.

Still, there are some occasions in which a judge's neutrality is viewed as callous or mean spirited, and deviation from neutrality is seen as an act of beneficence or heroism. For example, when neutral immigration officials judge someone's refugee claim to lack merit and order the person deported, their judgment is sometimes criticized as devoid of compassion. A significant number of such claimants appeal the judgment on compassionate grounds or seek the support of church and other sympathetic groups to assist in their appeal. Some of the claimants move to the sanctuary of church basements to avoid deportation, and their supporters phone the press. When deportation decisions are overturned on compassionate grounds, cheers and good news stories often follow. But the immigration officials may feel demoralized and frustrated. They may believe that they applied the rules fairly but were undermined by public opinion. Compassion may be a fine criterion to employ in assessing the merit of refugee claims. But the truth of arguments for compassion is fiendishly difficult to verify, and reliance on public support simply shifts the merit of each case from the procedures of immigration officials to the luck of finding soft hearts.

PRACTICAL IMPLICATIONS

We noted in chapter 1 that the case for allocating limited resources by judgments of merit gains most of its force from the presumed neutrality of the process. As the blindfold on the statues of Lady Justice signifies, judgments of merit are supposed to be made by weighing the evidence of merit objectively, blind to temptations of favoritism or bias. Double standards indicate that the blindfold has come loose, and the judgments generated by double standards quickly undermine observers' faith in the process. So in cases where double standards are anathema, one goal of any test of contest of merit should be to ensure that only one standard applies to all.

In order to eliminate double standards, they must first be detected. This is no easy task. Few judges line up to boast about the double standards they employ; indeed, many judges are likely unaware they are using double standards at all. Their ignorance likely stems from a common means for making merit judgments in tests and contests lacking clear criteria: merit criteria are constructed or emphasized on the fly to rationalize or justify judgments already made (Uhlmann & Cohen, 2005). Jack, for example, may come in distant second to Anita in work-related skills and barely exceed her in teamwork potential. So if Jack and Anita were applying for the same job, and if the two criteria were equally weighted, then a fair judgment would give Anita the advantage. But if the measures of skills or teamwork, or the weights given to these two criteria, are unspecified, a judge who does not like women or who wants Jack hired can adjust the weights or measures until Jack comes out on top. "This year the company really needs good team players, and Jack shows more team-player potential than Anita. So Jack gets the job." It is an effective cover for double standards.

If judges assess the merit of dozens or hundreds of applicants or performances, and if careful records are kept, it is often possible to detect double standards by statistical means. A multiple regression analysis of one judge's assessment of male job applicants who complete a standardized form can, for example, reveal how much weight the judge gives to different pieces of information on the form. If the same is done for female applicants, a comparison of regression weights would reveal shifts or discrepancies in the judge's weighting scheme—a good indicator of double standards. When the data are available, we recommend this procedure. We caution, however, that many prospective judges may be scared off by the prospect of such scrutiny. In addition, it is no simple task to collect, manage, and analyze relevant records. Organizations doing it are likely to require extra staff, space, and other resources. This is not a solution for the faint-budgeted.

If an evaluation of the evaluators can be conducted, and if double standards or other forms of bias are found, something should presumably be done to fix the problem. There are several possible solutions. One possible solution is to replace biased judges with neutral ones. Another is to train and to motivate offending judges to mend their judgmental ways. A third is to add more judges in hopes that their biases will counterbalance each other and produce a neutral group consensus. Each is worthy of brief consideration.

Indulging an instinct to cull bad apples or biased judges and replace them with fresh or neutral ones soon leads to the challenge of finding the desired replacements. Relying on chance is risky; replacements chosen by impulse or whimsy may be worse than those they replaced. So it seems reasonable to develop some means of judging the merit of prospective judges of merit that will detect double standards or other biases in a harmless way. One means is to adapt for prospective judges the multiple regression exercise discussed above. If previous applications cannot be found or used, hypothetical ones can be created that would suffice for statistical purposes (for examples see Hoffman, Slovic, & Rorer, 1968; Uhlmann & Cohen, 2005).

How would it work? Prospective judges would be asked to make merit judgments of a large number (50–100) of applications, real or hypothetical, that systematically varied in their information. One of the 50+ applications for a managerial job, for example, might come from a 27-year-old male with a B.A. in business, 2 years of relevant experience, and one strong reference letter. Another might come from a 32-year-old female with an M.A. in business, 6 years of relevant experience, and two strong reference letters. If prospective judges were told not to consider an applicant's sex, we would expect them to ascribe more merit to the female than to the male. If a prospective judge did the reverse, alarm bells should peal. Those who failed such a double standard and bias test would not be invited as judges.

It may be comforting to declare that all of one's judges have passed a neutrality test. But devising, administering, and scoring such a test takes time, effort, and money. The investment may well be worth it in some situations but probably not in all. And there is the nagging possibility that all prospective judges will fail a test of double standards or other biases, leaving no one neutral to do the job.

So why not train judges to be neutral? Those who believe in education are sure to be attracted to the possibility. Showing prospective or working judges any double standards and other biases that their tests or statistical analyses reveal can provide useful feedback to judges for improving their judgment processes. Other training techniques are available. Policy workshops, training sessions, procedural manuals, lectures, simulations, case histories, judgment games, and exercises are examples of a panoply of techniques available to form fair judges or to reform the unfair ones. Alas, research in judgment, decision making, and expertise suggests that none of the techniques provide a magic solution for dispensing with double standards and biases (see Larrick, 2007; Phillips, Klein, & Sieck, 2007). The success of each technique seems to be greatly influenced by a complex web of task, time, and personal variables. Training may reduce errors of merit judgment, but it is likely to take trial and error to find an effective training procedure.

If a judge who indulges in unacceptable double standards or biases cannot be culled or trained, he might still be neutered by a pack of judges with competing standards or reversed biases. Judgments of merit by committee are frequently justified this way. People who believe in the self-corrective tendencies of group decisions are attracted to this alternative. It often leads them to construct committees containing representatives of disadvantaged groups expected to serve as committee watchdogs for and antidotes to double standards and biases (recall the "token female" of committees in decades past?). But, as we discuss in detail in chapter 6, committee solutions also have complexities and limitations, including the logistics of organizing committees and the group dynamics that can detract from fair merit judgments.

A simpler possible solution to the problem of double standards is to eliminate information that would allow judges to apply whatever double standards they might possess. Photographs began to disappear from résumés and vitas in the early

1970s, in part to reduce the possibility that judgments of merit would be based on the sex or attractiveness of persons portrayed. Many orchestras began to hold auditions behind opaque screens to neutralize the double standards that previously prevented female musicians from receiving orchestral work. More recently, many application forms have dropped questions about age or date of birth to reduce unacceptable age biases. Such constructive censorship needs careful implementation to be effective. Eliminating photos, for example, does not eliminate sex discrimination if the sex of the applicant can still be deduced from his first name. Ethnicity cannot be eliminated if judges can guess it from a person's last name. And age discrimination cannot be eliminated if application forms still require year of graduation or dates of previous employment.

So we suggest a variation of the proposal we outlined at the end of chapter 3. Between the receipt of applications and the beginning of their assessment, cut them up! We are not suggesting the applications be shredded and thrown way. Instead, we propose they be cut carefully between the lines separating each item of the application form. In a case of job applications, the result might be a pile of paper slips containing only the names of applicants, another pile containing only dates of birth, a third containing education, a fourth containing relevant experience, etc. Now shuffle each pile so the order of applicants differs from one pile to the next. Better still, gather applicant information on computer forms and find software to do the virtual cutting and shuffling. Then give each pile to judges, one at a time, and ask for a merit judgment from the information on each slip. When all merit judgments are made, recombine the slips into the original applications and add or average the individual merit judgments of each person according to some predetermined weighting scheme—a single standard—to derive a single merit judgment for each applicant.

How does this eliminate double standards and other biases? It doesn't. But it eliminates their effects by eliminating knowledge about which features are associated with different applicants. A judge can learn that Mary Kawolski is applying but not know her age, education, experience, etc. Similarly, a judge can learn that some applicant graduated from McGill University but not know his age or experience or sex. By eliminating the personal context of information, we can eliminate the possibility that the context required for double standards and other biases will be utilized.

Our various suggestions for reducing or eliminating the discriminatory consequences of double standards and other forms of bias are likely to be more useful for large and repeated adjudications than for small or singular ones. Vast numbers of merit judgments are made in modest, one-off adjudications—the kind, for example, that small business owners conduct after posting a "help wanted" sign in their window. The owner may receive no more than a half dozen résumés, most delivered in person by the applicants, and may have no time or motivation to attend workshops on reducing double standards, carefully craft an application form, cut and shuffle the completed forms, or conduct interviews behind an opaque screen. Such solutions are either silly or impractical.

Can anything else be done to reduce the use of double standards in small and singular adjudications? Probably not. But we hazard one suggestion. If no applicant is clearly more meritorious than the others, or if none pass the socks-knocked-off test, then flip a coin. Random selection not only gets the job done but also provides an unassailable prophylactic against accusations of favoritism or corruption. And, as we shall see in subsequent chapters, it does not do that much worse than a lot of putative expert judgments.

5

Rules of the Game

Judgments of merit are made by the billions each day. Most are personal and informal, such as judging the merit of a child's request for dessert, a dog's response to "Sit!," a politician's pitch for votes, a proposal of marriage or reconciliation. Yet millions of others are made each day as part of organized tests and contests. Included are judgments of merit of applications for parole, loans, insurance claims, and welfare payments and in competitions for trophies, jobs, contracts, scholarships, time, space, attention, grants, and grades. In the United States alone, for example, there are about 5 million corporations ("Bizstats," 2006), most of which routinely hire, fire, promote, and demote their employees based on judgments of merit. In addition, there are thousands of granting agencies that incorporate judgments of merit in allocating charitable funds, scholarships, research grants, and other free money. Little wonder that judgments of merit attract considerable attention and debate. A visit to Google, for example, generates over 28 million hits for the phrase "résumé writing," 287 million hits for "scholarship," 399 million for "research grants," and 188 million for "winning."

In this and in the next two chapters we examine some of the common challenges facing organizations when allocating resources (usually money, but also time, jobs, publicity, status, trophies, and a wide assortment of other prizes) based on merit. We call these tests and contests *adjudications*. Organizations creating merit-based adjudications face dozens of decisions about how to run them. Application and judgment procedures must be determined. Contestants and judges must be found. Funding and accounting mechanisms must be set. Decisions about these procedures—about the rules of the game—are often based on past practices, convenience, organizational politics, whimsy, or mimicry of rules of other organizations. Such informal or haphazard tactics can get the job of adjudication done, but they by no means guarantee that the job will be done well. Indeed, sloppy construction of adjudication procedures is likely to accumulate legitimate charges of unfairness.

Consider, for example, a manager faced for the first time with adjudicating a pile of 100 résumés. How will she proceed? She might start at the top and read until she finds the first acceptable résumé—perhaps the third one on the pile—then stop. Or she might first scan all the applicants' names, notice that three of them have the same last name as the company president, and restrict her choice to one of these three. Either way would get the job of adjudication done. But the 97 applicants whose résumés were never examined, likely including more meritorious applicants than the three seen, would surely consider the procedure unfair. Conducting a fair contest takes considerable planning and effort, but it does increase the chances of attracting and rewarding the most meritorious applicants and reduce the chances of complaints.

Because the first purpose of adjudication is to reward meritorious applicants, the first task of adjudication organizers is to attract them. This is often done by promising big rewards to the winners, but big rewards do not always draw the best to a test or contest. Participation is influenced by several other adjudication features including the chances of winning, the amount of time and effort needed to apply, the length of wait to learn of contest results, and the perceived fairness of adjudication rules. There is no rational reason for a person to enter adjudication if the chances of winning are close to nil, if the time and effort necessary to prepare are unreasonable, if the wait for results is excruciating, or if the contest is seen to be rigged, corrupt, or otherwise unfair. Organizations conducting adjudications with these malodorous features are likely to develop a bad reputation, experience a decline in meritorious applicants, and face the embarrassment of rewarding the leftovers. No good can come of it, which is why organizations cannot afford to be naïve, haphazard, or cavalier about the way their adjudications are run and their judgments of merit are made.

Good adjudications are efficient and fair, and most can be made more efficient and fair by adopting sensible rules of the game. The rules fall into three categories. First are rules undertaken before merit judgments are made. These include rules for deciding what will be rewarded (topic eligibility), who will be considered (applicant eligibility), how merit will be determined (judgment criteria), and how applicants will be found (recruitment). Second are rules for the merit judgments themselves, including rules for selecting and training judges and rules of order for judgments made by committee. Third are rules that follow the merit judgments, including rules for mapping merit into reward (should the winner take all or should the wealth be spread?), and for offering or receiving feedback to or from applicants useful for improving the applicants or the adjudication. This chapter will consider the first of these three categories—the application rules that should be set before judgments of merit are made. Chapters 6 and 7 will consider the adjudication rules governing the judgments themselves and the provision of feedback and rewards.

In is no easy task to provide useful guidelines about all application and adjudication rules because many guidelines vary with the type of adjudication done (consider guidelines for choosing the best baseball pitcher versus a good church minister). Our challenge is to avoid two extremes. Homilies and platitudes such as "Choose judges with care" and "Try to ensure the rules are followed" are too general to be useful. So, too, are suggestions for specific situations such as, "In the semifinal round of a baroque lute competition, allow players with lutes of eight courses or more at least 30 minutes to tune their instruments."

Somewhere between these extremes we hope to find a useful median. To do so, we have chosen to focus on one kind of merit-based adjudication: competitions for research funding. These are competitions in which one group of scientists and scholars judge the merit of applications for money to do research, written by another group scientists and scholars, in order to determine who gets money and who does not—a venerated process called *peer review*. There are three reasons for our choice. First, most research grant competitions are formal and complex, and they include activities before, during, and after committee deliberations that are similar to other kinds of merit-based competitions. Second, many research grant competitions are well developed. Great care has gone into their construction and fine-tuning under the vigilant eye of competition organizers and judges sincerely interested in making the competitions as fair as possible. So a study of research grant adjudication rules can give valuable insights about how to do the job well. Still, cracks remain; most grant adjudications remain fallible to some degree. This suggests that even the best organized competitions are limited by something beyond their composition and procedures. We shall discuss these limitations in chapters 6 and 7.

Our third reason for discussing research grant competitions is personal. In addition to being grant applicants ourselves (sometimes successful, sometimes not), we have been studying peer-reviewed, research grant competitions over 20 years and now know more about them than about any other kind of merit-based adjudication. We have also listened to the opinions of several employees of funding organizations, program officers, about the research grant committee adjudications they assist and have learned as much from them about practical matters of judging merit than we have from any other source. The program officers have been, almost without exception, keen and sagacious observers with many useful suggestions, some of which we pass on here.

RESEARCH GRANT COMPETITIONS

Of the many inventions affecting the development of science in the 20th century, none has been more consequential than the invention of the research grant. Proliferating after World War II, research grants have become indispensable to the conduct of most contemporary research. They pay salaries; cover the costs of otherwise unaffordable equipment; subsidize travel, conferences, and publications; and help reduce university debts. They also transform little science into big science (Price, 1963), laboratories into research factories, academic cliques into institutes, and scientists into administrators. Grant holders accrue status, power, and political clout in direct proportion to grant size.

Research grants have become big business. Many governments are major supporters of scientific research. The National Science Foundation in the United States, for example, gives about $5.5 billion in grants to about 10,000 scientific projects each year. About 80% of the annual $27 billion given to the National Institutes of Health (NIH) goes to support about 50,000 medical and health research projects. Even Canada, through its NIH equivalent, the Canadian Institutes of Health Research (CIHR), now has an annual budget of about $660 million to fund about 3,000 medical and health research projects. There are hundreds more such agencies around the world, including the Social Sciences and Humanities Research Council and the National Sciences and Engineering Research Council in Canada, the Australian Research Council in Australia, the British Council and the Royal Society in England, and equivalent councils in almost every European country. Charitable organizations also offer money for research, including numerous cancer, heart, stroke, liver, lung, kidney, burn, brain, and rare disease societies. Private organizations also support research, including the Guggenheim, MacArthur, King Faisal, and Aga Khan Foundations. Some research money is even available from gambling revenues; for example, from the Ontario Problem Gambling Research Centre in Canada (see "Gambling Research," 2007).

There are hundreds of research funding agencies, and collectively they give away billions in research funding every year. Yet there is still not enough research money to go around—far from it. The proportion of scientists and scholars who are successful in their grant applications to any one agency rarely exceeds 50% and is much more often about 25%; typically, at least two thirds of applicants do not receive funding. Even when funding is obtained, it is never permanent. A typical grant provides money for 2–3 years, after which grant holders must again seek funding to continue research work. Large research projects typically pay the salaries of several scientists, students, technicians, and other specialists. When the money is gone, so are their jobs. Universities and other research factories often peg their prestige and operating budgets to the amount of money their scientists accrue. So the pressure to find more money is often extreme. Yet writing a proposal is hard work. Forty years ago it took perhaps a week to write one, but proposal requirements have proliferated and competition has become fiercer. Many contemporary applicants invest several months of full-time effort drafting, vetting, and revising proposals before submitting them. No one wants to invest such effort in a lost cause, so prospective grant applicants are understandably concerned about the fairness of funding adjudications.

So too are the funding agencies. The goal of any research funding agency is to spend its money on meritorious projects—sometimes known as "good bang for the buck"—predicted by considering project proposals and their authors. As previously noted, the goal can only be reached if meritorious proposals appear. These proposals do not grow on trees. Scientists are no different than most other prospective applicants; their decision to apply for funding from any given agency depends on dozens of factors, including the amount of money desired, the fit between the areas funded and the scientist's own work, the amount of time and effort needed to apply, how long it takes for a decision, and the chances of success. Their decision also depends on the reputation of the agency, in particular, whether the agency is viewed as efficient and fair. Many large funding agencies employ specialists to review and improve their adjudication procedures. It is a good indication of genuine concern for fairness and efficiency. The problems they face, and the solutions they try, can thus provide useful information for other organizations that judge merit for jobs, promotions, welfare, publishing contracts, trophies, or other prizes.

MAKING THE RULES OF THE GAME

Before a research funding agency opens for business, it must first address three questions: Who or what will be considered for funding? How will the merit of those considered be assessed? How will money be distributed among those with the most merit? Eligibility rules must be established to explicate which applicants, topics, goals, or research areas will be considered for funding and which will not. Merit criteria must be chosen to allow prospective applicants and judges to determine on what basis the merit of proposals will be assessed. Finally, budget regulations must be established to decide how much money will be spent, for how long, and how it will be concentrated or dispersed over a few or many projects.

Eligibility Rules

No research funding agency can afford to fund everything, so all agencies must specialize. Agencies often express their specializations in what are known as *funding priorities*, which, in turn, strongly influence eligibility rules: who or what will be considered for funding and who or what will not. Eligibility rules generate an organization's first line of merit criteria, because they establish who and what merits consideration for funding. Eligibility assessments thus become tests for a contest because only those passing the test of eligibility are allowed to compete (see chapter 1).

Eligibility rules are usually the result of several traditions and strategic interests—everything from the wishes of an organization's benefactors to the colonization of new funding niches to the politics of the day. Some eligibility rules are related to personal characteristics of applicants: citizenship, minimum education, and occasionally age, sex, ethnicity, geographic region, and the like. Most start-up research grants, for example, are reserved for young scientists and scholars; Iranian nuclear researchers are, as far as we know, ineligible for research funding from the U.S. Department of Defense. Other eligibility rules are related to the proposals of applicants. The most common such rule is *relevance*—the fit between the research topic proposed and the research topics an agency is born to fund. A proposal for research on the history of dance, for example, is likely ineligible for funding by the American Cancer Society or the Lupus Foundation. Other rules are set according to current laws and government regulations or in comparison to the eligibility rules of related organizations.

Funding organizations must not only consider the content of eligibility rules, they must also consider their consequences. A primary concern is the number of applicants who meet eligibility criteria. Organizations must ensure that at least some eligible and meritorious people will apply while also avoiding a flood of applicants. It is embarrassing for a funding agency to offer a pot of money only to find that nothing of merit meets its eligibility rules—rather like holding a party to which nobody comes. At the other extreme, it is nightmarish for a funding agency to offer a new pot of money that attracts far more eligible applicants than its staff and procedures can handle—like throwing a party that is crashed by the neighborhood. The former wastes the time and talent of administrators and judges and either leaves a budget surplus or squanders it on mediocre applicants. The latter stretches the time, stress, and cognitive limits of administrators and judges and exhausts the budget before all meritorious applicants can get what they deserve.

Adjusting eligibility criteria to strike a balance between a dearth and a deluge of applicants is a practical skill developed over many years of funding experience.

And it is a useful skill far beyond the rarefied world of research funding. Personnel officers of public and private corporations face the same balancing act when they try to fill job openings. So, too, do orchestra conductors seeking new players, philanthropic agencies seeking meritorious scholarship recipients, directors seeking actors to fill roles. We share some suggestions for mastering the art in our Practical Implications section below.

Like each funding agency, each scientist and scholar has her own research specialty, a field of knowledge cleared from a forest of ignorance and cultivated with effort and pride. Almost all scientists and scholars want resources to continue their clearing and cultivation, which means that almost all want money to do their work. Unfortunately, many scientists and scholars cultivate research areas ineligible for funding. One of us (WT), for example, has looked in vain for an agency funding young people in the Third World to collect oral histories of elders in their village, despite the cultural, historical, and educational merit of such a project. So the project languishes in the closet of good ideas. Other scientists and scholars may be eligible for funding from only one or two agencies—likely agencies with limited funds. Many meritorious Third-World scientists, for example, lack the citizenship to be eligible for funding consideration by otherwise relevant agencies and must repeatedly approach a handful organizations, such as Canada's International Development Research Centre, for a small chance at modest grants. Such scientists and scholars can only watch with envy their colleagues who have chosen areas to clear and cultivate that have become—to stretch the metaphor—prime real estate. There are, for example, well over a dozen agencies that fund research related to national security and over 100 agencies that fund research in various areas of health.

This presents underfunded scientists and scholars with a devil's trilemma: Do they continue working in poverty, quit their profession, or make a more fundable research choice? Some scientists choose the first and some the second, but not all. Willie Sutton, an infamous thief, once declared that he robbed banks because "That's where the money is." Many scientists and scholars are no less opportunistic, adapting themselves as best they can to the eligibility rules of new funding programs as they appear. It is rumored, for example, that soon after the 9/11 tragedy, the U.S. Department of Defense received over 23,000 applications for grants to support research on terrorism. While the proportion of meritorious terrorism researchers or projects among these 23,000 can be debated, the sheer number of applicants reflects the extent to which people, including scientists and scholars, are tempted or forced to follow the money. The result is a complex dynamic between funders and funded that can be altered by eligibility rules.

Once upon a time, eligibility rules were largely set by scientists and scholars themselves. The rules were minimal, most were personal (a Ph.D., a university affiliation, etc.), and as many meritorious proposals as possible were funded regardless of their topic. Retired scientists call these the good old days. They are gone. During the past few decades, those who control funding purses, usually governments and senior bureaucrats, have revived the famous adage about paying the piper and calling the tune. Funding priorities and the eligibility rules they introduce are now, more often than ever, set by politicians, governing boards, senior administrators, marketing departments, and such. NASA, for example, seems chronically embroiled in political struggles about the direction and extent of space research (e.g., see "Space Politics," n.d.), and the social sciences face similar political challenges (e.g., see "Federation," n.d.). Canada diverts an increasing proportion of its limited research funds to so-called strategic research areas and then changes the areas every 3–5 years partly to reflect the national mood and political weather. This is illustrated by the following announcement from Canada's Natural Sciences and Engineering Research Council.

> The objective of the Strategic Project Grants (SPG) program is to accelerate research and training in "targeted" areas of research in the natural sciences and engineering that could be very important to Canada's future. Given that these targeted areas change with new developments, NSERC conducts a major review every four or five years to determine the areas of research that will be the most pertinent for the program over the next cycle. NSERC is now completing such a review. In order to increase the impact of the funds available, NSERC will be narrowing the focus of the targeted areas for the 2006–2010 program cycle. The new targeted areas and priority research topics will be posted on the NSERC Web Site (NSERC–Strategic Project Grants) by late January 2006. ("Project Grants," 2006)

Funding priorities and their associated eligibility rules are now increasingly directed toward national economic advantage (think "synergistic public/private partnerships driving the global information economy"), demographic representation ("available only to Texan scientists younger than 35 and from a visible minority") and political compromise ("must have equal numbers of male and female research partners who represent at least five Canadian Provinces, four academic disciplines, three visible minority groups, two official languages"). The result is often one-shot funding competitions grafted onto unexpected crises or opportunities. Consider two examples, the first from Canada's Natural Sciences and Engineering Research Council and the second from the Ontario Problem Gambling Research Centre.

> Former weapons scientists in Armenia, Belarus, Georgia, Kazakhstan, Kyrgyz Republic, Russia, and Tajikistan are seeking Canadian scientists to collaborate with them on research in nuclear safety, biotechnology and life sciences, energy, environment, space technology, chemistry, physics, communications, materials, and instrumentation. The International Science and Technology Centre (ISTC) coordinates project funding with the objective of integrating former Soviet Union (FSU) weapons scientists into the international scientific community. Canada will contribute up to $18 million annually to fund FSU scientists through the ISTC. Although Canada is not presently funding Canadian scientists directly through this program, NSERC will ensure the peer review of proposals. This is an opportunity for Canadian scientists to work with highly accomplished FSU scientists and to potentially access and use the technology created in the process, thereby extending their own R&D budgets. ("International Cooperation," 2005)

> On January 20, 2005, the Ontario Ministry of Economic Development and Trade announced plans to introduce slots at the new Quinte Exhibition and Raceway (QER) in Belleville. In recognition of the unique opportunity afforded by this announcement, the Ontario Problem Gambling Research Centre (the Centre) is introducing a significant competitive award to study the effects of the new facility for a period of up to five years. ("Belleville Request," 2005)

While the sagacity of such competitions can be debated, the consequences of their proliferation cannot. When funding opportunities pop up unexpectedly, live a short life and then disappear, they create an unpredictable and unstable funding environment. We know from principles of evolutionary biology that organisms have great difficulty adapting to such an environment (see, for example, Levins, 1968; Real, 1980). Specialized species that evolved to thrive in small and stable environments have the greatest difficulty; when their environment changes, most specialists become extinct. Unpredictable and unstable environments favor opportunistic generalists, the jack-of-all-trades species that breed easily, move fast, and eat almost anything.

The same principles have their metaphorical parallels in the research world. Scientific and scholarly specialists tend to have more difficulty retooling for new research priorities and their associated eligibility rules than do opportunistic generalists. It takes time and money to acquire the knowledge, skills, and tools necessary to research something in depth. A typical Ph.D. student, for example, now spends about 6 years completing the degree. So specialists do not fare well when funding goes dry. Research generalists seem to fare better. The closest approximation to such generalists is people trained in research tools and methods—the hammers and chisels of research that presumably can be used to build anything someone is willing to pay for. It is one reason why laboratory research in psychology has declined, while questionnaires have proliferated like rabbits (Thorngate, 1990).

It is, of course, exceedingly wasteful of human capital to invest time and money educating specialists and then expose them to the dangers of a shifting funding scene. Many funding agencies are quite aware of the dangers and, seeking to avoid the waste they generate, have tried to reduce the dangers in at least two ways. The first is by reserving a portion of their budgets for programs with stable and predicable eligibility requirements, suitable for specialists. The portion is often called *funding for fundamental and normal research*—as distinct from the less stable and predictable funding for applied and strategic research. This creates two research environments, one favoring specialists and one favoring generalists. It is often a successful compromise.

Some funding agencies also try to reduce the dangers specialists face in unpredictable funding environments by encouraging the specialists to join forces. A primary result is the proliferation of applied and strategic funding opportunities for teams of specialists who pool their expertise. It is, we think, a brilliant adaptation of two of nature's most successful evolutionary strategies: communication and cooperation. Yet it requires each specialist to learn how to cooperate and communication with specialists from other areas. We discuss some of the ways to do this in our Practical Implications section.

Merit Criteria

Once research proposals and their authors pass the tests of eligibility, they must be judged for merit, so criteria of merit must be chosen and employed to get the job done. As we noted in chapter 2, it is often tempting—especially in small, informal, one-off competitions—to assess the merit of proposals by improvising criteria as the proposals are read. Judges who succumb to the temptation often justify it with a gut feeling, an intuitive sense, a holistic impression, or the popular pronouncement, "I'll know a good proposal when I see one." Chapters 2 and 3 have addressed some of the dangers in such informality and in making up criteria as judgments proceed. The criteria are likely to be neither explicit nor consistently employed. As a result, different proposals are likely be judged by different or double standards (chapter 4), some blatantly unfair. One proposal, for example, might be funded because it complements the work of a judge; another might be rejected because it is written by a judge's ex-spouse or printed in an ugly font. Criteria such as these are rarely defensible and are likely to sow bad feelings among losing applicants. To reduce the chances of embarrassment, litigation, and a bad reputation, a funding organization must explicate its criteria of merit before the judges begin deliberation and preferably before solicitation of proposals begins.

Although explicating merit criteria is a good thing, it has its dangers. When criteria are known, they can be scrutinized, and the scrutiny may lead to criticism. So it pays a funding agency to pay careful attention to the merit criteria it publicly announces and employs. Clearly, organizations should employ good and defensible criteria rather than bad and indefensible ones. But how many criteria are enough? And how can an organization tell the difference between good ones and bad?

In the world of research grants, good merit criteria are those that can predict the success of a research project—the valid predictors we noted in chapter 2. Success is usually defined by one of four Ps: publications, policies, patents, or profits. No one has yet found a single criterion of merit that will successfully predict any of the four Ps, so funding agencies usually resort to a handful of criteria with modest predictive validity in hopes that together they will do better than any singleton. It is no mean feat to assess in any scientific way the predictive validity of such criteria. The best way is to judge applicants on each criterion under consideration and then allocate grants at random, monitor the products of those who received the grants, and correlate judgments with productivity. If there is a strong relationship between judgments on some criterion and productivity, then the criterion should be included in the set of those for judging merit. If there is a weak relationship or none, the criterion should be chucked.

No agency would leap at the chance to allocate grants at random; the political fallout from angry applicants and sponsors would be too high. Some agencies do the best they can to monitor relationships between merit criteria and outcomes, but they are often constrained by privacy issues and restricted merit ranges of winning grant applicants. In the meantime, merit criteria are often selected according to their assumed links with one of the four Ps (face validity), selected according to the personal preferences of current judges or administrators, or selected from lists of merit criteria used in other adjudications. The criteria usually come in two flavors. One flavor of merit criteria is related to the researcher, most often her track record. The other flavor is related to the proposed research—logical derivation of ideas from previous theory and research, adequacy of research design, feasibility of procedures, justification of research budget, ethics, and the like.

The relative importance of these two sets of merit criteria is the stuff of a chronic debate about whether an agency should fund a person or an idea. Arguments for judging the merit of a person note that scientists and scholars who have consistently produced meritorious work are very likely to continue, so they should be trusted to continue and given the funding and freedom to do what they think is best. Arguments for judging the merit of the proposal go something like this: Grants are not prizes for good work already done but gifts for good work proposed; a proposal is the promise, so the merit of a proposal is a better indicator of good work than is the merit of its author. If an author has produced meritorious work in the past, then he is likely to write a meritorious proposal for future work. So let the proposal be the indicator.

Both arguments have strengths and weaknesses. Funding meritorious people gives great advantage to those who are meritorious, and it is probably true that most will continue to do good work. Explicating the criteria by which a person's merit will be assessed can be daunting. The devil, as usual, is in the details. Consider, for example, the following list heroically explicated by the Social Sciences and Humanities Research Council's (SSHRC's) standard research grant competition to evaluate the merit of an applicant's record of achievement.

> The record of research achievement refers to the tangible contributions made by the applicant(s) to the advancement, development and dissemination of knowledge in the social sciences and humanities. The focus of the evaluation is on the most recent six-year period of activity. In evaluating regular scholars, the committee will also take into account the five most significant research contributions (as identified by the applicant) from any period of an applicant's career. External assessors and adjudication committees evaluate the record of research achievement using these criteria:
>
> - quality and significance of published work (taking into consideration the quality of the chosen publication venues);
> - originality of previous research and its impact on the discipline or field;
> - quantity of research activity relative to the stage of the applicant's career;
> - demonstrated importance of other scholarly activities and contributions;
> - recentness of output (taking into account the nature of the applicant's career pattern and previous non-research responsibilities);
> - importance and relevance of dissemination of research results directed to non-academic audiences (as appropriate);
> - significance of any previous research supported by SSHRC or any other agency;
> - where applicable, the contribution to the training of future researchers; and,
> - efforts made, where appropriate, to develop research partnerships with civil society organizations and government departments ("Evaluation," 2006)

We commend SSHRC for listing these criteria but wonder how they can be used. How, for example, should quality, significance, and originality of published work (items 1 and 2, above) be measured? What counts as a demonstration of the "importance of other scholarly activities" (item 3)? Can efforts to develop research partnerships with civil society organizations (item 9) be rated or compared? There are, for better or worse, no objective measures of these criteria. This gives wiggle room for judges to use their discretion, which allows for differences of opinion and the possibility of shifting standards in the assessments of different proposals. Even so, providing the list to judges and applicants allows them to get a sense of what counts and what does not; to make suggestions for additions, deletions, or other improvements; and to commend SSHRC on its good intention to be fair and transparent.

Many judges try to eschew the vagaries of subjective judgments by relying on lengths, counts, and other crude indicants or by giving more importance to criteria with objective indicants than to criteria without them. It is a perilous strategy, rarely reducing bias or error. For example, perhaps the most popular objective indicants of academic achievement are (a) the length or thickness of a vita and (b) the size or number of past grants (see the "quantity" clause in item 3, above). But these are controversial indicants because they are subject to biases ranging from the rejection rate of journals in a scholar's discipline (about 25% for the hard sciences versus 75% for the social sciences), to the size of a typical grant in a scholar's discipline (biology and medical grants tend to be an order of magnitude larger than grants in the humanities), to country of origin (most Third-World countries do not offer research grants and require professors to teach 2–3 times as many courses as North American professors teach, leaving far less time to do research). Such indicators are further sullied by the rise of joint grants and publications that allow several scholars to share a big budget and its prestige and to expand all their vitae with a single article (one recent article in *Science*, for example, has 87 coauthors; see Terracciano et al., 2005). We are reminded of the old *New Yorker* cartoon showing one man, standing below Jesus on the cross, turning to another and saying, "Sure he was a great teacher, but did he publish?"

When competitions are repeated, biases are compounded. For example, if a scientist or scholar is chosen at random to receive a grant, while her peers are not, it is more likely that the randomly chosen one will produce more scholarship and science than the impoverished peers—this is, after all the reason that grants are given. In the next competition we should then see the chosen one to have (a) more grants and (b) a longer vita than the others, increasing the chances that the randomly chosen one will receive another grant. As competitions multiply, the first random success should breed further success, and the randomly unfunded masses would eventually fall away. In science as in life, the rich get richer, even when they are luckier and not more meritorious than their poor peers (see chapter 7 for a fuller discussion of this phenomenon). In short, grant size, vita length, and similar indicants of production are as likely to reflect chance as to reflect competence. The indicants are arguably better than nothing at all and they are, in principle, at least more public and standardized than the more subjective indicants derived from intuition and gut feelings. Yet they remain fallible measures of a researcher's merit and will never eliminate judgment errors.

Funding meritorious proposals rather than meritorious authors—"We don't care who you are as long as you have a good idea!"—tends to reduce the insidious effects of a researcher's background and luck. But it raises two more issues. First, it is possible that people with good ideas might not have the competence to execute them well. This leaves judges with an occasional dilemma: Should they give money to a good proposal of an unknown applicant or to a mediocre proposal of a well-established applicant? Second, the assessment of proposals rather than their authors still does not solve the problem of what should be used as criteria of merit or how assessments of proposals along these criteria should be made. As with criteria for an applicant's merit, there are dozens of possible merit criteria for grant applications. Consider the following list of criteria (at least 14 counting the "and" clauses) posted on the same SSHRC Web site:

> External assessors and adjudication committees evaluate the proposed program of research using these criteria:
>
> degree of originality and expected contribution to the advancement of knowledge;
> scholarly, intellectual, social and cultural significance of the research;
> appropriateness of the theoretical approach or framework;
> appropriateness and expected effectiveness of the research strategies or methodologies;
> feasibility of successfully completing the program of research and the appropriateness of the schedule of research, given the applicant's and/or research team's resources and commitments;
> suitability and expected effectiveness of plans to communicate research results both within, and as appropriate beyond, the academic community; and
> where appropriate, the nature and extent of research training; and
> contribution to interdisciplinary research ("Program Descriptions," 2006)

The same vagaries inherent in criteria for judging researchers, discussed above, can be seen in these criteria for judging their proposals. How, for example, should the degree of originality (item 1, above) or cultural significance (item 2) of a proposal be assessed? Should appropriateness of theoretical approach (item 3) be given more or less weight than suitability of plans to communicate (item 6)?

The issue of criteria weighting or importance (see chapter 3) prompts another set of vexing questions. Weights are usually employed when the merit of separate features of the applicants or applications can be combined as independent entities—a variation of "adding up the positives and the negatives." In such cases, good features of an application can compensate for bad ones, especially if the good features are weighted more heavily than the bad ones. This is why methods of weighing and tallying good and bad features are collectively known as *compensatory*. It might be possible, for example, that a proposal judged average for its innovation can rise above (compensate for) mediocrity if it is also judged excellent for its methodology, especially if methodology is weighed more heavily than innovation.

But some features of applications or proposals may not be compensatory; one flaw may lead judges to discount or ignore all strengths of a proposal. Many experienced judges believe, for example, that a good idea cannot compensate for a flawed methodology. Others believe that a good methodology cannot compensate for a bad idea. Few judges believe that an excellent proposal can save (compensate for) an author who has failed to complete the research promised in his previous three funded projects. Yet many judges believe that an author who has previously delivered the goods can compensate for his current mediocre proposal. There is no law that says the use of compensatory and noncompensatory judgment rules must be consistent. But it would certainly help prospective applicants to know the nature of the rules as a supplement to the list of criteria. Alas, these rules are likely to change from one judge to the next, as we shall discuss in the next chapter.

What can be learned from all this? It is usually fiendishly difficult to develop clear criteria for judging the merit of researchers and their proposals and clear rules by which judgments of individual criteria should be weighed and combined. The challenge is similar to wording a perfect law. Unforeseen exceptions will almost certainly appear after the criteria have been developed, as will ambiguities, complexities, and inconsistencies. Even so, almost any list of criteria and combinatorial rules is better than none because a list can help eligible applicants guess more accurately what they should address in their proposals and estimate how strong their proposals might be. It is prudent to assume that a list of criteria and rules will be polished by iteration, much like the iterative improvement of software or other feats of engineering. All organizations should strive to do this. But it is also prudent to assume that an infallible set of merit criteria will never be found. There is no shame in this. Knowledge of the inherent fallibility of merit criteria can be very useful in managing the development of adjudications over time (see chapter 7). And an admission of fallibility, like the listing of fallible indicants of merit, goes a long way toward preparing applicants for what they can and cannot expect to occur during the adjudication.

Budgeting Regulations

Funding agencies must not only determine who and what is eligible to be considered for their money, and determine how the merit of those eligible for consideration will be judged, but they must also determine how much money they will give away. Funding agencies have budgets they normally cannot exceed, so the bottom line sets an upper limit on how much money they can spend. This presents agencies with an important question: Should their money go to many small projects or a few large ones? The answer depends on a dozen important considerations, including expenses in the area to be funded, the needs and preferences of prospective applicants, and the burdens of vetting applications and administering funds. There is no sense giving $10,000 to 200 researchers if each is requesting a $2 million MRI machine. Nor is there much sense in giving $2 million to one person who requests only $10,000, leaving empty-handed 199 others with equally modest requests. Prospective applicants vary in their opinions about how concentrated or disperse funding should be, often according to their vested interests. Those with large grants tend to argue that only a few large grants should be given, while those with small or no grants argue that the wealth should be spread.

Facing no consensus, agencies often turn to their own concerns in making their budgeting decisions. In an era of shrinking budgets, increasing administrative burdens, and the pressures of accountability, many funding agencies have shifted more of their funds to a few large, visible, and safe projects rather than many small, obscure, and risky ones. This is often done by supporting research institutes or groups of researchers (teams) who promise to coordinate their activities in the name of a common cause. Though the money is the same, it is simpler to vet, say, five proposals competing for one $5 million grant than to vet five hundred proposals competing for 100 $50,000 grants. It is also easier to audit one large grant than hundreds of small ones; so funding agencies have reason to prefer the large and the few over the small and the numerous.

There are, however, some likely costs associated with a decision to fund a few large projects rather than many small ones. An agency that relieves itself of administrative burdens invariably increases the administrative burdens of others—usually applicants. It is much more arduous and tedious to write a funding proposal for a large project than for a small one, and the effort often increases exponentially as more scientists and their institutional bureaucracies become involved. One result is that scientists with little time or other resources will likely not apply, while rich institutes or other organizations with spare funds may hire professional proposal writers (retired personnel from funding agencies are popular choices) to get the job done. As decisions about proposed budgets are made, conflicts about who gets what are inevitable, and politics invariably enter into budgeting activities. Most scientists are smart, but this does not make them nice; nasty quarrels about proposed money distributions, equipment allocations, and research directions can ensue. These are as likely to be resolved by power struggles and ostracism as by rational debate and compromise. Prospective scientists wanting to be affiliated with a large project can be accepted or rejected on personal grounds, such as friendship with the proposal coordinator, opinions about research technique or direction, gender, or accent, rather than on competence. Most funding agencies have no mechanisms for controlling such prejudice or discrimination during the proposal development process. So any concerns an agency has about making the proposal vetting process fair can be scuttled before the vetting process begins.

Funding a few large projects rather than many small ones has a second insidious effect. Perhaps hoping to reduce the applicants' burdens of writing long proposals and the adjudicators' burdens of reading them, many funding agencies have implemented a two-step application procedure. The first step generally requires a submission of something called a *letter of intent* (LOI) providing a brief synopsis of the proposal to come and containing enough information for the funding agency to assess the prospective proposal's eligibility in some informal eligibility test. Authors of eligible proposals outlined in the letters of intent are then invited to submit a full proposal; the others are politely dismissed. Although this may streamline the adjudication process, it introduces a second judgment that typically is less transparent and accountable than the primary judgment of peers. Someone must make decisions about who gets invitations and who does not. The task is usually left to funding agency administrators, rarely to peers. Most of their decisions are probably based on a simple assessment of the fit of the proposal to the eligibility criteria of the funding program. But with no mechanisms for oversight or appeal, there is room for biases to grow. Consider, for example, a government funding agency seeking letters of intent for research to improve health of people in Africa. One letter comes from a national medical association whose members include funding agency administrators, a second from a multinational drug company that has contributed to the political campaign of the Minister of International Health, and a third from a team of junior professors who have previously criticized the minister in print. Which of the three letters might receive the most critical scrutiny? Would administrators refuse lunches and phones calls from any or all of the authors of ministerial staff? The answers would probably vary.

The letter-of-intent mechanism has recently recursed down another level to a new low. Some funding agencies now allow only one or two letters of intent to be submitted from any given organization, and some universities have responded by requiring an internal competition to determine whose letter of intent will be submitted for scrutiny. The internal competition typically requires a proposal requesting to submit a letter to submit a proposal. Consider the following 2006 message from an unnamed Canadian university considering letters of intent to submit a "Tier 2" (big money) proposal to the Canadian International Development Agency (CIDA):

> Please note that the lead Canadian institution (acting individually or as the lead of a consortium) may submit no more than two Tier 2 LOIs per competition. ... Because of this limitation, we will have to hold an internal competition to determine which [of the university's] projects are to receive the "go-ahead" to prepare a Letter of Intent. This competition will be co-ordinated through [the international office]. Therefore, interested applicants are requested to inform [the international office] of their interest to apply by sending a one-page summary of their proposed submission, along with a preliminary budget, to [the international office director] by February 24. This will allow sufficient time for an internal review of proposals, with a view to preparing LOIs prior to CIDA's deadline of April 25.

By adopting such a recursive mechanism, a third layer of adjudication is introduced. Unless a university is abnormally thoughtful and forthcoming, the criteria, procedures, and adjudicators for this layer are likely to remain obscure. It is not difficult to envision a small, ad hoc group of administrators trying to judge the merit of proposals to write letters to apply for funding, wrestling with incommensurable proposal outlines, internal vested interests, and friendship/rivalry networks, second-guessing funding agency agendas and the likelihood of prospective proposals-to-be winning the cash flow lottery. As new layers of the adjudication process are added, each less accountable and more mysterious than the last, prospective applicants must reserve more time and energy to prepare for them. As new criteria are added at every layer, the prospective applicants are faced with more hurdles to surmount and more people to please. The result is an adjudication environment that favors insipid conservatism, political maneuvering, and lots of free time over the husbandry of innovative mutations. Radical proposals are shot down, and the meek inherit the wealth. This is, of course, fully defensible if merit is to be judged by inoffensiveness and adherence to the status quo. Yet, as Frank Zappa once remarked, "Without deviation, progress is not possible."

Budgets for large projects now often exceed a funding agency's funding capacity. So another new twist to funding has recently emerged, called *joint funding* or *joint sponsorship*. A jointly funded project receives funding from at least two agencies, each contributing some proportion of the money needed for the project.

The division is usually based on an agency's specialization. One agency, for example, might fund senior scientists, another might fund graduate and postdoctoral students, a third might fund equipment, and a fourth might fund publication expenses. But agencies also mate for a rich variety of political reasons, including political jurisdiction (should a Third-World health proposal be funded by a ministry of health or a ministry of foreign affairs or both?) and the big-government/big-business compromise of public private partnerships.

The joint funding strategy has at least two advantages for funding agencies, which is probably why it is increasingly popular. By adopting joint funding requirements, agencies can specialize not only in the kind of research they fund but also in the parts of research they support, thus reducing the chances of embarrassment that occurs when two or more agencies compete with each other to support the same projects. In addition, joint funding allows one agency to short cut adjudication procedures by relying on the adjudications of cooperating agencies: "If it is good enough for the Department of Defense, it is good enough for us."

Such agency advantages, however, deliver new hardships to many prospective applicants. Writing one proposal to one agency takes considerable time and effort. Writing several proposals to several agencies takes enormous time and effort. Copy-and-paste functions of word processors help, as long as the proposal requirements of two or more agencies are similar. If they are not, a new set of application procedures must be mastered for each agency, increasing the chances that procedural errors will be made. The task of writing multiple proposals, each necessary to fund a piece of the action, is almost always daunting. To accomplish it, many good scientists reluctantly become full-time proposal writers, devoting most of their career to chasing money rather than to doing research.

Few scientists enjoy writing multiple grant proposals; a common word to describe the task is *toxic*. To ease the burden, some writers employ one or two popular grant writing strategies. The first strategy is to propose research that has already been secretly completed from a previous grant. This allows scientists to avoid most of the uncertainties of proposing research with an unknown outcome and reduces two common fears of funding agency administrators: financial risk and political risk. The second strategy is to engage in informal contact with receptive representatives of an agency that seems favorable to a proposal, hoping that their early funding commitment will prod the other agencies to pony up. Most government funding agencies now have rigid rules to prevent such informal contact; most private companies do not. So public-private partnerships present entrepreneurial proposal authors with a panoply of opportunities to play by private rules in order to increase the chances of public funds. Lunches and site visits are common, as are the traditional social functions arranged by consultants and lobbyists: cocktail parties, golf outings, and such. The technical term for this strategy is *priming the pump*, leading one to wonder how it is related to merit.

Budgeting for a few large projects can also have equally insidious effects after funding decisions are made. Consider this: If universities educate 100 talented Ph.D.s, and funding agencies ask them to divide into groups of 10 to submit 10 proposals for one $10 million research grant, then what happens to the 90 Ph.D.s who are part of the nine groups losing the competition? Do they go on welfare and try again next year? If so, how can they compete with the chosen 10 who will certainly have a better track record in their year of plenty (see chapters 6 and 7)? Marketplace thinking might lead us to conclude that the 90 losers are dross and should find other work or leave town. Evolutionary thinking, and we dare say common sense, would conclude that the loss of 90 scientists is an unacceptable waste of talent and that as many as possible should be somehow supported to pursue what they were educated to do. Whatever happened to those talented Soviet nuclear and rocket scientists when they were no longer paid by the Russian government? How many are now receiving consulting contracts from North Korea and the Taliban?

The concentration of funding may quicken or simplify the process of judging merit but, as evolutionary biologists would say, it inevitably constrains variety. If we plant 100 different species of flowers but water only one, 99 species will die. The one we water may be our current favorite, but if it should die, no others will remain to keep the field in bloom. It is a dangerous game, predicated on the belief that our favorite will forever produce what we desire. Variety may not be efficient, but it is necessary for adaptation in a changing or uncertain world. As a result, funding agencies are wise to ensure that at least some of their funds go to small, unusual projects. Most of the small ones will fail, but the few that show promise will likely replace those that currently receive the bulk of funds.

Many large granting agencies want to fund small projects as well as big ones and offer special competitions for the purpose. But competitions for small grants tend to be more costly to conduct than competitions for large ones, simply because the former attract more proposals for the greater number of available grants. Most funding organizations want to avoid the large adjudication costs that come with circulating thousands of proposals to hundreds of judges in scores of committees and coordinating all the activities that ensue. So many funding organizations now ask universities to do the work and absorb the costs through "in kind" (read *volunteer*) contributions. The scheme works something like this. Funding agency X has $1 million for small grants (no grant over $5,000). It gives $100,000 to each of 10 universities with the instruction that each university adjudicate small grant proposals from its own faculty. Agency X gives the universities some general guidelines and suggestions for conducting their adjudications (often based on their own in-house adjudications) but allows considerable latitude in how the job is done.

How might the job be done? Universities often constitute an ad hoc committee, give it some general instructions such as, "Choose the best 20 of these 157 proposals by next Monday" and, with as much goodwill as its members can muster, the work begins. Alas, the committee will soon find its job far more difficult than the equivalent job confronting specialized committees run by the funding organization. How can the merit of a proposal for sociolinguistic studies of Elizabethan puns be compared to a proposal for prototype development of an object-oriented programming language? With no common criteria of comparison that often appear when assessing the merit of proposals within a discipline, university committee members assessing merit across disciplines are likely to drift toward more prosaic or political criteria, signaled by questions such as, "Is it Philosophy's turn to get money?" "Why should we subsidize business school professors for their consulting activities?" "Is it true that Frank spent his last grant on dope?" or "Can this proposal increase our university's visibility?"

In short, if the task of judging the merit of many small grant proposals is transferred from a national organization with high adjudication standards to local committees with undeclared, hidden, or shifting standards, we should expect the biases of politics, prejudice, and discrimination to seep in. It is flippant to argue that these biases are tolerable in local competitions because little is at stake—an argument reminiscent of the wonderful, anonymous quip, "Everybody lies, but it doesn't matter because nobody listens." Indeed, we can argue the reverse, that attempts to limit bias are more important in small competitions than in large ones because the possibilities of bias in small competitions are more numerous.

SOLICITING APPLICATIONS

Prospective applicants cannot apply to a competition if they do not know it exists, and they are unlikely to apply without enough information to make an informed application decision. So when eligibility rules, merit criteria, and budgets are set, they should be clearly communicated to prospective applicants. Writing understandable criteria and rules is part of the art of the next phase of running a research grant competition: soliciting applications, an art expressed in documents called *funding announcements* or *calls for proposals* (CFPs in acronymic jargon).

The Internet has greatly reduced the costs and difficulties of circulating calls for proposals, of passing the word. Expensive brochures and stamp licking parties have been replaced by Web sites and E-mailing lists. Still, the challenge of clear communication remains. Translating the general goals of a funding program, its eligibility rules, merit criteria, and budget requirements into a clear call for proposals is a difficult and challenging art.

Wording

The most common error of calls for proposals is poor writing. Consider two remarkably bad but sadly typical funding announcements, the first from the Canadian Institutes of Health Research (CIHR) and the second from the National Science Foundation (United States). For fun, count how many times you reread them in the futile pursuit of understanding.

> The purpose of this Priority Announcement is to improve Canada's ability to investigate and intervene on those underlying forces that challenge global health, by enhancing, in a sustainable manner, the capacity of national and international researchers and research-users to collaboratively develop and apply global health knowledge for evidence-based public health practice. ("Global Health," 2006)

> This solicitation invites proposals for "information infrastructure testbeds", each of which would include the development of the next generation of cyber-tools applied to data from various sources collected in two areas of research fundamental to social and behavioral scientists: organizations and individuals. The tools that are developed on these platforms must not only change ways

in which social and behavioral scientists research the behavior of organizations and individuals, but also serve sciences more broadly. It is envisioned that proposals for the "organization information testbed" will address three specific components:

- the development of tools that facilitate the integration of qualitative and quantitative information from heterogeneous sources, multiple media, and/or multiple modes;
- investment in basic research that addresses the protection of the confidentiality of respondents in computerized, widely accessible databases; and
- the development of incentives, standards and policies for collecting, storing, archiving, accessing, and publishing research results using organization-relevant information. ("Cyberinfrastructure," 2007)

We are not sure how to intervene on underlying forces, nor do we understand how forces could challenge or investigations could enhance capacity of investigators. We are also baffled how an infrastructure testbed of cybertools in two research areas could serve sciences more broadly. Perhaps such code phrases are meaningful to a small clique of prospective applicants who see a good fit with their specialized research areas. To the rest of us, the phrases are gibberish. If a funding agency wants to appear inclusive while attracting proposals only from members of the clique, then the purpose of their gibberish has been served. If an agency wants to cast a wider net to attract proposals beyond the clique, their statements could be written more clearly.

Even when poorly written solicitations serve no political purpose, they can have at least three deleterious effects. First, they can repel prospective applicants who might have submitted good proposals. Second, they can attract proposals that should have been left in a drawer. Third, they can, and almost certainly will, increase the number of prospective applicants who write or phone the funding organization asking for clarification. As the letters or phone calls pour in, the program officers who answer them become harried and cross. The officers often must improvise answers to unexpected questions because they too do not understand the solicitation. Their improvizations might encourage friendly or polite prospective applicants and discourage assertive or frustrated ones. When prospective applicants compare answers and see discrepancies, multiple exchanges between officers and applicants are likely to ensue, wasting everyone's time and frequently amplifying the problems.

Many organizations respond to the frustrating consequences of their poorly written solicitations in three ways: (a) they post a Frequently Asked Questions (FAQ) page on their Web site; (b) they add more words below the funding announcement to clarify the confusing ones; and (c) they transport program officers to information sessions. All three responses have the potential to help but rarely do. By the time the frequencies of questions are tallied and standard responses to the popular ones are written and posted, solicitation deadlines have usually passed. To precede the deadlines, many organizations guess at the questions that might be frequent, sometimes based on previous competitions, and post them with answers the day the solicitation begins. Some of their guesses may be correct, but the questions are frequently unimportant and the answers—usually filtered through a timid committee—are frequently useless. Few FAQ pages contain what are probably the most important questions of prospective applicants: What are you expecting me to write? How many people are applying? What are my chances of funding? Is this competition truly open and fair or just another seen-to-be-fair exercise? FAQ pages have the potential to serve a useful function. But organizations must take them seriously and update them frequently as their application deadline comes near. All things considered, it is better to post every new question and answer that comes to a program officer, frequent or not, than to stick to the safe ones.

A second response to poorly written solicitations is to write more. The extra is usually called *clarification* but rarely is. Below is a representative example from the International Development Research Centre in Canada and la Facultad Latinoamericana de Sciences Sociales (FLACSO) in Argentina. It is one of hundreds of examples of a poorly written statement of purpose, followed by a poorly written clarification.

> *The Gender Unit at IDRC and Facultad Latinoamericana de Ciencias Sociales (FLACSO)-Argentina are* launching a research competition on the theme "Decentralization and Women's Rights in Latin America and the Caribbean." The aim of the competition is to support research that empirically investigates whether and how contemporary decentralization reforms, in practice, contribute to or on the contrary hinder the realization and protection of women's and girls' civil, political, social, economic and/or cultural rights. The competition is aimed at experienced researchers, who are strongly encouraged to work in partnership with women's rights organizations and/or with less experienced colleagues.
>
> For the purposes of this competition we define gender as one of several important social categories, that is also cross-cut by other axes of difference, including age/lifecycle position, marital status, ethnicity, race, religion, class and sexual orientation. We support gender research that explores the relational dynamics between men and women, as well as amongst different categories of women and amongst different categories of men. In addition, we understand gender to be shaped by political, economic, social and cultural relations and contexts …
>
> For the purposes of this competition decentralisation refers to political and administrative reforms that transfer varying amounts and combinations of function, responsibility, resources, and political and fiscal autonomy to lower tiers of the state (e.g. regional, district, municipal governments, or decentralized units of the central government). Decentralisation may also transfer functions and responsibilities to quasi-state or private institutions. In the contemporary context, decentralisation is frequently associated with privatization in areas such as service provision. Decentralisation is also linked to new forms of interaction between a variety of institutional actors (including NGOs, community groups, women's groups, etc.) at the local level, often characterized as "partnerships". What is important in analyzing particular cases of decentralisation is to be clear about the precise form that decentralisation takes, asking what is decentralized; how it is decentralized; to what extent

it is decentralized; who benefits from decentralisation and to look at fiscal arrangements for financing decentralized responsibilities, such as the design and functioning of local government systems for revenue-collection. ("IDRC," n.d.)

Organizations producing such putative clarifications likely assume that they help prospective applicants understand how and what to write in their proposals. We could find no evidence of any organization testing the assumption but think that tests would be worthwhile.

Flush funding organizations often try a third strategy of clarifying their poorly worded solicitations: the *information session*. To offer such a session, well-meaning program officers drive or fly to groups of prospective applicants on their own turf. PowerPoints in hand, the presenters normally restate what is on their organization's Web site while circulating an attendance sheet to audit the number of bums in seats. There is a break for donuts and coffee followed by a question-and-answer (Q&A) session. Popular questions include, "Who will be on the committee judging my proposal?" "What are my chances of getting money?" "Why was funding cut from my discipline this year?" and "Why does your electronic submission Web page cut me off after 3 minutes?" Popular answers include, "We are not permitted to tell you," "We can send you the information as soon as we return," "You will have to ask the president," and "We don't know." Officers and audience often leave slightly more confused than when they arrived.

In response to the residual confusions of FAQs, clarifications, and information sessions, many universities proffer two of their own solutions: grant writing workshops and peer editing. Most grant writing workshops are conducted by local professors who have served as judges on adjudication committees of relevant granting agencies. They offer an insider's view of a previous adjudication process, including which criteria were defined and combined in committee deliberations. Peer editors are usually drawn from the ranks of recently successful applicants who volunteer to vet penultimate drafts of their colleagues' current proposals. They offer an outsider's advice on writing style and budgeting based on their own success.

Workshops and peer editing are often more useful that FAQ Web pages, clarifications, and information sessions. But they, too, have their limitations. If the criteria for judgments of merit are confusing to applicants, they are almost certainly confusing to judges as well (see the following chapter for a discussion). Consequently, criteria are likely to shift among judges' multiple understandings from year to year, depending on the range of new applications and the orientations of new committee members. What is good advice about winning last year's competition may not be good for this year. Writing workshop participants usually have diverse and specific problems reflecting their research specialties. Solutions offered to one participant rarely apply to other participants, many of whom sit in boredom while their colleague's questions are answered. Workshops also suck time and energy from busy academics. Few workshop leaders continue to offer their services more than a few years; most of those who do soon fall out of date as new judges and judgment procedures and funding priorities emerge in the funding organizations. In addition, improvements in the quality of proposals that come from workshops and peer editing also make the proposals sound more similar. As all proposals evolve to sound stylish and polished, style and polish no longer distinguish them, and judges must look to other criteria to decide who gets money and who does not. As we shall see in chapter 9, not all of the remaining criteria concern the quality of research ideas.

FAQs, clarifications, information sessions, grant writing workshops, peer editing, and related tactics are supposed to increase an applicant's understanding of what will be funded and how merit will be assessed. The limitations of these tactics lead us to two old conclusions: (a) no one can make a silk purse from a sow's ear and (b) an ounce of prevention is worth a pound of cure. If a solicitation of a competition is insufficient, contradictory, or unclear, nothing stands much of a chance of patching it. A solicitation announcement can be worded to defend a funding agency against improprieties or law suits. It can be filtered through several layers of bureaucrats for political correctness and organizational consistency. But if prospective applicants are confused by a solicitation, then no one should be surprised if many choose not to apply or if those who do apply submit confusing applications in return.

Application Forms

Compared to the importance of writing solicitations clearly, it may seem trivial to comment on the design of application forms. Yet there are so many badly designed forms, and so many curses leveled against them, that comment is due. Few grant competitions still allow applicants to write as much as they wish in their own discursive style. Forms provide structure for what to write and how much is written. A well-designed form provides enough structure to assist applicants in writing, and judges in finding, information with minimum fuss.

Most current application forms are noticeably longer and more complex than those of decades past. This is largely because funding agencies' statistical and financial auditing requirements have proliferated. Most current applications now have more restrictive limits on the number of words for proposed work than existed 10 or 20 years ago. In generations past, an applicant might be allowed 5,000 words to make an intellectual case for funding. Over time, an increasing proportion of applicants felt compelled to meet or exceed the limit, making a judge's task of reading their collected works increasingly tedious. In response, limits were cut. The typical limit for a proposal is now about 2,500 words. Appendices are sometimes allowed. When they are, proposals tend to thicken to the old limits. But reading appendices is optional, allowing judges the welcomed relief of ignoring them.

In order to remain comprehensible as forms lengthen, careful attention must be paid to form design. Such attention seems rare. Surely everyone has suffered the petty annoyances of forms with a page-wide line to write the date and an inch-wide line to write the project title or forms requiring printed responses that must be aligned with computer printers through trial and error. As online entry of grant proposals becomes more common, several other design blunders are frequently seen. They include the following.

- Forms with software bugs that have not been discovered and removed;
- Forms with jargon ("How many standardized functional employment units are you requesting during your initialization phase?")
- Forms requiring code numbers that cannot be found on the forms (example: "Enter your discipline and subdiscipline RPTFQ codes below; see www.sillybuggers.org for the code list");
- Secure sites that automatically assign passwords that applicants cannot remember from year to year logins;
- Secure sites that invalidate passwords every few weeks, requiring applicants to change them before frequent deadlines;
- Time limits to enter information (some sites allow only 10 minutes before automatically logging out a hapless applicant);
- Unusual, nonstandard CV-résumé formatting requirements that do not match the discipline;
- Character, not word, limits on proposal length;
- No provisions for graphics or illustrations;
- No relation between the importance of criteria of merit and amount of information allowed for these criteria (example: limit your methods section to 200 words but give us 500 words justifying why you seek a travel budget).

Such design flaws make the normally unpleasant and time-consuming task of proposal composition close to intolerable. Most, perhaps all, of the flaws can be eliminated. The hard way is to tell a reluctant employee in an organization's IT shop to develop a Web site with an application form, wait for complaints about the form to accrue during a competition, and then modify it after a competition ends. The easy way is to hire people who know something about form design to develop the form, hire some prospective applicants to try the site and criticize it, and fix the site before it goes public.

BEYOND RESEARCH GRANT COMPETITIONS

Though we have discussed examples from research grant competitions, we believe the principles and phenomena they illustrate can be seen in many other kinds of competitions as well. Examples of eligibility rules, merit criteria, budget regulations, good and bad wording, and forms beyond research grant competitions can be found on thousands of Web sites. Some categories to Google (each with one example):

- civic awards (http://www.munileague.org/awards/default.htm)
- design awards (http://www.cooperhewitt.org/NDA/JURY/index.shtml)
- government contracts (http://contractscanada.gc.ca/en/busin-e.htm)
- scholarships (http://www.rhodesscholar.org/)
- jobs (http://www.monster.com/)

Many merit competitions are missing features of research grant competitions but include other features of their own. A common example is a reference letter requirement. While most research grant competitions collect reviews from peers after application, most job and scholarship competitions require reference letters with applications, presumably because the parent organizations believe that the letters give important or corroborating information about contestants. Letters missing from recent employers, for example, might signal that a job applicant had some problems with the employers, which might in turn lead to speculation that the applicant is prone to stubbornness or conflict. Judgment errors are, however, the most common outcome of such a speculative chain. Letters might also serve to assist lazy judges who are happy to bless an applicant endorsed by a famous person or a friend or to damn an applicant endorsed by an infamous person or a foe, without reading the content of the letter or the application it accompanies. Such a lazy procedure is, of course, the stuff of bias and error (see chapter 2), and it prompts laziness from letter writers as well. Why spend valuable time writing a reference letter that will likely not be read when it is now possible to copy and paste canned letters from the Internet (see, for example, "Instant Rec," n.d.)?

We can find no research testing the validity of reference letters in predicting job performance, scholarship, or anything else. Until such research is reported, we must rely on two indirect arguments to assess the utility of reference letters as merit criteria. First, they are, in their free-form ways, similar to unstructured interviews known to have severely limited validity in making personnel decisions (see, for example, Cortina, Goldstein, Payne, Davidson, & Gilliland, 2000). Second, glowing reference letters have shown an amusing but disturbing tendency to proliferate in the past decade. Perhaps because applicants now choose their referees carefully, or because many of the letters are no longer confidential, or because many of the letters are penned by applicants themselves, few are condemnatory; indeed, judging from modern reference letters, we seem to be basking in a generation of applicants who walk on water, a feat previously accomplished only by a few biblical figures (see Schneider, 2000). The result of such homogenous praise is to limit severely the variability, if not the sincerity, of information that reference letters provide. With no variability, there can be no predictive utility. So, unless the idiosyncrasies of a competition demand them, we believe that reference letters can be omitted with little loss of useful information.

A second difference between most research grant competitions and some other putative merit-based competitions is the appearance of skullduggery or cheating. Many prospective applicants shy away from a competition because they sense that it is a mere formality, a ritual necessitated by law or regulation that legitimizes or covers a decision already made. Common examples come from complaints about awarding contracts or employment offers, complaints stemming from a suspicion that the contract call for proposals or job description was tailor-made for an insider. It is likely dangerous for any organization to admit to such skullduggery, so most would argue strenuously that it had not occurred. Still, suspicion might be enough to dissuade good applicants from competing, thus limiting competitors to a few, including the prefavored one. No doubt, for example, the following composite, hypothetical advertisement is completely legitimate and unbiased. It does, however, illustrate how the wording, eligibility rules, and merit criteria of a job advertisement could suggest that the employer had someone in mind for the job.

Qualifications:

- Well-rounded individual who is politically sensitive with experience in policy and government relations management, with proven ability in the interpretation of political, legislative and regulatory policy development, and with established relationships with local levels of government and capital markets focused business.
- A thorough understanding of the process of policy decision making, and a minimum of five to seven years' experience in a previous leadership role encompassing policy development and implementation within the capital markets arena.
- Comprehensive understanding of capital markets and institutions operating in the financial sector, a thorough understanding of the capital-raising process in both public and private markets, and the regulatory framework in Capital Markets policy.
- Business degree with a focus on economics and finance, and completed Canadian Securities Course.
- An excellent understanding of tax and fiscal policy activity, as it relates to the Canadian economy, and comprehensive understanding of the debt and derivatives markets, including trading, financing, product development, equity etc.
- Exceptional ability and interest to represent the organization to the business community and association members.

Note as well that the advertisement above says nothing about how the criteria are assessed, weighted, or combined, nor does it say how many people will review the applications, when a decision will be made, or whether the losers will be notified. This is common in the employment world and prompts us to wonder why such information is not provided. There are likely several reasons. Advertising rates are often steep, and words might be spared to save money. The omission of information likely appreciated by applicants or competitors might simply reflect corporate habits or culture. Perhaps job description templates have no space for the information.

Equally likely, an employer might simply not know how the criteria will be assessed, weighted, and combined or not know who will judge the merit of applications or when a job offer will be made. When competitions proliferate, and when each competition is rather different than the rest, organizations must scramble to organize them. The chaos that frequently results can be seen when a new company must hire hundreds of people for new jobs or when a city passes a new bylaw that immediately requires new employees filling new and unprecedented jobs. Employers and competition organizers might clearly understand that fuller disclosure of information about their adjudications would increase applicants' feelings of procedural fairness and lead to a more organized competition, but the information might simply not be available to disclose. Indeed, while flying by the seat of their pants, many competition organizers are likely to desire the freedom gained by avoiding commitment to a clear set of rules of the game. What contestants call vagueness contest organizers may call flexibility.

The clear vision that many scientists have about criteria for judging the scientific merit of peers and their proposals is probably not duplicated in less lofty, improvised contests for sales staff or emergency sewer repair services. The latter are often handled on a case-by-case basis, by hiring the one who did a good job last year, having a gut feeling, or by "knowing a good contestant when I see one." As noted in chapter 2, ad hoc rules such as these are petri dishes of shifting standards, biases, corruption, and other unfair practices. Still, they reduce the paralysis of analysis and accomplish the task of making a decision when many contestants are perfectly acceptable and most of them look pretty much the same. Crusty employers and Survival TV producers might then ask: If contestants become accustomed to a dearth of information, if they lower their standards to tolerate opaque procedures, then why upset them with news about what really goes on?

Their question, though cynical, is critical. Prospective contestants in a sloppy or corrupt contest have three choices of action: They can avoid the contest; they can enter the contest with their own rules of fair play, hoping that good will triumph over evil; or they can cheat, expecting to gain a competitive edge. When the edge is gained, even by chance, cheating is more likely to be repeated (see chapter 7). This variation of Gresham's law ("Gresham," 2007), like the defecting choice in a Prisoner's Dilemma game, probably accounts for the growing popularity of books on how to be fake in a job or scholarship interview and for increasing reports of résumés spiced with self-serving lies (see, for example, Sahadi, 2004). It may also account for increasing incidence of cheating in sports, business, and finance (Callahan, 2004).

Two more differences between research grant competitions and other competitions deserve mention. First, many of the other competitions require application fees. These include competitions for university entrance and for arts trophies. Some competitions require information in their applications that can only be obtained by paying additional fees. Most graduate schools, for example, not only charge application fees but also require transcripts of grades, which are rarely free, and scores on standardized exams such as the LSAT, MCAT, TOEFL, SAT, or GRE, which are never free. Sometimes the fees are rationalized as a filter for seriousness, assumed to discourage dilatants and thus limit the height of the application pile. Sometimes they are justified as a payment for administrative expenses (the salaries of secretaries, the time of judges, etc.). Regardless of their justification, they do have at least one unfortunate, perhaps unethical, consequence: they discourage or prevent poor people from applying.

We illustrate with one example. Many universities charge about $100 to apply for admission. The Education Testing Service, which offers often-required exams such as the LSAT, MCAT, TOEFL, SAT, or GRE charges over $100 to take each. Transcripts might run $10 per copy. So an applicant must spend over $200 to apply to one university and over $400 to apply for three. Four hundred dollars is greater than the monthly family income of most students in poor countries and the monthly income of many poor students in rich countries. Perhaps this is why few of these students, including the talented ones, apply for admission competitions. We shudder to think how the difficulty will be compounded if companies begin to charge application fees for their job competitions.

Finally, some merit-based competitions differ from research grant competitions in their number. Most researchers looking for money can do little more than line up at a small number of government and private funding agencies holding a handful of competitions. In contrast, most students seeking university entrance or a scholarship, most general practitioners seeking a medical practice, most trilingually fluent Ivy League MBAs seeking an entry level management position, and many other prospective competitors have hundreds of competitions from which to choose. Indeed, some organizations, including universities and doctor-deprived communities, compete with each other for qualified candidates, leading to a reciprocated contest in which people compete for money or positions while organizations offering the money or positions compete for people. When good people are scarce and competitions to select them are plentiful, a buyer's market prevails. Then the merit of contests becomes as important as the merit of contestants and the perceived fairness and efficiency of contests cannot be ignored.

Practical Implications

As we noted at the beginning of this chapter, the rules of the game for research grant adjudications have been examined, evaluated, and modified more extensively than for perhaps any other kind of merit-based competition. As a result, many of the research grant adjudication rules have evolved to be as close to optimal as can be expected. Organizations wishing to start a new adjudication or to improve one already underway could thus do worse than mimicking what is done in the major research granting agencies. Finer points would likely need modification to suit the constraints of the adjudication. Football team tryouts and orchestra auditions, for example, do not require a list of publications. Job competitions usually require a résumé (equivalent to a scientist's curriculum vita) and an interview but do not require a proposal for work to be done if hired. Even so, general principles should transfer well. Here are a few of the general principles.

- The more planning and preparation done to establish clear and concise eligibility rules, merit criteria, and budgeting regulations before an adjudication, the better.
- The more prospective applicants and judges are informed of the rules of the game, the better. And the sooner, the better. Well-informed judges and applicants create fewer problems than do poorly informed judges and applicants.
- Clearly stated rules are more useful for everyone than are vaguely stated rules. Clear examples are better still. A torrent of queries from prospective applicants seeking clarification of the rules is a good indicator of wording problems. An ounce of clarity is worth a pound of clarification.
- Whenever possible, changes to the rules of the game should be made gradually and announced far in advance to allow prospective applicants time to adapt if they desire.
- Feedback from prospective, successful, and unsuccessful applicants can be exceedingly useful in improving adjudication rules. It should be regularly sought and used.

How can an organization develop clear and concise rules of the game? How can judges and applicants best be informed of these rules? What rules should be changed, and what is the best way to proceed in changing them? How can feedback best be solicited and used? It is difficult to overstate the usefulness of consultation in answering such practical questions. The trick is to determine whom to consult. One popular alternative is putative experts: long-time employees of personnel offices, retired judges, former winners—even authors of books on judging merit. Experts can be useful for many purposes; former winners, for example, often give useful opinions about how criteria should be judged and combined. But experts, by definition, are not new to the game (indeed, many no longer play it) and may overlook new problems facing new players. So it is worthwhile to look for the opinions of others as well.

As noted in chapter 1, organizations that conduct merit-based adjudications must serve at least four constituencies: First are the applicants, second are the judges, third are the adjudication staff, and fourth are sponsors and others who pay the bills. All four groups have the potential to offer useful suggestions about making or changing the rules of the game. Each group should be especially good at seeing the rules from their own perspective. All four perspectives are valuable. So organizations should seek improvements to their adjudications by quadrangulation—triangulation from four points of view.

The four constituencies may have varying interests in different aspects of the adjudication process and in different rules of the game. Sponsors, for example, likely have considerable interest in what they pay for and lesser interest in the design of application forms. Form design should be of greater interest to applicants and judges than to sponsors. It is sometimes advisable to allow one constituency to have more say in certain decisions than others. Employers, for example, would likely expect more say than would adjudication staff in what kind of job openings should be advertised, while judges would likely want more say than would applicants about eligibility and merit criteria. Even so, members of each constituency often provide good suggestions beyond their areas of interest. So it is worthwhile to seek consultation about all areas with all constituencies. The weights given to opinions about rules from different constituencies should be discussed and settled as consultations proceed.

It is usually infeasible to consult with all members of large constituencies. While sponsors and staff are normally few and easily identified, there may be thousands of prospective applicants and hundreds of prospective judges, and it may not be possible to identify more than a handful. Fortunately, it is not necessary; indeed, it is often not advisable. If normally distributed, we would expect half of constituency members to be below average in motivation, insight, and personal biases. Ask Frank, a prospective scholarship applicant, for his opinions about new scholarship merit criteria, and he may respond with no more than "Whatever" or "Dunno" Ask Mary, an anthropology graduate and prospective applicant for managerial jobs, for her opinions about eligibility criteria for the jobs, and she might suggest that the jobs only be open to anthropology graduates.

It may be difficult to find motivated and insightful constituents to vet ideas about new adjudications or rules of the game, but it is worth the effort. Large samples are unnecessary; three to five motivated and articulate members of each constituency should normally suffice. We have found the best evaluators to be sensitive to detail and quick to complain. These are the people who find fault with the time taken to complete an application form, the number of phone calls requesting clarification, or the quality of judges' notepads. Though obstreperous complainers can be annoying, a good complainer is most likely to spot the flaws that bedevil even the most well-intentioned adjudication. There is nothing more instructive, for example, than a straight-talking applicant or judge who can read a draft of adjudication rules, point a finger, and exclaim, "What in hell does this mean?" When good complainers are found, try to retain them as consultants, invite them to comment frequently, and pay them for their work. If larger samples of constituents are required for special, one-off evaluations, they can be collected as needed.

Despite the noble cause of perfecting the rules of the game, consultation can be lengthy and cumbersome. It can also breed conflicts. A consulting applicant for a music competition might disagree with a sponsor who believes that a special award should be created for the worst performance. A consulting staff member might disagree with a judge who suggests that scholarship applicants submit a handwriting sample. By placing a period of consultation between the creation or alteration of an adjudication and the public launch of the adjudication, new or improved, organizers must plan further ahead than usual to receive consultants' evaluations and to resolve the conflicts they may bring. There are dozens of means to resolve conflicts (see Deutsch & Coleman, 2006), and we encourage adjudication organizers to try some as the need arises. As a general rule, organizers should plan for 6–10 months of consultation before a new or improved adjudication makes its debut. They should also plan some workshops on how to run pretests and field trials.

Software developers have their beta tests and testers. Car manufacturers have their prototypes and test tracks. Marketers have their focus groups. Scientists have their pilot studies. Drug companies have their clinical trials. The idea of pretesting has a long and successful history. Pretesting adjudications and their rules among samples of people who will likely be affected by them might reduce future complications by half. Retesting adjudications regularly should reduce the complications by half again each time one is undertaken. New complications will surely emerge and some will never be eliminated. But they can be better managed with forethought than with afterthought.

6

Organizing Adjudication Committees

A fter applications for adjudication are collected, someone must assess their merit. Many assessments are made by one person; chapters 2 and 3 discussed some of the psychological mechanisms used to make these judgments and some of their pitfalls. Yet at least as many assessments of applications are made by committees of two or more people. Most large organizations have personnel committees to select or promote the most meritorious job applicants. University departments have admissions committees to select the most talented graduate school applicants. Almost all research granting organizations and peer-reviewed journals have committees to choose winning applications or manuscripts. The winners of many sports competitions such as figure skating, diving, and gymnastics are chosen by committee. Other committees can be found judging contestants in competitions ranging from music and art to Nobel prizes, from tenure to contracts for hospital food or building maintenance.

Formal arguments for judging merit by committee are hard to find, but anecdotal justifications reveal several popular themes. Many people believe that it is ethically desirable and politically correct for members of organizations who must live with the consequences of merit judgments to have their say in making the judgments. So committees are formed of members who might supervise, work for, share an office with, reward, pay, educate, or otherwise be affected by the results of merit judgments. The belief resembles the "consent of the governed" principle offered to justify democracy. Many people also form adjudication committees in hopes of dividing the labor among committee members, decreasing each member's judicial workload. Some people reason that committee judgments have more authority than individual judgments because more people make them. As a corollary, these people also reason that group judgments divide the responsibility for bad judgments among committee members, reducing individual guilt and blame. Committees also meet to judge merit because it has become a tradition or habit, part of organizational culture. The habit is sometimes reinforced by occasional junkets to nice locations for committee deliberations.

Other reasons for justifying committee judgments of merit concern the validity and fairness of the result. Many people argue that more valid and fair judgments of merit can be made by two or more people who discuss their opinions than by one person judging alone. The arguments resemble those favoring trial-by-jury over trial-by-judge and reflect the adage that "two heads are better than one." Committee members are assumed to bring different points of view to a meeting and triangulate a group judgment superior in validity and fairness to any individual judgment through the added value of committee deliberations.

The added-value argument deserves further consideration. Although there are several different kinds of validity, the most common, called *predictive validity*, is normally assessed by comparing a judgment with an objective criterion. If, for example, a sportscaster judges the Almonte Aardvarks to be a better hockey team than the Pakenham Penguins, and the AAs beat the PPs in 17 consecutive games, we might say that the sportscaster's judgment was valid. If Ian the investor judges that the Cash Cow, Inc., will flourish next year and the company goes bankrupt, we would say that Ian's judgment was invalid. In such cases there is an objective definition (game outcomes and financial success) that allows us to assess validity as the difference between what is predicted or judged with what is real.

Alas, as we discussed in chapters 1 and 2, there is no objective definition of merit, so predictive validation is hard to do. Merit is, to pilfer a postmodern cliché, a social construction with several arbitrary definitions prone to all manner of social and political influences. Without possible objective definition of merit, it is not possible to discuss the predictive validity of a merit judgment. However, we can sometimes discuss other forms of validity, including one called *construct validity*, which is one step removed from predictive validity and often equally important. To assess construct validity, we begin by explicating a definition of merit; however, we wish to socially construct it. Suppose, for example, that an organization decides to run a competition for the best Elvis Presley impersonator. Adjudicators define, however arbitrarily, one or more criteria for assessing how close each pretender is to the original: hair, paunch, costume, voice, accent, wiggle, and the like. If the most meritorious impersonator is the one judged closest to the real Elvis on these criteria, then we can conclude that the judgment of merit has high construct validity. In short, criteria of merit might be subjective and socially constructed, but once the criteria and their measures are set, they can be used to assess the validity of merit judgments and to increase the chances of improving them.

A third form of validity is called *consensual validity*. As noted in chapter 1, judgments of merit are defined as consensually valid if everyone agrees that they are valid. Everyone? Sometimes this means everyone who is involved in making judgments: judges, organizers, and sponsors. But it can also mean all these and others, including applicants and observers. Consensual validation is an ideal solution to assessments based on socially constructed definitions and criteria—everything may be arbitrary, but if everyone agrees on everything, then who cares? Clocks go clockwise and everyone in North America agrees to drive on the right side of the road. These rules are arbitrary but consensually validated; people do not argue they were late because clocks ran in the wrong direction or that they collided with an oncoming car because the right-hand rule is invalid.

Committee members judging applicants frequently reach consensus about their merit judgments; consensual validation is thus achieved. When it is not, the members usually resort to majority rule or fiat to resolve their differences. But their consensus is frequently not shared by the applicants whose merit was judged, especially among the applicants whose merit was judged to be lacking. Like players and fans who disagree with a referee's call, many applicants feel more anger than disappointment at what they consider a bad call, and some are sure to protest. One result is the growth of appeals, which, regardless of their outcome, drain the time and energy of everyone.

Disappointments in the outcome of a merit judgment often turn to anger when there is suspicion about how the outcome was achieved. The shift in emotions reflects a distinction between distributive justice and procedural justice. Distributive justice is said to occur when applicants receive what they believe they merit or deserve. Conversely, distributive injustice occurs when people do not receive what they believe they merit or deserve. Procedural justice is said to occur when people believe the criteria and procedures for deciding merit and distributing its rewards are, well, just or fair. Its converse, procedural injustice, occurs when people believe that unjust criteria or procedures were employed. Many people believe that fair procedures lead to fair distributions (e.g., see Lind & Tyler, 1988) and look to improving judgment processes as the best means for improving outcomes. The belief is not always correct, as we shall see in chapter 7. But we shall assume that it is correct here in order to make suggestions for guidelines to improve the fairness of judging merit by committee.

Gordon Hewart (1870–1943) gave us the venerable aphorism that "Justice should not only be done, but should manifestly and undoubtedly be seen to be done" (Andrews, Biggs, & Seidel, 1996). The same is true of fairness. Adjudication orgnizers face two equally important challenges: (a) designing a fair adjudication and (b) demonstrating the fairness of the adjudication to current and prospective applicants. Losing applicants are especially prone to criticize how the decisions were made. Few losers readily admit that they or their applications were inferior; instead, they seek to explain their loss by finding fault with the adjudicators or the adjudication process. A common but unhelpful response to these folks is to suggest that they "Trust us," "Suck it up," or "Get over it." Phrases such as these add insult to injury and frequently escalate bad feelings and complaints. A rarer but much wiser response is to give more information about how the judgments were made.

This chapter and the next one examine some of the factors that influence the validity of committee judgments and perceptions of the fairness of these judgments. Some of these factors sow their influence before a committee meets, factors related committee membership, judgment criteria, roles and workloads, the time and place of meeting, and the solicitation of outside opinions. We shall examine these factors in the current chapter. Other factors emerge from the structure and dynamics of committee deliberations, including procedural rules for considering applicants, resolving disagreements, and combining opinions, as well as social influence tactics and conformity pressures. Still others appear at the end of, or after, committee deliberations, when judgments of merit must be translated into prizes or rewards or letters of rejection. Because these many factors interact in complex and often contrary ways, attempts to improve committee judgments are as much art and craft as science. But it is not a tranquil art. Ask any organizer of a merit-based, committee adjudication and you will almost certainly hear hair-raising stories of conflict, compromise, and stress. Still, careful observation, a little research, and some common sense can be useful for directing attempts to improve deliberations.

As in the previous chapter, we shall again focus our discussion on peer-review committees judging applications for research grants. Our reasons have not changed. We have more experience participating in and studying these committees than any others. Most of our peer-review committee work has been in organizations that invest considerable time and money trying to improve the committee adjudication process. We believe that much can be learned from their trials, errors, and triumphs. Other scholars have studied other groups, including juries (for example, see Hastie, 1993; Hastie, Penrod, & Pennington, 2002), voters (Norris, 2004), personnel committees (Barclay & York, 2003; Posthuma, 2003; Stumpf & London, 1981), and organizational elites (Baron, 2005; Janis, 1972). The problems and pathologies of committees that they uncover parallel those we report here, as do many of the recommendations they propose.

To make the current chapter more useful, we ask you to imagine that you have recently been hired by a large granting agency to organize and administer a committee conceived to adjudicate research grant applications for some area of scholarship or science—software engineering, architecture, African history, diabetes, or any of hundreds of others will do. Adjudication organizers are usually responsible for solving the problems of committees. But successful solutions for the committee often create new problems for those whom the committee serves—namely, the applicants. Conversely, solutions to problems faced by applicants often create new problems for the committee. Much of the stressful art of managing an adjudication committee involves negotiating compromises to the competing interests of committee members and applicants. Here are some examples.

COMMITTEE SELECTION

Membership

Who should be on a committee and who should not? Put in different words, who merits being a judge of merit—what criteria for judging judges should be employed? In the ideal world of peer review, every committee would be filled with members who shared expertise in all areas relevant to all applications; who had no biases or inconsistencies of any kind; who were highly motivated to promote high-quality research; who filled the room with wisdom, held no grudges, and showed no more than minor disagreements, easily resolved. In our accumulated years of observing adjudication committees of all kinds, we have never seen such a committee. Some have been close, but most have had their personnel problems and these problems have occasionally been severe.

Peer review requires credible peers, which usually means that the peers exhibit proper expertise and an unbiased attitude. Hoping to increase committee expertise, most organizations look for established scholars, assuming they will have more expertise than lesser folk. The desire for expertise flows from a belief that people with expertise are better able to judge merit than people without it. The belief seems reasonable at the extreme. It is easy to argue, for example, that a high school dropout who rarely and barely reads would not have sufficient expertise to judge fairly the relative merit of three proposals for research on, say, stochastic topology, synaptic biochemistry, or comparative religion. On the other hand, there is no good reason to believe that a junior scholar in such areas will be any less competent at judging merit than a senior scholar. Beyond a minimal level of background knowledge, there is no consistent relationship between expertise and the validity of judgment (e.g., see Goldberg, 1969; Oskamp, 1965). Alas, neither group is stellar, as we shall discuss in chapter 8.

Senior scholars do add a patina of credibility to committee deliberations and often boost perceptions of fairness among those who believe that senior scholars can do no wrong. Adjudication organizers wanting good public relations cannot, therefore, be blamed for wanting senior scholars on committees. But senior scholars have their limitations. Many of them, for example, are too busy to serve or they face scheduling constraints because of other demands on their time. And many of them do not have the expertise desired. As knowledge expands, the subareas of any discipline proliferate. There are, for example, over 1,500 journals in psychology alone, representing over 500 subspecialties, each with its own variation of methods, concepts, and controversies. Over 90,000 research articles are published in psychology each year. A dedicated scholar has time to read perhaps 50 of these per year; busy scholars rarely read more than 25. So no scholar can hope to claim expertise in more than a handful of topics; beyond the handful, the topical expertise of a senior scholar may be no different from that of a well-read graduate student.

Some competition organizers still prefer senior scholars in the belief that their judgments will be seen as fairer than those of juniors. Perhaps outsiders would view them as fairer because of a mental association between grey hair and credibility. But there is little reason to believe that applicants would follow suit. Applicants are far more likely to assess judges according to their judgments than to assess judgments according to their judges. Most applicants would reason that an approving committee member is credible and that a disapproving committee member is not. It stretches our imagination to think of losers consoling themselves because they were rejected by a senior scholar. It is easier to believe that losers would question any critical judgment and rely on the credibility of the reasons given, rather than the credibility of their source, in assessing the fairness of the adjudication process.

For these reasons, attitude is probably more important than expertise in selecting committee members. The attitude of a committee member, how he approaches the task, can have a large effect on his judgments of merit. Consider a committee member who is apathetic and who adopts an attitude of minimal involvement in making fair decisions. Such a member would likely spend little time digesting every word of every application; he simply would not care. Indeed, an apathetic member, faced with the task of reading a stack of applications, might decide to skim only a handful of applications and ignore the rest, approving of those skimmed regardless of their merit. Or an apathetic member might read nothing, relying instead on the arguments other members give to support or criticize each application, and then vote according to the arguments. More extreme, an apathetic member might choose to trade favors with other committee members, voting for each others' friends or against each others' enemies.

If apathy is a dangerous extreme, so too is vested interest. It is possible that some committee members come to an adjudication committee with a personal or ideological agenda, an attitude toward certain kinds of applicants or applications that dooms them to rejection. Such an attitude might be secretly expressed as, "It's a waste of money to fund nursing applications!" or "Nobody who was supervised by Professor Beelzebub should ever receive a grant!"

Less extreme attitudes can also affect judgments. It is often claimed, for example, that many senior scholars become stuck in their old ways of thinking; their old ideas, after all, are the source of their expertise and reputation. A committee filled with senior scholars, however well respected, might thus prefer applications for research smugly similar to their own. There is at least one glaring problem with this: science progresses by mutation rather than replication, by challenging or abandoning the ideas of senior scientists rather than extrapolating from them. Senior scholars might prefer derivative applications, not because they are reactionary but because they, like most of us, prefer what they know. But the effect is the same. If applicants with mutant ideas are not supported, they are more likely than their traditional and supported cousins to direct their talent elsewhere, decreasing the chances of scientific progress.

We do not know what proportion of committee members approach the task of judging merit with such attitudes. No research we know has been done to estimate the proportion and, because few judges are eager to be scrutinized for biases, we doubt that such research could ever be done. We do know, however, that it is better to exclude such people from committees than to welcome them. The trick is to learn who they are. Curriculum vitae can be scrutinized for expertise, but CVs do not contain information about attitudes that might bias the adjudication process. Probably the best that can be done is to observe what committee members do during one adjudication process, looking for manifestations of apathy, vested interests, or other bad attitudes leading to unfair judgments—and then don't invite the bad apples back.

If committee members with bad attitudes cannot be excluded, then perhaps their harm can be limited. There are several ways to limit the harm they do. One way is to add new rules of order in the adjudication process whenever a hole is found that lets harm through (see chapter 5). Conflict of interest rules, for example, are almost always added for this reason; members are expected to leave the room when the applications of friends, students, or colleagues are being discussed. Another way to limit harm is to rotate committee membership so that no bad apple serves for more than a few adjudications. A third is to increase the size of committees, hoping that a few suspect committee members will be smothered by a host of good ones or that two opinionated committee members will have conflicting opinions and cancel each other out.

There are strengths and limitations in each of these possible solutions. Adding rules to plug holes could help if everyone knows the rules and abides by them. However, as rules accrue over years of activity, their number and complexity can become oppressive and frequently ignored. A classic example comes from Henry

Martyn Robert, author of the 1876 pamphlet, *Pocket Manual of Rules of Order for Deliberative Assemblies*, which grew malignantly over 10 editions into *Robert's Rules of Order*, an edition containing over 700 pages of procedural rules for group decisions requiring months or years of study (see Robert, Evans, et al., 2000). Few committee members enjoy reading lots of procedural rules, especially when they are difficult to understand. Many ignore them, believing that rules will be monitored and enforced by adjudication organizers and that any transgressions will be duly addressed. Others—known in the subculture as *bulldozers*—like to know the rules and use them to their own advantage, hoping to manipulate or intimidate other committee members to their own point of view.

Most peer-review committees meet repeatedly and, as the years go by, attrition takes its toll. Some members move, retire, or die; some face scheduling conflicts; some just lose interest in the committee work. Anticipating attrition, most adjudication organizers set limits on the tenure of committee members; 2 to 4 years is common. By staggering the beginning and end of tenure periods, committee membership can rotate; each year, for example, new recruits would replace perhaps a third of the old guard. This has the advantage of limiting to a few years the damage done by members with bad attitudes. Applicants who believe that they were unfairly treated by one generation of a committee can then wait it out, if possible, and try again when a new generation begins.

Alas, there is no guarantee that the new generation will be any fairer than the previous one. If this were the case, long-running committees would have evolved close to perfection by now. Bad apples are eventually eliminated by rotation, but so too are the good ones. And new recruits are often hard to find. Though there is some prestige associated with committee membership, committee tasks are usually time consuming, and membership can perforate an otherwise productive career. To avoid the perception of feathering their own nest, for example, members are normally not allowed to apply for funding while they sit on the committee. So many prospective recruits are forced to choose between a chance to get money for their own research or a funding hiatus for the honor of giving the money to others. Most go for the money, leaving a limited set of prospects for committee work.

Adjudication organizers must also worry about the relations among committee members. Young members may feel intimidated by old ones, especially the bulldozers. Personal rivalries, some decades old, may resurface. A contentious judgment lost one year may lead an otherwise staid committee member to even the score the next year. It is usually considered improper for organizers to ask prospective committee members if they have any personal objections to working with the other committee members, so most organizers make do with reminders to remain professional during the proceedings. A reminder usually works, and professionalism prevails but, when it does not, personal animosities can hijack committee work.

Committee Size

In view of the limits on the number and type of people interested in serving on committees, many competition organizers wonder about how big a committee should be. The organizers face conflicting pressures, some to make committees large and some to keep them small. There is pressure to increase the size of the committees in order to spread the workload. There is pressure to expand committees in order to smooth the rough edges of inconsistencies and biases produced by apathy, vested interests, and personal animosities. There is pressure to expand committees to include experts in increasingly specialized research areas or to make committees appear and be more representative of the range of applicants and the diversity of their proposals. Some of this has been done in the name of political correctness—the addition of community representatives to community research committees is a popular example. Their addition seems to increase public perceptions, and perhaps even applicants' perceptions, that the committee decisions are fair. And though many committee members once argued that such representatives were too naïve to be peers, their participation has arguably more often improved committee judgments than sullied them.

Yet increasing the size of committees also increases the logistic problems of organizing them and of getting their judgment job done. Scheduling problems, for example, increase exponentially as members are added. It is rarely easy to schedule even a handful of busy people to meet at the same place and time. Prior commitments, some scheduled months in advance, make it unlikely that all committee members will share the same free time sooner than perhaps 2 months in the future. Add a few more to the committee and the first common free time may be 6–12 months away. During the interim, chance events such as sickness, accidents, or other personal emergencies may force some prospective members to withdraw, leading contest organizers to scramble for last-minute replacements. The larger the committee, the more likely this would happen, and the more likely that suitable replacements would not be found.

There is never enough time during committee deliberations for committee members to read applications while sitting at the table. A typical member may be responsible for reading 10–30 applications, each 10–30 pages long, so perhaps 500 pages of material must be ingested and digested for judgments of merit to be made The task can take 50 hours, far longer than anyone can sustain attention in one committee meeting. So when committee members are chosen and a meeting time is set, the members must be given application materials far enough in advance to read and assess them before committee deliberations begin. The applications must be included, of course, as well as the rules of the game (chapter 5).

The larger the committee, the greater the headaches of circulating applications and instructing judges in a timely way. Many applicants complain about rigid submission deadlines set far in advance of an adjudication. The complaint reflects a general frustration with the delays that inevitably increase when members are added to committees (including external reviewers; see below). This creates special difficulties for researchers who want to study unpredictable events such as the spread of disease or responses to natural disasters. Researchers cannot book a disaster a year or more in advance in order to meet distant application deadlines. So researchers are inclined to eschew studies of the unpredictable world for a more controllable laboratory climate. As a result, the study of unexpected phenomena declines.

The size of committees also affects the dynamics of their deliberations. Large committees take longer to deliberate than do small ones, in part because more people choose to speak. But committee time is limited, and time pressures often dictate the nature of deliberations. When time is limited, the larger a committee, the higher the proportion of its deliberations that are dominated by a few (Bales, 1950, 1953). Members of two-person committees, for example, tend to share their words almost equally; members of 12-person committees tend to split between a clique of two to four people who generate 80% of discussion and the remainder who frequently nod or grunt approval but rarely speak. The value of nods and grunts for making fair judgments of merit remains dubious, inviting us to wonder what purpose the extra members serve.

For these and other reasons, there seems to be a practical upper limit on the size of an adjudication committee. Few function well with more than seven members (Gabel & Shipan, 2000; Karotkin & Paroush, 2003; Manners, 1975). Often, a committee with seven members functions no better than a committee with three. Though generalizations are risky, we believe that a smaller committee with fair and active members is better than a larger committee with unfair or passive members (Francis, 1982). Many adjudication organizers realize that it is usually better to put more effort into selecting members with care than into adding members with abandon. But small, well-functioning committees might not pass Hewart's "seen to be done" test of fairness as often as larger, more inclusive committees, even though the latter is likely to be more unwieldy and fractious—another dilemma for organizers.

External Opinions

There remains the nagging problem of specialization. Faced with the possibility that no member of a peer review committee would have sufficient background to give a fair assessment of some grant applications, research granting organizations often rush to one solution: sending applications to putative experts, who are not on the committee, for review. The experts, usually called *external reviewers*, are sometimes selected from a long list of volunteers with self-declared specializations and sometimes selected from a shorter list of specialists given by the applicants themselves. They are usually asked to submit their reviews by mail several weeks prior to committee deliberations, further delaying judgment proceedings.

Most organizers are lucky if half of the external reviewers contacted for judgments of merit send their judgments in. Hoping for three such reviews per proposal, organizers are usually happy to receive one or two. External reviewers rarely face the same procedural constraints that lead committee members toward consistency and fairness. So the external reviews are much freer to express whatever biases they have. Though most external reviews we have read indicate that their authors do their serious best to be objective and fair, a stubborn minority give the impression that bias is there. Despite instructions to be polite, some external reviews are vicious—"No redeeming merit! Written by an idiot!" When these are written by reviewers whose own work is being challenged by the proposed research, a motive for bias is easily attributed. At the other extreme are praises so glowing, yet so short, as to suggest that the external reviewer did not put critical facilities into second gear. Some of these reviews come from external reviewers who are too busy to complete their voluntary review task and choose to be laudatory as a face-saving ploy. In short, just because an application is sent to experts does not mean that experts will give it a serious or fair review.

Even when external reviewers are as fair as they can be, they are no more likely to show consensus in their judgments of merit than are members of the committee they assist. Indeed, the more external reviewers who judge an application, the greater the chances that at least two of them will disagree. Disagreements among external reviewers are common, as are disagreements between external reviewers and committee members. How should these disagreements be resolved? If external reviews call for numerical ratings, it is hard to resist the temptation to average them. But most external reviews call only for a verbal assessment, leading a committee member to three temptations: (a) condemn any application that receives at least one bad review and/or no glowing review; (b) attend only to the reviews that agree with his own assessment; (c) ignore all reviews and go with a personal opinion.

In short, external reviews of grant proposals are as likely to make a merit judgment more difficult as they are to make it easier unless there are very clear procedural rules for incorporating them into committee judgments. The same, we should note, is true of reference letters for jobs, scholarships, and university admission, especially now that almost all reference letters are glowing and thus have lost their utility in distinguishing meritorious applicants from the rest. Perhaps realizing the mixed utility of external reviews, the Canadian Institutes of Health Research now allows applicants in many of its competitions to decide whether or not they wish to have them.

Committee Subdivision

If adding committee members to increase committee expertise makes committees unwieldy, and if adding external reviews muddies waters as often as it clears them, what else can be done? Some granting organizations try a third strategy: they create many small and specialized committees in preference to few large and general ones, packing each with as much specialized expertise as they can. The Canadian Institutes for Health Research again provides a good example; in 2006 it had no fewer than 46 committees covering topics ranging from metabolism to respiratory system, social dimensions in aging to palliative and end of life care.

There is much good to be said for this alternative but, as usual, there are dangers as well. Small and specialized committees are likely to work more efficiently, if not more fairly, than their larger and more inclusive cousins. Packing each of the small committees with members who cover most of their specialized field can reduce the anxiety of soliciting and processing external reviews. But the care and feeding of many small committees can be an administrative nightmare. Problems can occur when, for example, two members a three-person committee fall sick just before deliberations, leaving a committee of one. More problems can occur when all committee members personally know most of the applicants in their specialization and are ethically bound to excuse themselves from deliberations about these applications. A committee cannot function when all of its members must leave the room. Additional problems can occur when a small committee must assess a large number of applications. With fewer colleagues to spread the workload, members are liable to become overwhelmed, perhaps reducing the fairness of their judgments and discouraging them from serving on the committee again.

There is another and equally troublesome problem linked to the small committee solution. When should a new committee be created or an old committee disbanded? Decisions about the creation of new committees or disbanding of old ones are almost always made by adjudication organizers, and a political component almost always looms large. Like decisions about which sports are given representation in the Olympics, decisions about forming new specialized committees can become the caldron of intense lobbying and debate. The most common reason is money. Research granting, peer-review committees exist to distribute research money, so they must have some to distribute in order to serve their function. The money must come either from creating new wealth or from raiding the budgets of other committees. In good years, budgets expand and it is relatively easy to seed new committees with startup funds. In bad years, budgets remain stable or decline and money for new committees must be taken from the budgets of others. When budgeting becomes a zero-sum game, conflicts escalate. If, for example, a new committee were established to fund research on the health benefits of pets, and if money for its budget were taken from the prostate cancer and HIV research budgets, it would not be hard to envision the wars that followed.

To avoid such wars, it is tempting to consider disbanding existing committees and using their funds for new ones. Selecting criteria for deciding which committees should be disbanded brings another recursive set of problems. Obvious criteria such as a declining number of applications or high rejection rates are likely to lead some committee members to chase more applications or to lower their standards. The recent trend toward funding strategic themes or applied topics deemed to be socially important (see chapter 5) with designated 3- to 5-year funding limits offers one way to minimize the conflicts and maneuvering that can occur when existing committees assume that they will judge merit for money forever. And it suggests that no specialization, and no committee, should be immune from regular scrutiny and limited lifetimes.

TIME CONSTRAINTS AND DIVISION OF LABOR

Peer-review committee members rarely have a lot of time, so it is advisable for organizers to limit the time they require of members to prepare for committee deliberations. This is not difficult when a committee must review a half dozen short proposals. It can be challenging when a committee is faced with reviewing, say, 100 long proposals, each requiring 1–3 hours of concentration.

There are two popular ways to limit review time. The first is to limit the length of grant proposals. Almost all major funding organizations now do so, although most still allow generous appendices, which many applicants attach in hopes that adjudicators will find the time to read them and be duly impressed. Imposing length limits often stimulates waves of protest among applicants, especially those whose proposals are rejected because they did not provide sufficient information. A common response is to suggest that the applicants take a workshop in concise writing. Some may indeed benefit from the experience. However, the frustrated applicants often have a fair point. It is, for example, much easier to write a short proposal to extend existing work using well-known theories and methods than it is to write a short proposal for new work using new or little-known theories and methods. The new or obscure parts require explanation, but page or word limits make this impossible. As a result, new ideas are less likely to be proposed than the old ones.

The second most common way of limiting review time is to divide the labor. Most research proposals, including the short ones, are dense and thus require considerable concentration to ingest, digest, and assess. It can easily take at least an hour to read and evaluate one proposal in detail. Few committee members want to spend more than 20 or 30 hours at the task. Asking for more pushes the limits of goodwill by exceeding a committee member's available time and motivation.

Many organizations do not require every committee member to read every grant application. Instead, members Frank and Mary might read proposals 1–20 in detail and skim the rest; Ann and George might read proposals 21–40 and skim the rest, and so on. More sophisticated divisions are possible; for example, Frank and Mary read proposals 1–7, Frank and Ann read 8–14, Frank and George read 15–21, Mary and Ann read 22–28, Mary and George read 29–35, and Ann and George read 36–42. In any case, the goals are the same: to ensure that each proposal is read by at least two peers while limiting the task of judging the merit within reasonable time limits. The tradition of assuring that each proposal is read and judged by at least two peers gives tacit recognition to the long-standing observation that judges of merit, including peers, frequently disagree (see chapter 1). If they did not, there would be no need for committees; a single peer would do.

There are, not surprisingly, many ways to distribute proposals among committee members. One of the most common is by alphabetical order: Frank and Mary read proposals written by applicants Adams–Dunlop; Ann and George read proposals written by applicants Elridge–Kravitz, and so forth. Another way is to divide the proposals according to expertise; all the cat proposals go to the two cat experts on the committee, all the dog proposals go to the two dog experts, etc. Though the second makes more sense, it brings the possibility that some research topics or areas attract far more proposals than others, leading experts in popular areas to be stuck with far more proposals to evaluate than experts in others. Some way must be then found to spread the burden equally, which inevitably leads to some proposals being assessed by members with less expertise or by more external reviewers.

A committee member faced with a stack of applications is likely to want some guidelines for how to judge them. It is easy for competition organizers to instruct members to "use your better judgment" but the instruction is almost a license for inconsistency and bias. In our era of accountability, it is best to give members the written list of criteria for judging merit that was given in the solicitations for applications and then to teach how to apply these criteria to the applications they read (see chapters 3 and 5).

We have noted in previous chapters how vague criteria can befuddle applicants. Vague criteria can also befuddle judges. How does a committee member assess an application's innovativeness, methodological relevance, contribution to the field, or potential for sustainability? How does a member judge the applicant's track record, advanced training focus, or capacity for successful completion of the project? And how should assessments related to these criteria be weighed and combined into one judgment of an application's merit? The questions have their parallels in church committees assessing the merit of applicants for minister (weighing spiritual leadership, pastoral credibility, etc.), scholarship committees assessing the merit of music students (execution, phrasing, seriousness of purpose, etc.), and wine judges assessing the merit of merlots (body, nose, pretension, and the like).

In view of the inconsistencies and biases that can intrude on competitions with vague criteria, it is logical to suggest that vagueness should be banished, and that only precise criteria of merit should be used. But most competitions simply do not have precise criteria, vitiating the suggestion. Still, some try. Among the most fallible criteria in the rare world of research grant applications we find *objective indicators*, a fancy term for numbers. To assess research competence, for example, counts are made of an applicant's vita weight or of her publications, publications in the past 5 years, or publications in journals that themselves have been scaled for prestige by counts of the number of citations. In this way, no committee member need read the publications or try to understand them. The result is rather like judging musical performances by counting the number of wrong notes or judging a dancer by average leaping height.

When faced with a choice between vague criteria that are relevant to merit versus precise criteria that have no relevance, it is logical to choose the first but tempting to choose the second. An irrelevant criterion will, by definition, have no relationship to merit no matter how precisely it is measured. But a vague criterion has potential to predict merit as long as it is consistently applied. Alas, our experience suggests that many judges weigh precise criteria more heavily than vague criteria in making their assessments—like the drunk who looks for his lost keys under the street lamp because "That's where the light is." This causes applicants to promote their careers with countable fluff rather than readable substance, a topic discussed in the next chapter.

Training

If committee members can be taught to improve the fairness of their judgments using criteria provided (chapter 3), how and when should their training occur? Knowledge of pedagogy tells us that scant learning will occur unless clear cues and clear feedback are provided. Nothing can be learned if there is nothing to learn. If none of the criteria employed are predictive of merit, then it is more efficient to teach judges how to flip a coin than to expose them to criteria lists and adjudication guidelines. On the other hand, if some criteria do seem to predict merit, then there is hope that practice with feedback can improve a member's judgments. This rudimentary insight leads to visions of judges practicing their tasks before the competition, perhaps in an online exercise that allows them to obtain feedback about how they are weighing the information given and how their judgments compare with those of other judges. In this way, judges would at least have an opportunity to mold their assessments more closely to the guidelines and to become more consistent with their peers. Indeed, judges who try such a pedagogical procedure and fail might be excluded from the committee.

Training judges seems reasonable, but it is rarely done. All peer-review committees we have witnessed prepare their peers with no more than a cheat-sheet of criteria and instructions. Perhaps training is minimal because it consumes time, money, and patience, and it lengthens the wait for an adjudication to begin. Perhaps it is because judgment, like teaching, is (incorrectly) assumed to mature as a happy side effect of learning to do research. Pity. As the sports homily tells us: good players rarely make good referees.

Although the vast majority of organizations do not offer training for their adjudicators, most of them tacitly acknowledge that previous experience in judging merit is useful and important. The acknowledgement is evident from asking committee members to serve multiple terms. As noted above, most of the organizations also rotate membership so that each year fresh troops can mix with, and presumably learn from, the seasoned ones.

Such learning does occur, so it is important to question what is learned. New committee members are as likely to learn bad judgment habits by watching their seasoned peers as they are to learn good ones. Organizations relying on the old guard to teach the abecedarians on the job relinquish control over the training process. This can be dangerous, especially when the old guard perpetuates inconsistencies or biases. It would be nice to believe that the bad habits of committees— for example, a bad habit of giving money to most applications considered early in deliberations and rejecting most of the ones left over when members are tired and bored—die out as committees pass from one generation to the next. But without intervention, they do not (see, for example, Weick & Gilfillan, 1971).

Scheduling

Applicants for research money normally want to learn of committee judgments of the merit of their proposals as soon as possible. Many applicants live with considerable pressure to find research money and do not appreciate waiting month after month for feedback. Much of this pressure comes from universities who hire a large proportion of their new faculty members with the expectation that they will, like sales staff in a used car lot, bring income to their employer. Some of the income is spent to hire research assistants and support staff, all of whom are anxious to learn if they can continue their specialized work. Some is spent on overhead, defined as loosely as university debts can stretch. Many prospective applicants, facing a wait of 6 months or more to learn whether their 200+-hour effort to write a winning proposal succeeded or not, are likely to seek funding elsewhere. Justice delayed is justice denied. Organizations taking too much time for their adjudications could face the embarrassment of declining applications and the resulting possibility of future funding cutbacks.

How often should committees meet and when? Applicants understandably prefer committees to meet frequently. Quarterly meetings with four separate deadlines each year, for example, allow applicants much more flexibility than do biannual meetings in timing their submissions. They also reduce the number of applications considered at each meeting. But there are three problems with frequent meetings. The first problem is budgetary. Organization budgets are normally given once a year. If more than one competition is held each year, then an organization faces the possibility that it will award most of its money in the first meeting and have little left for the remaining adjudications. This can be especially embarrassing if applications submitted later in the year are better than those funded from the first competition. The reverse can also occur. A committee that is reluctant to award money in the first adjudication might discover that rejected applications from that competition are better than those submitted in the remaining competitions. In either case, the committee would likely be seen as unfair.

The second problem with frequent competitions is logistic. Adjudications are not easy to organize. Organizers need time to publicize competitions, answer the questions of confused applicants, and calm the nerves of anxious ones. They need time to solicit new committee members; cajole and nag external reviewers; receive, file, and duplicate reviews; and plan for meeting dates, flights, venues, and the personal requirements of committee members. Applicants, reviewers, and committee members sometimes disappear, get sick, suffer personal crises, lose their instructions, miss deadlines, chew hard disks, forget return addresses, and otherwise cause delays. They also complain. Between 2 weeks before a proposal deadline and 2 weeks after a committee's judgments have been made, chaos prevails. Those of us who have watched the efforts of most funding agency staff to control this chaos are full of praise for their efforts to do their thankless, Sisyphean tasks. If pushed too hard for the sake of frequent competitions, the best ones are likely to quit. They need time to recover and more praise for their work.

The third problem with frequent competitions is motivational. Most people who have been on a peer-review committee will attest that the romance of adjudication wears off after about 3 hours; after that, only the drudgery of the task remains. By the end of a second or third 10-hour day of judging merit, the task can become onerous. It is thus presumptuous and risky to ask prospective adjudicators to repeat the task several times a year. Like staff, committee members also need time to recover. Push them too hard and adjudication fatigue would likely rise. Many prospective committee members would refuse to continue. Those who dragged on would likely lose motivation to judge applications carefully. Errors would then increase.

Faced with budgetary, logistic, and motivational difficulties, most organizations favor the wishes of committee members, administrators, and staff and hold their adjudications once a year, usually early in winter. Winter meetings allow applicants the preceding summer to prepare their application, assuming that most applicants are professors with nothing better to do in the heat. The autumn months are then devoted to circulating applications and rules of order among committee members and external reviewers in preparation for the committee deliberations.

This yearly cycle has become a tradition and most applicants have, albeit reluctantly, adapted to it. But there is at least one major drawback to this lock-step, yearly cycle. If an applicant is not funded, he must wait another year to try again. The year may be crucial to his career as well as the jobs of those who would be funded by the grant. Applicants who can apply to two or more funding agencies for support naturally prefer the agencies to stagger their deadlines and adjudication meetings rather than to clump them. So, too, do applicants whose proposals are rejected by one organization and who wish to try another without delay.

PRACTICAL IMPLICATIONS

The challenges of organizing committee-based adjudications that we have noted above are not the only ones facing research grant adjudication organizers. We have omitted many others, including arranging accommodation for committee members who travel to the adjudication and handling food requests, daycare, and complaints. Even so, our notes lead us to several practical suggestions about managing the logistics of adjudications. Here is our first suggestion: Anyone wanting to avoid a stressful and thankless job should not become an adjudication organizer. Hats off to those who are.

It is important to remember that adjudications of research grant proposals undertaken by large funding organizations are more formal and complex than the vast majority of adjudications. There are, of course, some organizations that exceed the formality and complexity of research grant adjudications. Many political bodies ranging from congress or parliament to city councils, for example, run applications for legislation (bills) through labyrinths of committees, commissions, legal councils, public hearings, opinion polls, and other forms of vetting before their judgments of yea or nay. But most adjudications, such as those leading to decisions about jobs or promotions in small businesses, bursaries for students in financial need, or certificates of recognition given by chambers of commerce and service clubs, are far less formal and complex.

To be honest, our above exposition of some of the backstage problems confronting organizers of research grant adjudications may have few practical applications for small and informal adjudications. A local service club might feel more pressure finding just one volunteer for its high school bursary committee than deciding how to pick the best three from a dozen eager volunteers. High school coaches might benefit less from advice about choosing the best consultants for assessing team tryouts than from dealing with the angry parents of the kids who do not make the cut.

Still, our exposition does emphasize a much overlooked aspect of most adjudications, especially moderately large to very large adjudications based on committee deliberations. The logistics of these adjudications are much more complex than most people appreciate. Inside the black box, between the submission of applications and the announcement of successful and unsuccessful ones, a lot happens—and a lot can go wrong. The logistic complexity is sufficiently great that problems are statistically guaranteed to arise, many of them unexpected. Most seasoned organizers know this and pray, not for perfection, but for small imperfections rather than large ones. To borrow Herbert Simon's word, organizers are satisfiers not optimizers, especially before and during committee deliberations. Reforms of the adjudication process tend to occur between adjudications, after dust settles and nerves calm.

So what? Frazzled organizers and committee members are quite right to seek ways to improve the efficiency and decrease the stress of their work. Sponsors are unlikely to dispute their resulting reforms. But we believe that the fourth constituency (see chapter 5) tends to be overlooked in the process. Most reforms help sponsors, committee members, and organizers more than applicants. What is good for organizers and committee members is often not good for applicants. Shifting from semiannual adjudications to annual adjudications, for example, may save wear and tear on organizers and committee members. But, as noted above, applicants almost always find it less convenient and some find it troublesome. Limiting the length of proposals or increasing the amount of information required on application forms may lift the cognitive, motivational, or accounting burdens of organizers and committee members. But the burdens are usually transferred to applicants who do feel their weight.

Which leads us to variations of the principles of consultation we outlined in chapter 5. It is generally better to include all constituencies in the processes of designing and reforming adjudications than to include only a few. So there is benefit in encouraging articulate applicants, some who won and some who lost an adjudication, to suggest how the adjudication process can be reformed to streamline or otherwise improve the application process. Some organizations do this now. For example, after consultation with applicants, the Canadian Institute of Health Research encouraged applicants to list their preferred external reviewers. This not only helps organizers and committees find experts in areas beyond their expertise, it also makes applicants feel a bit more control of their adjudication and less likely to cry foul if they receive bad external reviews. It may be worthwhile to extend the example. Though it may be impractical, consider, for example, what might occur if applicants were allowed to vote on committee membership. Consider the possibility of improving the application process by allowing applicants to add items to the application form (example: "In the following space please make any suggestions for improving this application process"). Or consider how happy applicants would be if application forms could be standardized across organizations or if one application could be reviewed by all relevant organizations.

If reforms are made to reduce the burdens of applicants, it seems reasonable to expect applicants to reform their thinking in return. In our experience, most applicants across a wide variety of adjudications have few, if any, realistic conceptions about the adjudication process. Some applicants have unrealistically high expectations about the purity of committees and their deliberations. Others have unrealistically low opinions of committees that miss the merit of their applications. Both extremes are fed by rumor and gossip about adjudications and adjudicators from origins unknown.

Ignorance in this case is not bliss, but it is often perpetrated by adjudication organizers and committees who believe that their work—like the deliberations of courtroom juries—should be secret, lest some embarrassing truth be revealed and unleash a flood of outrage and disdain. But alternatives to full secrecy deserve consideration, especially in light of comments of former applicants who later serve on adjudication committees. Most of them say that switching roles opened eyes. Yes, it was sometimes unsettling to learn of the compromises and improvisation that often occurred before and during committee deliberations. But it was also comforting and sometimes inspiring to see how well almost everyone adapted and how sincere most organizers and committee members were in being fair. Few declare that they had great respect for committee work until they became a committee member. Most declare that they had far more respect for the committee after their membership than before.

The lesson of their experience is sad to lose on applicants who wait so anxiously for a judgment that could change their lives. We think that applicants would benefit from the lesson and believe it would not take much to learn. Some organizations have invited small groups of applicants to watch committee proceedings, with good success. The committees they watch are not those judging their own applications. Even so, what they learn from watching similar committees gives them well-deserved respect for committees that work well and good suggestions for committees that do not. It is often logistically impossible to set up a gallery and potentially tacky to turn deliberations into a spectator sport. But videos of live or simulated committee meetings might serve as a useful substitute, as might simulations of adjudications that prospective applicants could play. In sum, anything that reduces the mystery of committee work among highly anxious applicants is likely to bring more benefits than costs.

7

Committee Deliberations

*T*he rules of the game have been set (chapter 5). Preparations for the adjudication are over (chapter 6). We continue our analyses of research grant competitions by examining the next step in the adjudication process: the committee meetings where the winners and losers of grants are decided.

With sufficient effort and good fortune, a time will come when peer-review committee members are all gathered in one place to deliberate face-to-face about their merit judgments of the applications they were previously asked to review. Normally, 6–8 committee members are flown to the headquarters of the funding organization, put up in a local hotel, and kept in meetings for 2 or 3 full days. The meetings usually occur around a large table in a hotel meeting room and in the presence of an organizational representative (program officer) who keeps meeting records. In large funding organizations, meetings of different committees are held concurrently, so 10–50 meetings rooms of a hotel might be booked to house as many committees for deliberations. Each day of deliberation is generally long, intense, and tiring, typically beginning at 8:00 in the morning and lasting 8–12 hours, with breaks for meals. As people arrive, those who know each other—and most do—exchange news and gossip about colleagues, families, and universities. Friends usually sit together. Everyone arrives with a full briefcase of applications they were assigned to review.

When the meetings begin, it is customary for the program officer to welcome and introduce everyone. Often the first to be introduced is the leader of the meeting, one of the peers previously designated by the funding agency as the head of proceedings. This person, usually called the *chair*, is typically a peer with gray hair who has attended deliberations in previous years. The chair is responsible for conducting the meeting, often with the help of the program officer.

During the introductions, the program officer and chair give a brief summary of how the meeting will proceed and answer questions about the activities of the day. Among the more common questions are "Where are the bathrooms?" "When is our first break?" "Is this decaf coffee?" "How can I access the Internet for my e-mail?" "What arrangements have been made for lunch and dinner?" Occasionally, idiosyncratic questions, such as, "May we begin with my applicants so I can fly home early to visit my sick mother?" will also be answered.

Now deliberations, the heart of judging merit by committee, begin. How will the committee proceed? Procedural rules must be chosen and followed to bring some order to committee discussions and judgments. The traditional candidates of consensus and majority rule cannot on their own get the job done. Consensus, for example, gives no guide for resolving conflicts before consensus is reached, and majority rule gives no procedure for deciding what will be voted on. Other procedures are necessary, and there are hundreds to choose from. Variations range from a simple "Each committee member selects his three favorite proposals, and we fund alphabetically until the money runs out" to complex sets of dozens of rules about time limits for discussion, common criteria of merit, averaging rankings or ratings, etc.

Alas, rules are not neutral. Just as process can influence product, committee procedures can influence the outcomes of committee deliberations. The influence can be illustrated by the consequences of two popular procedures used to judge the merit of research grant proposals: the Three Pile procedure and the Rate-Discuss-Rate procedure.

THE THREE-PILE PROCEDURE

Sometimes rules spontaneously emerge in committees faced with time pressures for making judgments. Barbara Carroll and one of us (WT) observed such emergence in 1991 when we were kindly permitted to watch and analyze the in-camera deliberations of peer-review committees in the Social Sciences and Humanities Research Council (SSHRC) as part of an SSHRC-funded research project (Thorngate & Carroll, 1991). Tradition set the procedures for predeliberation assessments. Committee members were paired to be the primary assessors of 10–20 of the 50–100 applications submitted to their committee and to present their assessments to all members of the committee during deliberations. The program officer tried to solicit at least two external reviews of each application and send them to the two primary assessors in advance of deliberations. Each of the two primary assessors made independent assessments of merit based on personal reactions and on the reports of external reviewers. Assessors had to make two judgments of merit for each, one based on the scientific merit of the proposal and one based on the track record of its author(s). In addition, assessors had to provide the committee with written reasons for their judgments.

Although these premeeting procedures were well established, when deliberations began, improvised rules spontaneously emerged. Most committees spent their first hour or more developing a procedure to get through their pile of applications in 2 days. The most common emergent procedures were minor variants of the following:

- Applications would be considered alphabetically by author's last name.
- The two primary assessors of the application under consideration would identify themselves, announce their ratings, and read their reasons for giving them.

- If the two scientific merit ratings and the two track record ratings were all highly positive, the application would be put in a pile called "Definitely Fund" with little or no committee discussion.
- If the four ratings were all highly negative, the application would be put in a second pile called "Definitely Reject" with little or no committee discussion.
- If the ratings were middling or mixed, the application would be put in a third pile called "Discuss Later if Time Permits."

During the first morning of deliberations, considerable time was often spent debating finer points of differences between scientific merit or track record ratings and clarifying which criteria of merit should be applied in making these ratings. Should a proposal pursuing a fresh idea with a debatable methodology be rated higher than a proposal pursuing a stale idea with a well-tested methodology, or vice versa? Should the woman who stopped publishing for 10 years to raise children be penalized for her hiatus? Should the man who insisted on adding his name to all publications of his many graduate students be credited for his thick vita? The debates were sometimes heated, especially in interdisciplinary committees vetting proposals from different disciplines with different standards. As debates dragged on, someone on the committee eventually noted in frustration that time for considering the remaining applications is running short. "We've debated criteria of merit for 3 hours and finished only four applications. We have 92 more to consider this afternoon and tomorrow. Let's get going!"

By the afternoon of the first day of deliberations, committees usually developed their own routines and rhythms. It then became clearer that what began as an exercise in group judgment has become an exercise in persuasion. Primary assessors, quite naturally, tended to assume that their judgments of merit were valid, or at least more valid than those of committee members who gave the proposal under consideration no more than a cursory glance. So the task of primary assessors evolved from presentation to persuasion as the assessors tried to convince the other members that their judgments should prevail. Though most of the persuasive attempts were pedantic, rhetorical flourishes were frequently seen. One such flourish was to argue that a proposal lies outside the terms of reference of the committee ("I am sure this is a great proposal, but are we supposed to be funding what appears to be commercial research?"). Another was to argue that what may seem a bias is merely a concern for the integrity of the committee ("I am concerned that this good committee would be crucified by the press if it were to fund this project on urination latencies"). Others included bombast ("Surely you must all agree, as I pound the table with no apologies, that this research is, in my judgment as the world leader in my discipline, a brilliant extension of my own cutting-edge work that must be funded") and ethical twists ("How could we possibly fund this proposal when we rejected two similar proposals yesterday?") and the selective use of external reviews that supported a primary assessor's conclusion ("If you don't believe me, read the scathing criticism external reviewer F gave this proposal").

What to do? Faced with spending too much judgment time in rancorous debate, most committees tacitly agreed to put any contentious proposal in the third pile, Discuss Later. By doing so, grant proposals could be vetted quite quickly and time lost in debate could be recovered. Proposals and authors with consistently high merit judgments from their two primary assessors would be put in the Definitely Fund pile with few comments beyond "Agree," "Looks good to me," or "I'll go along with your judgment." Proposals or authors judged to have serious deficits would quickly be put in the Definitely Reject pile with little more than a caustic comment or chuckle. Every other proposal would go into the Discuss Later pile as soon as even modest disagreement was shown. Even a question such as, "Does anyone recall if this is the same proposal we received two years ago?" or "Does this proposal belong in our committee, or should it be sent over to the Pastoral Studies Committee?" was enough to send a proposal to the Discuss Later pile. The procedure became a form of triage, and it was usually very efficient. With practice, members of one committee were able to triage an application, likely taking the applicant(s) over 100 hours to write, in about 5 minutes.

Like all groups assigned a task, peer-review committees soon developed specialists who played emergent but predictable roles. For example, the program officer might come to play the role of procedural expert ("I'm sorry but the rules do not allow us to discuss the applicant's drinking habits"), while others might play the role of the moralizer ("How can we call ourselves fair if we reject this proposal just because no outside expert read it?"), the whiner ("I just can't continue until the hotel gives us better coffee"), or the observer ("Sorry, I was dozing. Is it time to vote? Just put me down with the majority"). Bulldozers frequently emerged ("Now that I have the floor, I am going to bully you into accepting my decision. Does anyone want to fight with me?"), and conflicts sometimes arose among those who came to dislike each other in or out of the roles they had chosen. These roles, and the people who played them, could greatly affect committee deliberations, often setting the stage for lenient decisions or for harsh ones. As a result, the same committee members playing different roles could reach different decisions. Alas, once the roles were set, it was almost impossible to extract their players from them. Program officers who watched the resulting group dynamics and their consequences often exchanged stories of tough and tender, notorious and exemplary committees emerging from the interactions among members and their roles.

A common example of this dynamic can be imagined by considering how normal peers might react to each other's recommendations. If John, a primary assessor of Alice's proposal, strongly recommends funding it but Frank, a committee member, roundly criticizes John's recommendation and votes against it, the stage is then set for retaliation. When Frank recommends Martha's proposal, should we expect John to agree? Or might John wish to exercise his own critical skills in finding flaws with Frank's recommendation? It is reasonable to assume that criticisms of a recommendation are frequently confused with criticisms of an application, and that tit-for-tat criticisms do, at times, emerge. They may also escalate, increasing the number of proposals reviewed by John and by Frank that generate disagreements between them, disagreements resolved by additions to the Discuss Later pile. To avoid retaliation and possible escalation, Frank might keep his mouth shut about assessments of proposals in John's application batch, expecting John to return the favor; tacit, mutual back-scratching may prevail. When it does, a committee of several peers reduces to several committees of two peers: the two primary assessors who currently have the floor, with passive peers awaiting their turn.

The heights of the three piles were never equal. Definitely Fund and Definitely Reject piles tended to be thin. In between them was the thick and tottering Discuss Later pile, often five times as high as its two neighbors. When all applications had been triaged, usually by the end of the second day of deliberations, committee members would look at the Discuss Later pile with dread, many fearing a return of the rancorous debates still unresolved.

Faced with only a few remaining hours and a pile of perhaps 50–75 Discuss Later applications, committees grew tense. Members tried to reduce their tension by asking the attending SSHRC program officer how much money they had promised to those in the Definitely Fund pile. Almost always, the officer announced that the committee had already overspent its budget ("exceeded the funding envelope" was the jargon of the day) and must concentrate on reducing their funding promises. The sigh of relief was generally enthusiastic. Committee members could avoid reexamining proposals in the Discuss Later pile and instead spend their final hours chopping equipment, travel, and assistantship budget items of proposals in the Definitely Fund pile. Simple suggestions such as, "Let's just cut 12% of everyone's budget to get down to our spending limit" were usually approved with gusto as committee members checked their watches and flight schedules.

Only one task remained: Composing rejection letters to authors of proposals in the Definitely Reject and Discuss Later piles. SSHRC hit upon what many committee members considered an elegant solution, though many applicants described it as crass. Program officers produced a printed list of numbered sentences, each describing a common application flaw—sentences similar to "The proposal did not contain sufficient methodological detail" or "The assessors judged your literature review to be inadequate." Committee members then suggested relevant sentences based upon the primary assessors reasons for concern. A sample discussion: "Let's send Dr. Zamboni sentences 4 and 12. OK, replace 12 with 17." The program officer was left to draft the letters with the usual "We regret to inform you ..." head and "Thank you for your submission" tail. A few years after our observations, and in light of considerable protests from unfunded Discuss Later authors who received no more funding than authors in the Definitely Reject pile, SSHRC modified its procedures. Instead of sending rejection letters to authors of Discuss Later proposals, most were sent a different letter, stating, in essence, that the committee found their proposal fundable in principle but ran out of money funding better ones. It was assumed that this felt better than a rejection.

Two days of sometimes intense and sometimes painfully boring proceedings thus came to a close. Most committee members felt that they had done a good job of judging merit. In many defendable ways, they had. Most members admitted some inconsistencies and biases and agreed that changes to membership or procedures would likely change some of the decisions. Yet their task of judgment, though imperfect, was at least done on time. Most members sincerely believed that the funded proposals deserved their happy end and that the bad ones were justifiably rejected. The rest? Rare was the committee member who anguished about proposals judged between the good and bad extremes and unfunded, in part because no committee member needed to feel completely responsible for the decision.

What is wrong with the Three Pile procedure? Despite its efficiency, the procedure contains at least two major flaws. First, it offers no mechanism for ensuring that each application is assessed according to the same standards. Like the bias-infested judgments produced from judging anything on a case-by-case basis, criteria for judging merit in the Three Pile procedure tended to vary from one application to the next. Member A might find fault with the statistical analyses proposed in Application 1; Member B might bristle at an anathematic methodology in Application 2; Member C might become cautious after reading the words of an external reviewer of Application 3 who wonders whether similar studies were once done in Ukraine. In all such cases, one flaw, even one question, could kill a proposal. The criteria would thus become noncompensatory; no set of strengths could overcome any single question or doubt in preventing a proposal from the purgatory of the Discuss Later pile.

The second major flaw of the Three Pile procedure followed from its reactionary nature. Almost all the funded proposals were those that made no waves. They were safe, conservative, predictable, regular science proposals, almost guaranteed to break no new intellectual ground. They were the proposals that slipped by after a heated debate about the previous proposal caused temporary shell shock. They were the proposals modeled after last year's winning proposals, one more year out of date.

THE RATE-DISCUSS-RATE PROCEDURE

Funding organizations have invented or borrowed hundreds of different procedures for judging merit by committee. The Three Pile procedure discussed above falls at the informal/unstructured end of their spectrum. Toward the formal/structured end are dozens of other procedures, most of them complex, that have usually evolved in response to calls for more consistency, accountability, and fairness and in response to embarrassing holes found in less formal procedures. Among these formal/structured procedures is one developed by the Canadian Institutes of Health Research, an organization noted in the previous chapter for its openness to improvements of its peer-review processes. Because of this openness, one of us was able to undertake extensive studies of various aspects of CIHR research grant adjudications (Thorngate, Faregh, & Young, 2002; Thorngate & Wang, 2004; Thorngate et al., 2004). CIHR adjudications are always evolving, but their procedures remain typical of the formal/structured group approach to judging merit, so we discuss them here. CIHR maintains a detailed description of their current procedures; see "Peer Review," 2007. We note that their current procedures may have changed from those reported here.

At the time of our studies, CIHR was organizing over 40 committees to judge over 2,500 grant proposals twice a year; the numbers have since increased. Most committees had between five and nine members, scientist peers flown to Ottawa from across Canada, housed in local hotels and sequestered for 2–3 days in hotel meeting rooms to judge merit. Each committee also had a chair, who conducted the meeting, and a program officer, who kept notes of deliberations. Prior to their arrival, all committee members were sent a box containing copies of the 40–80 applications to be judged by their committee and a list of the 8–12 applications in the box that they, and one other committee member, were responsible for presenting to the committee as primary assessors. In preparation for the committee meetings, members were asked to read these 8–12 applications, to rate each of them on a common rating scale, and to write justifications for their ratings without consulting one another. Members were also asked to familiarize themselves with another 8–12 applications in the box in order to serve a secondary role as a reader. During committee deliberations, readers were asked for their comments in hopes of breaking occasional deadlocks between the two primary assessors. Current peer-review practices, small variations of those described above, can be found at the CIHR Web site; see "Grants Committee," 2007.

The rating scale for assessing the quality of applications, itself the subject of considerable debate (Thorngate et al., 2004), ranged from 0.0 to 4.9 with assorted ranges tagged by adjectives. CIHR assumed that primary assessors would avail themselves of tenths of a point when using the scale, thus making the scale with a 50-point range. Below is the description of the scale and how it should be used by committees, as taken verbatim from the CIHR Web site.

> To ensure consistency, committees must adhere to a common scale. It is particularly important that committees use the full scale and apply the same convention in assigning ratings. To facilitate this, the following scale and descriptors should be utilized:
> ° Only applications rated 3.5 or higher are eligible for CIHR funding. The range 3.0 to 3.4 should be used for applications which, while technically and conceptually acceptable, are not considered to be a high priority for CIHR funding, perhaps because the topic is not considered relevant to an important health issue, or because the work proposed seems unlikely to yield major advances in knowledge, or because the approach is not particularly innovative. Please note that applications rated 3.0 to 3.4 are not eligible for CIHR funds, including those from partnership programs; however, these applications are discussed by the committee and applicants are encouraged to re-apply after addressing the reviews. Applications rated below 3.0 are so flawed in some respect that they do not represent a good investment of public funds, and would require significant rewriting to be considered acceptable. Such applications will normally be triaged, and not be discussed by the committee. ("Grants Committee," 2007)

Now, as when our studies were done, CIHR provides a list of features of applications that should be considered when assessing application quality but does not require committee members to rate them individually and does not state how assessments of the features should be weighed or combined. Quoting again the CIHR Web site, the features are

The Applicant's Productivity, Experience and Training
How appropriate is the training or track record of the applicant(s) to the
        research proposed?
How important and original is the recent productivity of the applicant(s)?
How confident are you that the applicant(s) can do the work proposed?
The Research Proposed

How important and/or original are the hypotheses or the questions to be addressed, and how clearly are they formulated?

How important and original are the contributions expected from the research proposed? What is the potential for important new observations or knowledge that will have an impact on the health of Canadians?

How well will the proposed experiments address the hypotheses or questions? How appropriate are the methods to be applied and the proposed analyses of data? How well will the applicant implement new methods which are to be introduced and/or explored? How well have the applicants anticipated difficulties in their approach and considered alternatives?

Is the rationale for the proposal well-grounded in a critical review of the pertinent literature?

Depending on the type of research, does the applicant have a plan for the dissemination of the research finding so that they can be translated into improved health, more effective products or services, or a strengthened health care system?

The Research Environment

Are the facilities and personnel available that are required to do the work?

Is the applicant able to commit the amount of time that is required to do the research well?

Are appropriate collaborations in place? ("Grants Committee," 2007)

CIHR also developed relatively detailed rules for how meeting should be conducted. Highlights include the following:

Applications are considered in random order.

The two primary assessors (called internal reviewers by CIHR) of the application under consideration first state their rating of the application. If both ratings are less than 3.0, the application is rejected. If one or more rating is above 3.0, the primary assessors then read to the committee their written comments justifying their rating; any external reviews are also read or summarized at this time.

The Chair leads a discussion of the full committee regarding the application, ratings and comments while the Scientific Officer takes notes.

The Chair asks the two primary assessors to reach a consensus rating. If they cannot read consensus, the Chair averages their two ratings for the consensus.

All members of the committee, including the two primary assessors, then privately rate the application; their ratings must not deviate more than 0.5 points above or below the consensus rating.

The private ratings are then averaged. This average becomes the final committee judgment of the quality of the application. ("Grants Committee," 2007)

The final committee judgment of the quality of an application, essentially its judgment of merit, was then passed to another committee for a funding decision. Though each committee could be assured by CIHR of controlling some of its own funding, it did not control all. One funding pot was reserved for rating competitions among all committees, a policy that became quite controversial and caused considerable intercommittee tensions. More will be said about this policy in the next section.

Does the formality and structure of such a Rate-Discuss-Rate procedure for judging merit produce more consistent and fewer biased judgments than a more informal and unstructured approach such as the Three Pile procedure? The Rate-Discuss-Rate procedure certainly appears to be more rigid and standardized, and this appearance probably gives it a stronger claim to procedural justice. No research comparing the judgments of Three Pile versus the Rate-Discuss-Rate procedures has been done, so we do not know if one is significantly better or worse than the other. However, we do know something about the inconsistencies and biases that creep into the Rate-Discuss-Rate procedure because we observed the CIHR committees while they were using it and because we examined the archives of past committee deliberations.

CIHR contracted one of us (WT) to undertake an archival study of the deliberations of several CIHR research grant funding committees. After observing seven of the committees during the September 2001 adjudications to become familiar with how the Rate-Discuss-Rate procedure was practiced, WT and two graduate research assistants signed confidentiality agreements and obtained special security clearances to enter the CIHR building and sit among the archives of thousands of files containing the written records of all committee deliberations of thousands of research grant applications.

Our research had three purposes. The first purpose was to determine what might account for varying success rates of different adjudication committees. The second purpose was to determine the value of committee discussion in changing the ratings of committee members. The third was to see how the opinions of external reviewers influence primary assessors and other committee members.

The first purpose requires explanation. CIHR was born on April 13, 2000, from the ashes of the Medical Research Council (MRC) with an expanded mandate to fund research beyond MRC's biomedical domain. The expansion included health areas such as pubic health, health promotion, aboriginal health, and nursing. Applicants for research grants in these health areas soon noticed that a greater percentage of biomedical grant applications (about 25–35%) were being funded than were their own (about 20–25%). The difference was especially noticeable in cross-committee competitions for common funds and prompted rumors of double standards (see chapter 4). To simplify slightly, CIHR put its funds into two pots. Pot A had the money for the research budgets of all committees; each committee was given its own money to spend from this pot—like the funding envelopes of SSHRC committees. The second pot was up for grabs. CIHR's procedural rules of the day allowed each committee to fund its own highest rated applications to the limit of its own budget (pot A), but required each committee to submit the ratings of its second-tier (aka second-rate) applications to a committee-wide competition for money in pot B. The second-tier applications from biomedical committees tended to have higher ratings than those of the health committees. As a result, the biomedical committees received more than their proportional share of the common funding pot.

Was the disproportional success of the biomedical committee applications the result of bias? Many health grant applicants and committee members believed it was, so justice was not seen to be done. A few speculated that biomedical researchers raised on MRC budgets were protecting their empires. In rebuttal, some biomedical applicants and committee members argued that their higher ratings simply reflected better proposals and better science. It was also possible that the biomedical and health subcultures had different interpretations of the rating scale; for example, despite the adjectives anchoring the rating scale, above, perhaps biomedical members would rate a mediocre proposal as 4.1 on the scale above, while health researchers would rate a mediocre proposal as 3.6. It was also possible that biomedical researchers artificially raised the ratings of their second-rate proposals in the belief that second-rate biomedical research deserved to be funded more than did second-rate (or even first-rate) health science. Fearing this, health committees had begun to raise their ratings from one adjudication to the next, prompting biomedical committees to reciprocate and triggering rounds of rating inflation similar to the grade inflation that now gives even mediocre students an A average.

Hoping to resolve the debate about biomedical bias, and to determine the value of committee discussion and external reviews in changing ratings, we examined 306 files of grant application adjudications. About one third came from the September 2000 competition, one third from the March 2001 competition, and the remainder from the September 2001 competition. The committees and competitions were chosen with the advice of CIHR staff. Of the 306 files, 145 came from five biomedical committees: biochemistry and molecular biology, cancer, cardiovascular system, experimental medicine, and neurosciences. We randomly sampled 28–30 files from each of these committees, 8–10 from each of the three competitions. The remaining 161 of the 306 files came from six health committees: behavioral science; health, ethics law, and humanities; health information and promotion; health services intervention and evaluations; public, community, and population health; psychosocial, sociocultural, and behavioral determinants of health. We randomly sampled 24–29 files from each of these committees, 5–10 from each competition. The small variations in sample sizes occurred because the archives were being moved while we were trying to access them, and during that time the locations of files were not always known.

We coded each file for 74 features, some used to determine how committee discussion changed ratings, some to determine how external reviews were or were not used, and some to find patterns that might address the issue of biomedical favoritism. A few features were also used to explore other aspects of the deliberation process. Of the latter, two of the most interesting were the ratings of the two primary assessors. Each of the two members playing the primary assessor role had to evaluate their assigned applications without knowing each others' evaluations, so any similarity between the ratings of a proposal would result from agreement on the merit of proposal rather than from social influence. We correlated their ratings as a measure of inter-judge reliability. Had two assessors agreed completely in their ratings of all proposals, a statistical indicator called r (a correlation coefficient; see "Correlation," n.d.) of their agreement would be at the maximum of $r = +1.00$. Had the two assessors shown complete disagreement, the statistical indicator would be at the minimum of $r = -1.00$. Between these extremes is a range of r values; for example, if one assessor's ratings of merit have no relationship at all with those of the second assessor—a relationship that, when plotted, looks like a random sample of stars in the night—then $r = 0.00$.

We hoped that the judgments of assessors would have a high correlation. People are different, so we could not expect a perfect correspondence ($r = +1.00$) between their ratings. It would, however, be reassuring if their correlation were +0.90 or above, comforting if their correlation were $r = +.80$ or above, increasingly worrisome if their correlation dropped below $r = +0.70$.

We correlated the judgments of assessors for 143 of the 145 applications sent to biomedical committees and 158 of the 161 applications sent to health committees, excluding the few with incomplete records. The correlation between pairs of biomedical assessors was $r = +0.49$. The correlation between pairs of health assessors was $r = +0.46$. This is roughly the same correlation as the heights of parents and their same-sex children or the IQs of husbands and wives. It indicates that there is at best a modest relationship between peers in how merit is judged, and that disagreement is common. This was worrisome.

How big was the difference between pairs of assessors in their judgments of merit? There was more disagreement between pairs of health assessors than between pairs of biomedical assessors. On the rating scale shown above, the average difference in ratings between pairs of biomedical assessors was 0.41 points. The average difference in ratings between pairs of health researchers was 0.59 points. The difference is statistically reliable.

Did the primary assessors in biomedical committees rate their assigned applications more or less positively than the primary assessors in health committees? The average consensus rating reached by primary assessors of biomedical applications was 3.66—in the "very good, may be funded" range on the scale described above. The average consensus rating reached by primary assessors of health applications was 3.25—in the "acceptable but low priority, not funded" range on the scale. This was also a statistically reliable difference. The lower consensus ratings of health applications could, as noted above, be the result of inferior proposals, harsher readers, subcultural norms, or any combination of these. We don't know. But the rating difference partly explains the lower proportion of health proposals that biomedical proposals were not funded in the free-for-all competition.

One of the most important purposes of committee discussion is to resolve disagreements between adjudicators, especially between the two primary assessors. Sure enough, when primary assessors disagreed, discussion frequently followed. At the beginning of deliberations, when a committee was fresh, the discussion was often long and animated; members asked lots of questions, challenged assumptions, worried about precedents, and debated contentious points about the importance of flawless methods, track record, creativity, etc., in judging merit. Such discussion all but vanished by the middle of the first afternoon. By then, committee activity usually became routine, even humdrum, and pairs of primary assessors who had the floor at any moment were normally allowed to debate each other while other members listened in silence.

Debates became shorter and more tranquil because routines evolved to resolve them quickly. A bit of data detective work gave us important clues about the nature of these routines. One clue was distilled from examining the relationship between the point spread of ratings given by the pairs of primary assessors and the mean of the private ratings of all committee members given after the committee reached consensus. The correlation between the point spreads and the biomedical committee private rating averages was $r = -0.41$; for the health committees it was $r = -0.23$. Though modest, both negative correlations were statistically reliable and indicate that the greater the disagreement between primary assessors, the greater the chances that committee deliberation would lower judgments of merit. In short, committees tended toward conservatism; when assessors disagreed, committees were more likely to side with the skeptic than with the enthusiast. We previously noted that the average point spread between ratings of assessors in health committees (0.59 points) was higher than the average spread between ratings of assessors in biomedical committees (0.41 points). This is likely one reason that the average of final ratings in health committees (3.24) was significantly lower than the consensus ratings in biomedical committees (3.64).

Another clue about evolving deliberation routines and their conservative consequences came from our informal observations of the committee deliberations. Over half the disagreements occurred because one of the two assessors claimed to find a conceptual or methodological flaw in the application under discussion. Perhaps this acute assessor would almost always link the flaw to his low rating, leaving the obtuse assessor who had missed the flaw in an awkward, sometimes embarrassing, interpersonal pickle. The obtuse assessor risked looking foolish for denying the flaw or for arguing it was trivial. The acute assessor risked look foolish for withdrawing his criticism. So there was usually more pressure for the obtuse assessor to capitulate than for the acute assessor to withdraw his criticism. Compromises were therefore closer to the judgments of the critic.

One consequence of resolving many disagreements was the creation of on-the-fly precedents. Despite the best efforts of CIHR to include rules for all occasions, based on precedents from adjudications past, committees would almost always encounter a few unusual applicants or applications during their deliberations. Should an application for collecting data in Iran be approved by an Iranian ethics committee even though none exists? Should an applicant be considered for funding if a headline in the morning paper reports that she has been charged with embezzlement? When someone on a committee asks such questions, and when answers are debated and resolved, the resolution normally becomes a precedent for assessing all subsequent applications. Ironically, however, we have yet to see the precedent used for reassessing applications that preceded it. Committees do not have the time or energy to begin again whenever a new rule is established. If the new rule is stringent, applications judged before its creation benefit. If the new rule is lenient, applications judged after its creation benefit. In either case, the two groups of applications are judged by varying standards, violating the principle of equal justice for all.

THE DUBIOUS VALUE OF COMMITTEE DISCUSSION

If discussion resolved disagreements, we would expect that there would be little or no variability in the private ratings once the consensus rating was reached.

Moreover, we should expect there would be no relationship between the spread of the primary assessors' ratings and variability of the private ratings. Alas, our expectations were dashed. The correlation between the assessors' point spread and the spread (standard deviation) of the private ratings around the consensus rating was $r = +.28$ in medical committees and $r = +0.18$ in health committees, both statistically reliable. In short, the more primary assessors disagreed about merit, the more the committee members disagreed about merit, despite the opportunity to resolve disagreements through discussion.

Perhaps it didn't matter. The correlation between the average rating given by pairs of primary assessors in biomedical committees and the average of private ratings of all committee members following discussion and consensus (the final committee judgment of merit) was $r = +0.92$. The corresponding correlation in health committees was $r = +0.82$. The high correlations indicate that final committee judgments could be predicted with high accuracy from the average of assessors' judgments. Which leads us to ask: What is the value of committee discussion?

THE INFLUENCE OF EXTERNAL REVIEWS

Of the 306 applications we examined, 101 had no external reviews, 61 had one review, 87 had two reviews, 49 had three, and 8 had four. Reviewers were not asked to rate the quality or merit of the proposals they reviewed. As a result, many interesting comparisons between external reviewers' assessments and primary assessors' assessments could not be done. Even so, we could examine how the number and length of reviews might influence the ratings of primary assessors. Suppose, for example, that each external review—verbal assessments written by people designated as topic experts—affected the two primary assessors in the same way. We would then expect that the more reviews the assessors read, the more their own assessments would converge: "The two of us didn't agree at first, but after we both read all the reviews of experts, we reached the same conclusion." Alas, the correlation between the number of reviews and the distance between the ratings of the two assessors was $r = -0.01$, essentially zero. Pairs of assessors were just as likely to disagree after reading four reviews as after reading three, two, one, or none. Similarly, the length of reviews had no reliable influence on resolving disagreements. The correlation between total words in all reviews and the distance between ratings of primary assessors was $r = +0.06$, not a statistically reliable relation. Which leads us to ask: Why solicit reviews at all?

PRACTICAL IMPLICATIONS

Our analyses of two kinds of committee adjudication procedures, the relatively informal Three Pile procedure and the far more structured Rate-Discuss-Rate procedure, pull us toward several conclusions. The analyses offer no evidence that committee deliberations produce more valid judgments of merit than do individual judgments summed or averaged without committee discussion. Nor do the analyses support that argument that the benefits of external reviews outweigh their costs, since no consistent benefits were found. With both procedures, committee deliberations did little more than lead committee members to resolve uncertainties or assessment differences with caution, sending applications to the Discuss Later pile or pushing the committee rating toward the lower of the two assessors' ratings.

In short, there appears to be no demonstrable added value either in committee deliberations or in external reviews. Group judgments are as likely to be valid (or invalid) when obtained by averaging the judgments of independent assessors without external reviews as they are when obtained by discussing the judgments in light of external reviews. Furthermore, it is much less troublesome and costly for judges to sit at home and review a stack of applications without group discussion or external reviews than it is for judges to fly to a hotel and sit around a table talking for 3 days. We thus have good reason to recommend that committee deliberations and external reviews be abandoned.

Our recommendation is perhaps too radical for those steeped in the traditions of peer review. No doubt some would argue that we have examined only two of hundreds of possible deliberation procedures and that there is surely a set of procedures that would increase the value of committee deliberations and external reviews. Some committee apologists, for example, might suggest that committee deliberations could be improved rather than chucked by ensuring that every application is rated by all committee members along a set of predetermined dimensions and discussed only in reference to these dimensions. Others might suggest that external reviews could be improved if the reviewers were asked to rate applications along the same dimensions used by the committee and that reviewers be paid for doing their job on time. Still more might suggest that both committee deliberations and external reviews would improve if committee members and external reviewers were given far more training and selected with more care.

Such suggestions parallel those made for decades to improve the judgments of clinicians, doctors, and other experts (see chapter 3). They have, alas, met with mixed success. There is little doubt that making anything related to judgment more logical and consistent will improve the fairness and quality of judgments made (see chapter 3; Hastie & Dawes, 2001). The challenge is to induce judges to adopt more logical and consistent procedures. The procedures must first be found and then explicated and taught to the judges who should use them. Training takes time and motivation. Neither is likely to be in great supply prior to committee meetings. And even if training were possible, we do not yet know how much improvement in merit judgments would come from it. If someone could demonstrate that judges trained to use the best procedures made, say, 80% fewer judgment errors than they did in the old days, then we should happily recommend getting on with the job of improvement. But if judges and procedures reduced errors by, say, 3%, then we would ask if the costs of these changes might exceed their insipid benefits.

That said, we admit that the abandonment of committee deliberations and external reviews might generate at least two problems. One possible problem concerns the perception of fairness. Applicants might believe that it is fairer to make a traditional submission to a traditional committee than to make a submission to a disparate collection of online assessors who never discuss what they do. No doubt those who are experienced and successful in milking the traditional committee procedures would want to retain them, despite their costs. The stripped-down procedures we recommend would not result in more successful applications—budgets limit success rates, not procedures. But they would likely generate a few different acceptances and a few different rejections. Those who benefited from new procedures would probably prefer them, and those who suffered would not.

A second possible problem with abandoning committee deliberations and external reviews is motivation. Committee members must have some source of motivation to undertake their thankless tasks, and short meetings with peers offer a paid-for occasion to work in a room that likely has several old friends. What would motivate a committee member to sit at a computer, facing a deadline, reading and rating dozens of applications? Probably not money and probably not some abstract notion of serving the community of scholars (the community became endangered around 1962 and now is extinct in almost all campuses). The perks of travel, friends, and gossip associated with committee meetings and the dinners that accompany them are hard to beat. So we offer a compromise.

Most committees now discuss almost every proposal in their docket. There is no great reason to do so. Applications consistently judged before deliberations by two or more committee members to be either outstanding or terrible will almost certainly be funded or rejected respectively; no amount of discussion is likely to change this outcome. The applications that might benefit from discussion are the most controversial ones—those with the highest disagreement among assessors. So we propose that adjudicators submit their independent judgments to the funding organization before meeting, that the organization calculate which applications have generated the greatest disagreement among judges, and that meetings then be held to discuss only the controversial ones. Averaged independent ratings would thus serve as a form of triage: applications with the highest and with the lowest average ratings would escape debate; meetings would be held only to discuss those with the most divergent reviews. After excellent applications are funded, the funding organization would know how much money remains to allocate to the controversial ones; if no money remained, then no meeting is needed.

Any money that does remain after the independently assessed, excellent applications have been funded is likely to be scant (cf. the Three Pile procedure), and two types of applications would compete for it: first, the controversial applications (those generating a large differences in assessments among two or more assessors); second, the mediocre ones (applications generating agreement among assessors to be good but not great). It might happen, for example, that 100 applications are submitted to a competition that can fund 25. Fifteen of the proposals might be independently assessed as excellent, 12 as terrible. The former would receive funding, leaving money to fund 10 more applications of the remaining 100 − 15 − 12 = 73. Of these 73, 63 might be consistently judged by all independent assessors as having varying degrees of mediocrity, and 10 might be judged by different assessors at the excellent/terrible extremes. A meeting would then be held to determine which, if any, of these 10 controversial applications might be better than the best mediocre ones and thus deserving of one of the 10 remaining grants.

If the committee members do not consider the 15 excellent applications and 12 terrible ones in their meeting, more time remains to debate the relative merits of the 43 mediocre applications and the 30 controversial ones. But the extra time can only be fruitful if rules are established to compare these proposals and resolve the debates. What might these rules be? We offer a few suggestions. First, if the highest rating given a controversial application is lower than the lowest rating (one variation: the average rating) of a mediocre application, then prefer the mediocre one. For example, if a mediocre proposal were rated by two assessors as 4.2 and 4.0 on the CIHR scale noted above, and if a controversial proposal were rated as 4.0 and 2.9, then choose the mediocre proposal. Second, if the highest rating (variation: the average rating) of a mediocre application is lower than the lowest rating of a controversial one, then fund the controversial one. Thus, if a mediocre proposal were rated 4.1 and 4.0, and a controversial proposal were rated 4.1 and 4.6, then choose the controversial one.

Decisions become more difficult when ratings of mediocre and controversial applications overlap. What should be done, for example, when a mediocre proposal is rated by two reviewers as 3.9 and 4.1 on the CIHR scale and a controversial application is rated 3.2 and 4.8? There is no universally acceptable rule for stating a preference. Results from the CIHR study suggest that discussion would move a committee to prefer the mediocre proposal because discussion seems to focus on proposal weaknesses more than strengths and thus lead committees toward the lower ratings. The result is consistent with speculation that committees are more worried about funding a bad proposal than about not funding a good one, a topic discussed at length in chapter 8. There is no logical reason to fear funding a potential dog more than not funding a potential gem, but there are several psychological reasons to do so. They include the general conservatism of scientists to new ideas, the desire to avoid angering a skeptical committee member, and an aversion to looking foolish by giving money to a debatable project. Let us not forget, as well, the usual Catch-22 often invoked for rejecting a controversial application: If the application really is good, then the applicant could polish it and seek funding elsewhere, implying, of course, that the application consistently judged mediocre is more worthy of immediate funding.

When a committee often faces the dilemma of funding mediocre versus controversial applications, we think it is important for the committee to set a policy for resolving the dilemma well in advance of its deliberations. The policy can then be announced to prospective applicants to help them decide whether to bother applying or not. Indeed, we should like to go one step further. In the interests of perceptions of justice, we encourage competition organizers to poll prospective applicants about their preferences for funding controversial versus mediocre proposals and to abide by majority rule. By doing so, funding organizations would allow applicants more say in policies for judging merit, and adjudication committees would be relieved of possible accusations that they are setting policies in their own self-interests. The more that prospective applicants assist in the formation of rules of order for committee deliberations, the greater the perception of procedural justice there is likely to be.

A MATTER OF SCALE

If funding organizations choose to use a rating scale for assessing merit, they should give careful consideration to the scale they use. The three-point Three Pile scale and the 50-point CIHR scale noted above are only two of hundreds of variations. Consider a few others:

- 10 = *top notch*, 9 = *the cat's meow*, 7 = *cool*, 5 = *average*, 3 = *worthless*
- 5 = *fabulous*, 4 = *outstanding*, 3 = *worthwhile*, 2 = *promising*, 1 = *flawed*, 0 = *no good*
- 4 = *exceptional*, 3 = *above average*, 2 = *average*, 1 = *below average*, 0 = *failing*
- 1 = *1st rate*, 2 = *2nd rate*, 3 = *3rd rate*, 4 = *unacceptable*
- 1 = *top 10th percentile*, 2 = *11–25th percentile*, 3 = *26–75th percentile*, 4 = *lowest 25th percentile*

There are at least three important rules for selecting a scale to rate merit. First, do not use more than seven points on the scale because people cannot distinguish more than about seven gradations of anything, including merit. Second, when possible, use anchor words that have comparative content such as *among the best 15% of all applications received* rather than adjectives with vague and various meanings such as *highly meritorious, inspiring, flawed,* or *potentially fundable.* If adjectives must be used, make sure that all judges share a common meaning of each, even if it means training the judges with dictionary definitions, or with standardized examples from previous competitions, before they begin their own assessments. Also, make sure that the rank order of the merit implied by the adjectives corresponds to the rank order of the numbers they anchor. Should a scale be "1 = *exceptional*, 2 = *outstanding* ..." or "1 = *outstanding*, 2 = *exceptional* ..."? If one judge's definition of *exceptional* is another judge's definition of *outstanding*, then a scale with both words for anchors will cause undue inconsistency and confusion.

The third rule for selecting a scale of merit is as least as important as the first two: If merit assessments of two or more adjudicators are averaged, then the subjective distances between equal numerical intervals on a scale should also be equal, or as equal as possible. If the subjective distances between anchor words are not the same as the objective distances between the numbers these words represent, then averaging the numbers will likely produce biased results. Suppose, for example, that judges were asked use the following top-heavy scale to assess the merit of applications:

- 5 = *exceptional*, 4 = *outstanding*, 3 = *good*, 2 = *fair*, 1 = *marginal*

But suppose the psychological distance between the five anchor words was thus:

- 5.0 = *exceptional*, 4.8 = *outstanding*, 3.2 = *good*, 2.6 = *fair*, 0.7 = *marginal*

Three judges who respectively considered application A to be outstanding, outstanding, and fair would generate an average scale rating of (4 + 4 + 2)/3 = 3.33. If the three judges respectively considered application B to be exceptional, good, and good, they would also generate an average scale score of (5 + 3 + 3)/3 = 3.67. The rating scale averages would therefore indicate that application B was superior to application A. But the psychological average of application A would be (4.8 + 4.8 + 2.6)/3 = 4.07 and the psychological average of application B would be (5.0 + 3.2 + 3.2)/3 = 3.80. Psychologically, A would be superior to B. Embarrassing reversals such as this do not always occur, but the more distorted the rating scale, the more often they will.

There is, to our knowledge, only one small study that has tried to evaluate verbal descriptors of the kind used on rating scales to determine which descriptors have approximately equal subjective distances and low inter-judge variability. Thorngate et al. (2004) asked 23 former CIHR peer-review committee members to complete a simple task designed to scale 47 verbal descriptors such as extraordinary, competent, flawed, mediocre, uninspiring, and awful. Table 7.1 shows the average estimates and the standard deviations of these estimates given by the descriptors used on the 2004 CIHR rating scale and an alternative selection of descriptors with more evenly spaced averages and lower standard deviations.

CIHR did not adopt the alternative and perhaps should not until more research is done, including research related to descriptors in French and other languages. Even so, the results suggest that the descriptors on the 2004 CIHR scale have a worrisome gap between *excellent* and *very good* spanning the cutoff point for funding, that judges have shown low consensus in their interpretation of *very good*, and that better scales can be constructed.

It is a statistical certainty that committees with lots of judges, or with lots of applications to judge, will find most of their average application ratings humping around the overall average and showing only tiny differences between them. If, for example, a committee of six judges evaluates 100 proposals on a 5-point scale, the difference between the average ratings of proposal ranked best and the proposal ranked 2nd best might be 0.5 rating points, while the difference in average ratings between the 40th best and 60th best might be less than 0.10 rating points. These tiny differences around the middle often seal the fate of an application. A middling

TABLE 7.1   Ratings of CIHR Descriptors and Alternative Descriptors

CIHR descriptors			Alternative descriptors		
Descriptor	Mean	SD	Descriptor	Mean	SD
Outstanding	4.55	0.18	Extraordinary	4.62	0.17
Excellent	4.34	0.19	First-rate	4.13	0.35
Very good	3.41	0.84	Strong	3.68	0.38
Acceptable	2.80	0.60	Good	3.12	0.68
Needs revision	2.21	0.91	Average	2.56	0.46
Needs major revision	1.39	0.84	Weak	1.55	0.73
Seriously flawed	0.85	0.74			

proposal with an average rating of, say, 4.06 might be funded but one with an average rating of 4.05 might not.

Are there really significant, or even noticeable, differences in merit among proposals with such tiny differences in their average ratings? Any classically trained statistician would likely address the question using a standard analytical technique, called the *analysis of variance*, that attempts to determine of the differences between two or more averages are reliable/reproducible or are simply a matter of sampling error or chance. When the variability of judgments among judges is large relative to the difference in average judgments—and it almost always is—many judgments must be collected (sampled) before a decision about the reliability of any difference in average judgments can be made. As a ballpark figure, perhaps 20 to 60 merit judgments of each middling application would need to be collected in order to determine whether a difference in average ratings between any two applications was reliable and reproducible. This number of judgments is an order of magnitude greater than the number (2–6) collected from most committees.

It is, of course, logistically impossible to convene a committee of 20–60 peers to adjudicate applications. Even if it were possible, it is still quite presumptuous, and arguably unfair, to fund applications that are perhaps only one or two one hundredths of a merit rating point higher than applications given no funds. It is far more honest and fair to conclude that applications with highly similar average merit ratings are indistinguishable. But this honest and fair conclusion presents a dilemma: If the applications are indistinguishable and only a fraction of them can be funded, how will the winners be chosen?

To answer the question, we offer an unusual but defensible recommendation: Choose the winners at random by lottery. Consider, for example, a committee adjudicating 100 applications to determine which 30 most merit its limited funding. If the average merit ratings of 18 applications are clearly superior (however determined) to the remaining 82, and if merit ratings of the next 45 of these 82 are clustered closely together, then fund 30 – 18 = 12 of these 45 proposals at random. This would have at least four desirable effects. First, it would formalize what is, in essence, done now when committee members cannot distinguish the merit of similarly rated proposals. Second, it would relieve committee members of the agony of nit-picking through proposals, haphazardly seeking various reasons to reject them. Third, it would likely reduce the number of complaints from losing applicants about the unfairness of judges making such haphazard decisions beyond their discriminative abilities. Fourth, it would likely limit the smugness of funded applicants, knowing that their good fortune was in part the explicit result of chance rather than entirely an anointment by peers.

We must note, however, at least one danger of choosing winners by lottery. Winners tend to have a competitive advantage over losers in subsequent competitions. Consider Maria and Alice, who audition for a play. Both are equally talented, so the director chooses Alice by flipping a coin. Alice then has more opportunity than Maria to practice her craft and perfect her talent. If Maria and Alice again audition for a part in another play, we would expect Alice to stand a better chance than Maria of getting the part because of her additional experience. If Alice got the part, she would have a second opportunity for more experience than would

Maria, making Alice even more likely to get the parts in subsequent auditions. Alice may become a star, and Maria may drift into obscurity, despite the fact that they are equally talented, all because of a chance event. Had the coin flipped to the other side, Maria would have had a similar competitive advantage over Alice. We discuss the phenomenon in more detail in our next chapter under the section Track Record.

It is probably controversial to suggest that people of equal merit should receive equal outcomes. But those who endorse the principle should be concerned about the cumulative and amplifying consequences of coin flips or other random events. How can these effects be attenuated? Two suggestions come to mind. First, whenever possible, reward all equally meritorious applicants. In the case of Maria and Alice, invite both to share the part in the first play in order to give both an equal opportunity to perfect their talent. Of course, the possibility is rare and often impractical (we wonder, tongue in cheek, what might have happened if George W. Bush and Al Gore were allowed to share the presidency because the vote in Florida was too close to call). So we offer a second suggestion: If it is not possible or practical to divide rewards among equally meritorious people, then divide these people among equal opportunities for rewards. One way to accomplish this goal is to make winners of one competition temporarily ineligible to compete in one or more similar or subsequent competitions. If Maria and Alice are tied for talent, and if Alice gets the first role, then allow Maria to audition for the next play without competition from Alice.

Impractical? Perhaps. But we note that one variation has become sacrosanct in countries from the United States to Iran: A president is not allowed to serve more than two terms, in part to allow others a better chance of winning subsequent presidential competitions. We also note the widespread criticism, especially among the young, of the elimination of mandatory retirement—a criticism based on the idea that old and established workers have unfair competitive advantage over young applicants in the job market. The examples remind us of an anonymous quip, "The ultimate solution to all social problems is to take turns being oppressed."

8

Competitions Small and Large

J udgments of merit are fallible. Whether the result of limited time, limited attention, mental fatigue, shifts of standards or criteria, biases, group dynamics, or something else, judges are prone to be less than perfectly consistent in their merit assessments. Likewise, those whose merit is judged are prone to be less than perfectly consistency in the products or performances they present to the judges. Athletes sometimes stumble or miss. Job applicants sometimes overlook important information on their résumés or in their job interviews. Anxious students often forget answers to questions they know, while others make lucky guesses as answers to questions they do not know.

These deviations from true merit are collectively known as *error*. As we have noted elsewhere in the book, adjudications with relatively small amounts of error are likely to be judged as fair. Adjudications with relatively large amounts of error are likely to be judged as unfair. So error should be reduced in order to increase fairness. Some errors can be reduced. We would not be writing this book if it were otherwise. Yet because the sources of error in judging merit are numerous and persistent, it is safe to assume that no amount of effort will eliminate all errors. Like cockroaches, some errors will always find ways to resist extermination.

Sometimes errors do not matter because they do not change the outcomes of a competition. Consider, for example, a contest to select one person for a violin scholarship. Three scholarship judges assess the merit of contestants after listening to their rendition of the Bach chaconne from the Partita #2 in B minor, rating the quality of performance on a scale from 0 (*awful*) to 10 (*wonderful*). Now assume that there are only two contestants. Glenda has studied violin with Pinkus Zuckerman for 14 years and baroque violin interpretation at Julliard for 3 years, she has practiced the chaconne 700 times, and she has played it in 17 competitions for an average performance rating of 8.8. Bruce has studied violin from Mr. Fiddlehead, the high school music teacher, for 3 years and has sight-read the piece 11 times, 2 of them before judges who gave average ratings of 1.9. It should not stretch your imagination to think that Glenda is a shoe-in for the scholarship. Perhaps the three scholarship judges are in a good mood and give Glenda 9.2, 8.6, and 9.9 for her performance. Perhaps they are in a bad mood and give her

7.3, 6.7, and 7.2, or perhaps she fluffs a few notes to deserve these ratings. But even in a good mood, the judges are unlikely to give Bruce much more than a 2.5. So, despite disagreements in the ratings of the three judges (one source of error), despite mood swings that would alter their assessments (another source of error), and despite Glenda's fluffs (a third source of error), the degree of difference between them virtually guarantees that even large errors will not matter and that Glenda will win.

Not so if Glenda competes for the scholarship against Harvey, another seasoned Bach specialist who has played the chaconne in 21 previous competitions for an average score of 8.2. Our best estimate of Harvey's true merit (8.2) is lower than our best estimate of Glenda's true merit (8.8). But assume that Glenda plays just before lunch, when judge A is tired, judge B is hungry, and judge C needs a bathroom break. She fluffs six notes, and the judges give her ratings of 8.9, 7.9, and 8.1 for an average of 8.3. Assume that Harvey plays just after a good lunch when all three judges are happy and refreshed. He fluffs five notes. They rate Harvey's performance as 8.9, 8.2, and 8.2 for an average of 8.4. Harvey would thus win the scholarship. Glenda, the long-run better player, might then give up the violin, squandering her talent.

Small competitions, such as the one between Glenda and Bruce in which even large errors are unlikely to affect the selection of a clearly superior contestant, are relatively rare. More common are competitions such as the one between Glenda and Harvey in which two or more contestants have similar merit and small errors are likely to influence outcomes. Indeed, as we shall see below, they are especially common in contests with dozens, hundreds, or thousands of contestants. The first purpose of this chapter is to investigate the relationships between the size of competitions (measured by the number of contestants), the amount of error in judges' assessments, and the chances that the best people win. Knowledge of these relations will give us a better idea of when we should be concerned about even small errors and of what the consequences of these errors might be. The second purpose of this chapter is to investigate what happens to competitions when the merit of two or more contestants is high and judges find it difficult to distinguish who is best. The investigation will lead us to speculate about the evolution of contests and to prescribe when contests should and should not be held.

TRUE MERIT AND ERROR

If we want to answer the questions above, we need a way to think of error and its relation to what we call a "true" assessment of merit. Remember that, because merit is a subjective reaction to something and subject to social influence, it is strictly improper to talk about true merit in any absolute sense. But it is acceptable and useful to talk about a consistent assessment of merit, a word or number that always results from consistently applying a well-defined set of criteria. And it is useful to talk about a best estimate of merit, one that comes, say, from averaging 500 independent assessments of the same person or thing in order to cancel out the random variation in these 500 estimates. So we shall adopt these conceptions of merit here.

By doing so, we can make good use of an idea handed down both from engineering and from psychological testing, introduced in chapter 2. Radio engineers analyze the quality of radio reception as a combination of signal and noise, the former being, say, the clear music or speech that comes from a recording or microphone and the latter being the hissing sound that we hear on top of the music or speech when we try to tune in a distant station. Psychologists similarly analyze psychological test scores, such as scores in an IQ test, by assuming they have two components: a true score—think of your "true IQ"—and error—variations around the true score resulting from all manner of random and transient events such as mood swings, sleep deprivation, lighting, moment-to-moment variations of anxiety, random memory losses, lucky and unlucky guesses on an IQ test. True scores are similar to signals; errors are similar to noise. Like signals and noise, true scores and errors are assumed to be independent of each other. In addition, true scores and error, like noise, are assumed to be normally distributed—referring to the bell-shaped curve we so often see when we plot scores on the x-axis against frequency of scores on the y-axis. Fortunate errors such as lucky guesses, "giving it 110%," or the good mood of a judge produce a score above a person's true score. Unfortunate errors such as fluffs, the effects of illness, or a judge's bad mood, produce a score below the true score. Because errors are normally distributed, the larger the error, the smaller the chances it will occur.

We will adopt this "true score and error" conception to consider how judgments of merit are related to true (consistent) merit, modifying a simple and well-known formula used to characterize what we hear on the radio or how we perform on a psychological test. The modified formula is this:

$$\text{judged merit} = \text{true merit} + \text{error} \qquad (8.1)$$

What does this equation mean? Consider a student who has received only Bs in her previous 38 undergraduate courses and needs only two more courses to graduate. Her record strongly suggests that she is a B student or, to rephrase a bit, that her true merit (as judged by grades) is B. Suppose the student receives a C in one of her two last courses, and an A in the other. In the first case, her judged merit (C grade) is equal to her true merit (B grade) minus what we call error, which, in this case, might be the result of any combination of dozens of factors, ranging from the hard-nosed attitude of a randomly chosen professor to a chance contraction of a flu bug that kept the student home for 3 weeks to a smudged copy of the final exam that left the student guessing at the wording of several exam questions. In the second case, her judged merit (A grade) is equal to her true merit (B grade) plus error, which might be the result of the student's inspiration to do well because of the charisma of the professor, or an easy grading scheme, or a lucky guess at the four practice questions that appeared on the final exam, or any of dozens of other influences.

All this would be academic if errors did not exist or if they had no effect on the outcome of contests. Ideally, contestants would always reflect their true merit in their presentations, and judges would always assess this true merit without error. The ideal is equivalent to hearing a radio signal with no noise. Because the ideal never occurs, errors happen, sometimes causing judged merit to be higher than true merit, sometimes causing judged merit to be lower than true merit. As a result, it is possible that one contestant with lower true merit and good luck will be judged superior to another contestant with higher true merit and bad luck. Consider, for example, Glenda, Bruce, and Harvey, now competing in a scholarship contest with eight other contestants, shown in Table 8.1. Column A shows the true merit of each contestant; Glenda remains the best of the lot. If small random errors (column B) are added to the true merit to produce a merit judgment (column C), Glenda still wins the contest. We would then say, "the best person won" and deem the contest to be fair—at least in its outcome. As the random errors become larger relative to the differences in the true merit of contestants (column D), there is an increasing chance that the best person will not be judged as best and that someone else will win (column E)—in this case Harvey.

It is also possible for contestants other than Glenda to shift their positions as the result of errors. Bruce, for example, who has the lowest merit of the all 11 contestants (Table 8.1), is judged as second lowest when the error increases, thus missing his expected booby prize. And Alice, who should be in third place, is judged in fourth place when small errors are added and in fifth place as the size of the errors increases. Keep in mind that the errors we report in Table 8.1 are assumed to be entirely random. If the same contest were held on the day following, the error amounts for each contestant would likely be different, perhaps leading to different contest outcomes.

How often would the person with the greatest true talent be judged as such in such contests? Phrased differently, how often does the best person win? Thorngate and Carroll (1987) provided a preliminary answer to this question with a series of simple computer simulations that varied (a) the number of contestants in a contest, (b) the amount of error added to or subtracted from true merit to render a merit judgment, and (c) the rules of the contest to see how each would change the chances that the best person would win. Alas, the article appeared in a journal now long out of print, and is now almost impossible to find. So we shall reproduce

TABLE 8.1   How Random Error Can Affect Contest Outcomes

Contestant	A "True" merit	B Small error	C True + error = judged merit	D Larger error	E True + error = judged merit
Alice	7.2	−0.5	6.7	−1.0	6.2
Bruce	2.0	+0.5	2.5	+1.0	3.0
Carl	4.6	+0.4	5.0	+0.8	5.4
Denise	3.3	−0.3	3.0	−0.6	2.7
Earl	6.2	+0.6	6.8	+1.2	7.4
Fiona	5.0	+0.0	5.0	+0.0	5.0
Glenda	9.1	−0.2	8.9	−0.4	8.7
Harvey	8.2	+0.5	8.7	+1.0	9.2
Iona	5.0	−0.1	4.9	−0.2	4.8
Jim	6.1	−0.2	5.9	−0.4	5.7
Kathy	7.0	+0.3	7.3	+0.6	7.6
Winner	Glenda		Glenda		Harvey

some of the simulations here to illustrate the technique and to show you some of the surprising results.

HOW OFTEN DO THE BEST PEOPLE WIN?

There are at least two ways to answer the above question. One way is to find a good mathematician willing to derive the formulas that answer it analytically. Another is to approximate the answer by running thousands of simulated contests, randomly sampling numbers representing the true merit of, say, 10, 100, or 1,000 contestants, randomly sampling different amounts of error to associate with each of these contestants, and counting how many times the contestant(s) with the most true merit win(s). We chose the second way, known in the literature as a *Monte Carlo* simulation (after the casino). Having no time to do them by hand, we undertook the simulations using a programming language wonderfully suited for our purpose. The language is called Euler, developed by Professor R Grothmann, and is freely available (see Grothmann, 2006). Euler is similar to the commercial language Matlab®. The program we used in the simulations described below is listed in Appendix A.

The program allows us to determine quickly how (a) the number of contestants in a contest and (b) the amount of random error added to or subtracted from each contestant's true merit are related to (c) the chances that the most meritorious or "best" contestant will win. In Figure 8.1 and Figure 8.2 we illustrate some typical findings based on 5,000 simulated contests for each of several combinations of number of contestants and amounts of error. The amount of error is, of course, inversely related to the correlation between the true merit and the judged merit; the greater the error, the lower the correlation. Because readers are more likely to understand correlation coefficients than error amounts, we report true-judged correlations on the x-axis.

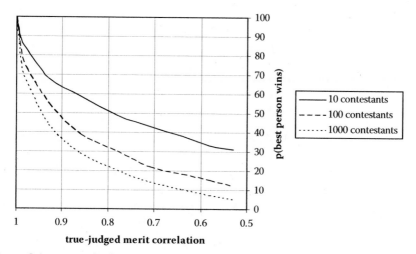

Figure 8.1   True-judged merit correlation (r) and the probability that the best person wins.

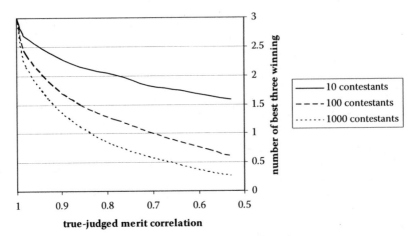

Figure 8.2   True-judged merit and average number of best three contestants winning top three prizes.

The results illustrated in Figure 8.1 and Figure 8.2 lead us to two disturbing conclusions. First, relatively small amounts of error can lead to large reductions in the chances that the most meritorious contestant(s) will win. Second, the insidious effects of error increase as the size of the competition increases. Even in relatively small competitions with only 10 contestants, small amounts of error, causing imperfect correlations between true merit and judged merit, generate significant declines in the chances that the best person wins. As interpolated from Figure 8.1, for example, an extremely high true-judged correlation of $r = +0.95$ reduces the chances of the best person winning a 10-contestant competition to about 75%. A true-judged correlation of $r = +0.90$ reduces the chances of the best person winning a 100-contestant competition to about 50%. If the correlation declines only to about $r = +0.85$ in a 1,000-contestant competition, the chances of the best person winning plummets to about 25%. Recall from chapter 7 that the correlation between pairs of judges assessing grant applications was about $r = +0.50$, a correlation we would expect between two independent judges if each of them had a correlation with true merit of about $r = +0.71$. Interpolating from Figure 8.1, if the judges were adjudicating 100 applications submitted for just one grant, the most meritorious application would have only about a 22% chance of receiving it.

Of course, many competitions award more than one prize. A common number is three: a prize for first place, one for second place, and one for third. How many of the three most meritorious contestants are likely to walk away with one of these prizes? Again, it depends on the numbers of contestants in a competition and the amount of error in merit assessments. Still, Figure 8.2 illustrates the same disturbing trend. As interpolated from Figure 8.1, in a small competition with only 10 contestants, judgments with a correlation of about $r = +0.8$ with true merit will, on average, reward about two of the three most meritorious contestants. In a competition with 100 contestants, judgments with a correlation of $r = +0.8$ with true merit will reward about 1.3 of the three most meritorious contestants. The equivalent average in a competition with 1,000 contestants is about 0.8 of the top three. Many of the research grant competitions described in chapter 5 assess about 100 applications for about 30 grants. Using the $r = +0.71$ correlation between true and judged merit estimated in the paragraph above (equivalent to an error number of 15 for the Euler program in Appendix A), we would expect about 20 of the 30 best applications to receive one of the 30 grants; the remaining 10 grants would be awarded to applications that had higher judged merit but lower true merit than 10 others as a result of random errors, as illustrated in the case of Glenda and Harvey shown in Table 8.1.

In sum, the brute force of these computer simulations illustrates the mathematical truth that the capability of competitions to separate the best from the rest degrades rapidly with even a small injection of judgment error and more rapidly as the size of the contest increases. There are two reasons why. First, judgment error becomes increasingly influential as the range of merit of eligible contestants contracts. Even sloppy assessment methods can correctly distinguish outstanding contestants from truly awful ones. But even the most meticulous assessment methods cannot guarantee to distinguish reliably among two or more outstanding contestants. Second, large competitions normally have a greater number of meritorious contestants than do small competitions. Judging the relative merit of the two outstanding contestants who may appear in a 100-contestant competition might lead the one who is marginally more outstanding than the other to win the competition 70% of the time. Judging the relative merit of 20 outstanding contestants who may appear in a 1,000-contestant competition might lead the one who is marginally more outstanding than the 19 others to win the competition 10% of the time.

Consider an example. Suppose we could magically invent an infallible and errorless way to assess merit: the True Merit test. Suppose we standardized our test so that the average merit score among millions of people is 65% and the standard deviation, a measure of variability or range, is 10%. And suppose we selected 10 people completely at random and asked them to complete our True Merit test. Here would be a typical result:

Exhibit A:
True Merit scores = 59.1, 61.0, 64.4, 64.6, 67.3, 67.9, 69.8, 75.6, 82.0, 87.8
Average = 69.9
Range = 87.8–59.1 = 28.7

Now suppose we gave our True Merit test to 100 people at random and examined the scores of the top 10. Here is a typical result:

Exhibit B:
True Merit scores = 77.8, 78.6, 79.3, 79.5, 80.3, 81.2, 88.5, 89.7, 90.0, 91.7
Average = 83.7
Range = 91.7–77.8 = 13.9

Finally, suppose we gave our test to 1,000 people at random and examined the scores of the top 10. Here is a typical result:

Exhibit C:
True Merit scores = 89.3, 89.4, 90.4, 91.9, 92.4, 93.8, 94.8, 94.9, 95.6, 96.9

Average = 92.9
Range = 96.9–89.3 = 7.6

Notice two trends. The more people we sample to meet our quota of 10 (and thus the smaller the proportion of them we pick from the top), the higher the average true merit score in our quota. Equally important, the more people we sample (and thus the smaller the proportion of them we pick from the top), the smaller the range of true merit scores in our quota. Lacking a True Merit test, even a poor indicant of merit—an unreliable or insensitive measure, a sloppy judgment, etc.— would probably distinguish correctly among persons in Exhibit A; it would almost certainly distinguish between the person with a merit score of 59.1 and the person with a merit score of 87.8. But the same unreliable, insensitive test or fallible judgment would likely not distinguish between the persons with merit of 89.3 and 96.9 in Exhibit C, much less between persons with merit of 95.6 and 96.9.

Fallible measures can correctly detect big differences but not small ones. When a merit-based competition is crowded at the top of the scale and the differences between contestants are increasingly small, measures of merit must be exceedingly sensitive and valid to distinguish the very meritorious. No one has invented such a sensitive measure. We have not come close to a True Merit test, which is why judgments of merit are increasingly prone to error when making fine distinctions.

When a competition allows more than one winner, those hovering at the lower limit of winner's circle are equally affected by competition size and error. Suppose, for example, that 100 job applicants are competing for 10 or 20 jobs. What are the chances that the 10th or 20th most meritorious applicants would be hired? We can modify the program in Appendix A to answer the question. If the true-judged merit correlation is $r = +0.95$, then the chances that the 10th most meritorious of 100 applicants will get one of 10 jobs is about 45%, and the chances that the 20th most meritorious will get one of 20 jobs is about 46%. If the true-judged merit correlation is at a more realistic $r = +0.70$, then these two chances decline to about 32 and 37%, respectively. In short, a contestant just above the cutoff is more likely to be a loser than a winner, largely because there are many others just below the cutoff who could rise above the slightly superior contestant if random errors work in their favor.

BIASES

Deviations from true merit can come from at least one source other than random error. They can also come from one or more biases (see chapter 2). Some biases exclude a subset of prospective contestants from a competition, as do eligibility criteria (see chapter 5). A medical school admission bias, for example, might exclude anyone over 30 years of age from applying. Other biases systematically add or subtract merit points to the judged merit of each member of a subset of contestants. We will concentrate on additive and subtractive biases. An additive bias would occur if a teacher boosted by one letter grade the exam mark of each student who presented the teacher with a $100 token of pedagogical appreciation. A subtractive bias (aka handicap) would occur if all professional tennis players in a pro-amateur tennis match were required to play using their nonpreferred hand. These biases are represented in the following pair of equations:

$$\text{judged merit} = \text{true merit} + \text{error [for a normal subset of contestants]} \quad (8.2a)$$

$$\text{judged merit} = \text{true merit} + \text{bias} + \text{error [for a biased set of contestants]} \quad (8.2b)$$

How much do biases distort the outcomes of competitions? The answer depends on numerous variables, including the amount of bias, the proportion of contestants judged with bias, the number of winners, and the amount of judgment error. The effects of some of these variables can be explored with a modification of the contest simulation program—the modification listed in Appendix B. The "biased" function shown in this appendix generates true merit scores for a set of contestants accruing no biases and true merit + bias scores for another set of contestants who enjoy a positive judgment bias (for example, +3 extra merit points) or suffer a negative one (−3 merit points). It then adds judgment error to all contestants and tallies how many of the contestants with a positive (or negative) bias are among the winners.

Consider a few outcomes of the simulation. Suppose we ran a prototypical 100-contestant competition to determine which contestants would be among the top 10 winners. Suppose the average true merit of these 100 contestants was 65 and the standard deviation of their true merit was 10. Now suppose 50 contestants are judged without bias, that 50 are judged with a bias of +3, adding 3 to their true merit scores. Finally, suppose the standard deviation of judgment error was 5. Entering these values into the program in Appendix B shows us that about 62% of the top-10 winners come from the biased group. If the bias were 0 (if there were no bias), we would expect about 50% of the top 10 to be from this group. So a bias that added 3 units of merit under the conditions above would increase the chances of being a top-10 winner by 62 − 50 = 12%. Conversely, a bias that subtracted 3 units of merit would reduce the chances of being a top-10 winner by 12%, from 50 to 38%.

Now let us vary some of the parameters of the above prototypical competition, one by one. If we reduce the number of winners from 10 to 1, the winner would be a member of the biased group in about 66% of the competitions, rather than the expected 50% if no bias were present. If we increased the bias in the previous paragraph's settings from +3 to +10 (the size of true merit standard deviation), about 84% of the top-10 winners would be from the biased group; if there is only one winner, it will be a member of the biased group about 91% of the time. And if we changed the proportion of biased contestants from 50 to 20%, then the proportion of biased contestants in the 10-winner circle would rise from 20 to about 28%.

Ironically, but not surprisingly, an increase in judgment error mitigates these outcomes. For example, if there were no judgment error in prototypical competition above, only true merit and (for half the contestants) an error of +3, then 63% of the top 10 would be from the set of biased contestants. If the judgment error were 10, the proportion would decline to 59%, and if the error were 20, then the proportion would decline to 56%. The decline reflects the increasing importance of error over bias in competition outcomes as error increases.

These variations of the prototypical competition can be interpreted in different ways. The one we prefer is that bias, when attached to people who are spread across the whole range of true merit, has a noticeable but relatively modest effect on the outcomes of competitions, especially when mitigated by random judgment errors. The effects of bias, however, multiply among the most meritorious contestants whose range of true merit is far smaller than the range of the entire population (cf. Exhibits A, B, and C in the previous section). Consider a competition with only 10 very meritorious contestants whose mean merit score is 90 and whose standard deviation is 2 (producing a range of about 8 as shown in Exhibit C above). Adding 3 merit points to one of the 10 contestants would increase that contestant's chances of winning top spot from 10 to about 50%, and reduce the remaining nine contestant's chances from 10% to 50/9 = 5.5%. The result illustrates again that when differences between merit are small, little things—bias as well as error—mean a lot.

HIERARCHICAL COMPETITIONS

The significant role of chance and bias in selecting winners of large contests is chillingly demonstrated in what we call *hierarchical competitions*. Hierarchical competitions proceed in rounds, each round eliminating some contestants while allowing others to compete in the next round. Many music performance competitions are held this way; winners of local or preliminary contests are allowed to compete in regional contests, winners of regional contests are allowed to compete in provincial/state contests, and so on until one winner is finally chosen at a national or international level. So, too, are many sports playoffs in which round-robin "regular season" play determines which teams will begin elimination matches (hierarchical competitions) to determine which person or team is the last one standing. Thorngate and Carroll (1987) showed that the outcomes of hierarchical competitions are statistically the same as outcomes of one large "free for all"—in this case, the structure of a competition does not matter. But there are enormous structural and psychological differences between the two.

Hierarchical competitions have notable advantages over free-for-all competitions for judges, for organizers, and for the viewing public. It is, for example, probably impossible for any judge to assess differences in the merit of 100 or more contestants in a free-for-all competition. It seems difficult to make fine distinctions among more than a dozen candidates; indeed, the number is likely even lower (see, for example, Miller, 1956). Beyond some relative low number of contestants to be judged, habituation and fatigue overtake sensitivity and sensibility; judges lose their edge. In 1968, one of us (WT) sat behind two judges in an audience of a Canadian national violin maker's competition, both of whom were doing their best to assess the sound quality of about 200 violins, each played on stage for about 3 minutes by a bored violinist who repeated the same scales and musical excerpts 200 times. After listening to about 12 violins in this free-for-all competition, the younger judge turned to the older judge and said, "I feel badly, but my ears are tired and I just can't tell the difference between these violins anymore. Can you?" And the older judge replied, "Heavens no! But don't worry. Just rate all of them somewhere in the 'Good' range unless one of them knocks you over with its sound." None of them did. Hierarchical competitions make it possible to divide the labor of adjudication among several judges in hopes of relieving a judge of such boredom, fatigue, satiation, or waning motivation that can reduce the validity of his judgments.

Hierarchical competitions can also become popular spectacles and money pumps. Many professional sports and talent competitions, for example, entertain millions of fans who pay good money to organizers for contest tickets or for betting on outcomes or for the products and profits of competition advertisers. Consider the number of people who watch, and pay for, the Stanley Cup playoffs, the World Series, the NBA championships, or the Super Bowl. Alternatively, think of the advertising revenues accrued to various Idol and other talent shows as they glitz through their hierarchical eliminations. Few free-for-all competitions of all contestants attract such followings.

Alas, the benefits of hierarchical competitions for contestants are far less clear. Hierarchical competitions by definition require reassessments of the merit of winners of the previous level, continuing in this way until contestants lose a round or win the final one. Each round requires its contestants to invest time, energy, and, more often than not, money. In addition, some contests hold rounds months or years apart, requiring months or years of dedication, practice, anxiety, and expenditures, fueled by the fear that all could be lost in the next competition.

Any young person pursuing dreams of the big leagues, be they in an Olympic or professional sport, a literary or scientific prize, even a higher education, knows this well. Consider Mary, a hypothetical entrant to a hierarchical sports competition. Mary's first encouragements are likely to come from proud parents or local coaches who believe Mary's figure skating performance is noticeably better than the wide range of performances among local peers (see Figure 8.3, white bars). These are the judges who anoint Mary with the cliché of *potential.* Using an older cliché, Mary is a big fish in a small pond. Promoted to the next level, Mary no

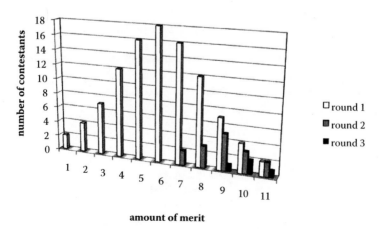

Figure 8.3   The distribution of merit in a three-round hierarchical competition.

longer competes with the locals who lack the talent or motivation to perform well. These local losers have dropped out or been eliminated, leaving Mary to compete with big fish from many small ponds, the moderately to extremely meritorious, all of whom probably have potential (Figure 8.3, gray bars). A few months or years of practice to develop potential at this second level, combined with larger investments in equipment, coaching, transportation, tutoring, etc., should prepare Mary for competitions to advance to level three (Figure 8.3, black bars). If Mary loses these competitions, then a few months or years of life, and a few thousands of dollars of investment, would be lost in the name of experience. If Mary wins, then everything escalates to the next level, where most of the smaller big fish are gone, where few of the moderately meritorious remain. Now Mary must compete with a shrinking population of winners whose range of merit has also shrunk to toward the top end. More practice, more money, more fear of the losses that would accrue if Mary, inexperienced in the ways of a normal life, were to lose. Each step up the ladder makes the fall more frightening. So it would not be surprising if Mary and most of her peers at this level turn interest into obsession, recreation to compulsion, and normal life into a neurotic climb for the last rung.

Perhaps such competitions build character. Perhaps they keep young people away from psychoactive drugs (though they may tempt them with performance-enhancing drugs; see below). On the other hand, hierarchical competitions are remarkably similar to social and temporal traps (Messick & McClelland, 1983; Platt, 1973) that can too easily lead the talented to tragedy.

Why? Primarily because the requirements for winning change with each escalation in the hierarchy. Mary, for example, might stand out from her local competition because of her superior natural ability. When she escalates to the next level, most of her new competitors will have superior natural ability; indeed, our best guess is that Mary will have an average amount of superior natural ability. Winning at this level will require more, perhaps, for example, 4 hours a day of dedicated practice. If Mary does practice 4 hours a day, and if her competitors do not, then she is likely to win at this level as well and be promoted to the third level. Yet each competitor at the third level is likely to have superior natural talent and to practice 4 hours a day, leaving Mary as just another talented and dedicated competitor. Now what might distinguish Mary from the others in this third-level group? Perhaps it would be double the amount of practice. Perhaps it would be hiring a personal trainer, a choreographer, or a sports psychologist. Perhaps it would be money to buy better equipment or costumes or to take more trips for more experience in more competitions. Of course, while Mary is considering her options, so are all her naturally talented and dedicated competitors. As a result, whatever option seems to be working for one competitor will likely be copied by the others, decreasing the chances that it will lead to a competitive advantage. So we should not be surprised if competitors begin to keep secrets.

As competitors rise in hierarchical competitions, whatever they did to give them competitive advantage at the previous level is less likely to give them competitive advantage at the current or subsequent levels, simply because a greater proportion of the remaining competitors are doing the same. Competitors must maintain whatever previously gave them competitive advantage; they cannot "let go" of motivation or practice or coaching or travel or anything else that everyone at their level employs and still hope to remain competitive. As competitors try to control their destiny, each step up the hierarchy means increasing or adding something else.

Where does it end? Contestants try to control the judgments of merit they receive in competitions by doing whatever they can to stand out from, to be noticeably better than, their competitors. But each step up the hierarchy decreases the variability of competitors, so they become not only increasingly good but increasingly similar. As a result, it becomes increasingly difficult for any contestant to stand out from the rest. When they are all talented, dedicated, motivated, practiced, experienced well coached, well dressed, and artistic, what is left to distinguish them? In a word: *error.*

It might be the random error of a fraction of a second when the ice conditions cause a tiny wobble in a skate to magnify into a fall. It might be the random error of a facial muscle that causes a painted smile to yield to fatigue. It just as likely might be the random error of a judge who blinked when the smile faded or another judge whose mood had soured by judging the previous contestant higher than did other judges or a third judge who was slightly influenced by the applause of the audience during a performance. These and a hundred other possibilities are likely to play their final part in deciding who the ultimate winner is, simply because all of the finalists are, in truth, indistinguishable in their merit.

Let us review. Because each round of a hierarchical competition tends to exclude more contestants with lower merit than with higher merit, each round reduces the variability of merit as it increases the average amount among those who remain. Unless judgment errors are also reduced at the same rate as the variability of merit, judgment errors come to play an increasing role in determining which contestants may proceed to the next level. There is no reason to believe that judgment errors are reduced at this rate. So there is more reason to accept the increasing role that random errors play in determining winners of each round of a hierarchical competition. Stated another way, the more contestants rise in hierarchical competitions, the less their fate is determined by their talent or skill or motivation or knowledge or creativity or anything else that might be meritorious. All of these may be necessary but none are sufficient to guarantee success. In the beginning of a large and hierarchical competition, meritorious qualities make a difference. In the end, it is luck.

Why would people invest a large portion of their life for an opportunity to let luck determine their fate? Behavioral psychologists would explain the investment as the consequence of shaping behavior through partial reinforcement schedules, rewarding contestants with decreasing frequency as they persist in their activities and watching the well-known consequence: increasing persistence of the activity and increasing resistance to extinction, the same phenomenon observed in compulsive gamblers (Keller & Schoenfeld, 1950). Adaptation level theorists (Helson, 1964) would note that contestants would probably adapt to slow escalations of suffering from one level in a hierarchical competition to the next, which, like the apocryphal frog boiled alive in slowly heated water, would lower the chances of a contestant leaving an otherwise insufferable situation. Social comparison theorists (Festinger,

1954) would point to escalating aspirations adjusted to the current reference group of competitors, the kind of peer pressure that leads people to accept foolish dares. Decision theorists (Arkes & Blumer, 1985) would discuss the continued investment as a good example of the sunk cost fallacy, leading people to throw good money (or time, effort, self-esteem) after bad in hopes of recovering what had previously been lost. And we must not forget hubris, the excessive pride that surely keeps many contestants in competitions far longer than common sense would prescribe. All of these reasons, and likely several more, contribute to meritorious people pursuing a chance to take a chance in hierarchical competitions.

There is a great potential for tragedy in all this. It comes most often in the popular and populated hierarchical competitions that stir the dreams of young people or their pushy parents, the famous and arduous national or international contests that promise the winner fame, fortune, or both. But the potential for tragedy can also be seen in more common competitions such as those that prompt millions of students to pursue ever more degrees seeking ever higher marks and ever larger scholarships in hopes of accruing a "competitive edge" in job interview committees controlling the gates to high-paying, secure, and personally rewarding careers. Or the laughable academic competitions that prompt ever more neurotic professors to write ever more grant proposals with ever more trendy topics in hopes of generating ever more publications in ever more "high-impact" journals that ever more colleagues cite but ever fewer people read.

The tragedy is of two kinds. One kind occurs when exceptionally talented, creative, skilled, dedicated, or similarly meritorious contestants who lose a competition are discouraged or prevented from offering their gift again. The second kind occurs when the gift they are discouraged or prevented from offering is useful to their society. Many fine musicians who are just as good as the winners but who rank third in an international competition are never heard of again. The same often happens to outstanding and perfectly capable students who make all but the last cut to medical schools or other advanced programs simply because they are fractionally and unreliably lower in judged merit than the one(s) who were accepted. Despite common but insensitive pleas to "suck it up" or "get over it," such losses usually produce gut-wrenching reactions, often rendering many enormously gifted people unable or unwilling to offer again their gifts to the world. Most such gifts are useful to society; consider, for example, why it is better to have 10 excellent doctors than to have one superb doctor to serve 100,000 patients. Someone once remarked that civilizations decline in direct relation to the squandering of their talent. No society can be well served by competitions that waste more talent than they reward.

TRACK RECORD

In most competitions related to skill or talent, judgments of merit are based on predictions of future performance. This occurs, for example, when employers judge job applicants to predict who will do the best job, when house owners judge contractors to predict who will do the best home renovations, when scouts or directors judge professional athletes or actors to predict who will give the best performance, and when scholarship or research grant committees judge applicants to predict who will produce the best work. Judges in such competitions are naturally inclined to seek good predictors of future performance. And one of the most tempting predictors is a record of past performance, also known as previous experience or *track record*.

Though still fallible, track record is usually a better predictor of future performance than are indicants such as lines in palms, signs of the zodiac, national exam scores, lists of hobbies, reference letters, or interviews; indeed, recent past behavior is usually a better predictor of future behavior than anything else. So it seems reasonable, even seductive, to use information about the merit of past performance in assessing future performance. The seduction has been embraced by several research granting agencies that are quite explicit in weighing, sometimes heavily, the track record of the applicant in assessing the merit of his application. (e.g., see "Grants Committee," 2007).

Alas, track record reflects far more than the skill or talent that is normally attributed to it. It also reflects opportunity, motivation, and luck, all of which can, in turn, be influenced by good connections. Sons of Texas oil millionaires, for example, probably have more opportunities to accrue an impressive track record than do daughters of immigrants. Mothers who begin university while raising children are probably more motivated to get good grades if their family praises them and helps with housework than if their family complains.

Then there is luck. We have shown above how large competitions tend to have large numbers of highly meritorious people who vary so little in their merit that their differences are effectively indistinguishable. In these cases, judgment error accounts for almost all of the final decisions, and the winner is distinguished from the other finalists almost entirely by chance. If such good luck provides the winner with more opportunities or motivation than the other finalists have for improving track record, then the winner would have an advantage over the finalists in subsequent competitions. And if, as the result of the advantage, the winner of the first competition also wins the second, then the winner would accrue even more opportunities and motivation to improve his track record, giving even more competitive advantage over equally skillful or talented finalists. Over several iterations of this cycle, the track record that began by chance will accumulate, increasing competitive advantage, much like compound interest. One person would accrue a track record all out of proportion to differences in talent or skill (for example, 1% more skill than others could yield 1,000% more experience), while others who have indistinguishable merit but no track record might fall by the wayside, perhaps after wasting years to develop a talent that could otherwise be put to good use.

To illustrate how track record can amplify chance differences, consider two young job applicants, Samantha and Earl, both finishing their third year in premed biology at the same university with the same high grade average, having equally meritorious grade-point averages and no track record. Assume that they are competing for the same summer job as a biology research assistant, and that the committee members judging them cannot decide who is superior. In desperation, the committee flips a coin, Earl wins the toss, gets the research job, and finishes the summer coauthoring a published scientific report, while Samantha spends the summer serving fries from a chip wagon.

In their fourth year of university, what would we expect of Earl and Samantha? If Earl did reasonably well in his summer job, we could reasonably guess that he would be more motivated in his studies than would Samantha and would have developed more research skills. In addition, Earl would probably have more professional connections among biology professors and better reference letters. Earl would also have one more publication than Samantha. So it would not be surprising if Earl received better grades in his fourth-year courses than would Samantha. Even if they continued to receive the same grades, Earl would have a competitive edge over Samantha in applying for medical schools and scholarships simply because he had the better track record in biology research. Indeed, if Earl's track record led him to accrue more scholarships and more education, he would have more opportunities to improve his track record even than would Samantha. Samantha might then have good reason to become discouraged and perhaps drop out of biology or suffer rejection from medical school. Because of the flip of a coin, one of two equally meritorious students would then be lost from medicine, causing Earl to turn away new patients for lack of time to see them.

The rich get richer and the poor get poorer. Billy Holiday once paraphrased a line from the Book of Matthew in song, "Them who's got shall get. Them who's not shall lose." Similarly inspired, Merton (1968b) coined the term *Matthew effect* to discuss the insidious influence of track record on scientific productivity, leading scientists with research funding to publish more than scientists without, which, in turn, leads to more funding and jealously guarded empires. The Matthew effect exemplifies what is now known as *cumulative advantage* (DiPrete & Eirich, 2006), the effects of which are beautifully and depressingly illustrated by Frank and Cook (1995) in "winner-take-all" societies. Here is one example. *Forbes* magazine (Kroll & Fass, 2006) estimates that in 1985 there were 140 billionaires in the world. In 2003 there were an estimated 476. In the current year there are an estimated 793, and their estimated cumulative worth is about 2.6 trillion dollars. This is approximately equal to the cumulative worth of the poorest third of the world's population of about 6.3 billion. In short, $793 = 2.1$ billion, or $1 = 2.65$ billion. We doubt that many of the 793 billionaires have over 2.5 million times the talent or skill of each of their poor cousins. When people can deposit their track record, or the track record inherited from their rich family, in the bank, the distribution of rewards can escalate toward obscenity.

Is it fair to consider track record? A clear answer can only be given after answering another question: Fair for whom? Most self-serving judges looking for the best deal for themselves or those they represent are unlikely to care about the people they reject, even if these people are just as skillful as the people they select. Instead, they are likely to ask, "If track record is a good indicant of merit, then why ignore it?" The question has several rhetorical variations. Would someone, for example, rather have a medical operation done by an experienced surgeon with an excellent track record or by an inexperienced surgeon with excellent potential? For those with a vested interest in the outcome of a competition, consideration of track record is usually considered justifiable, important, and fair.

In contrast, those with talent and skill equal to or better than those with a good and long track record would surely argue that track record is unfair. Most people looking for their first job know the conundrum: In order to get a job they must have experience, but in order to get experience they must have a job. The conundrum is painful because talented people with no track record fare no better in competition with experienced contestants than do untalented people or those with a bad track record. So, they may ask, why stay in the game? We shall address this question in the next chapter.

Some organizations attempt to surmount the conundrum with special competitions that do not incorporate track record as a criterion of merit or that do not allow those with long track records to compete. Such contests go by many names, including amateur nights, Idol contests, cattle calls, peewee or bush leagues, co-op summer programs, new scholar and new scientist research competitions, etc. Most give smaller prizes to their winners than do competitions among contestants who have track records to flaunt. The smaller prizes are often justified by noting that wins offer the beginning of track record and thus a valuable ticket to a chance in the big leagues. We suspect that organizations also wish to reduce the consequences of what they assume would be increased risks of failure among trackless winners.

PRACTICAL IMPLICATIONS

Our reasoning and demonstrations above show that hopes for improving the fairness of a competition by reducing judgment error are vitiated by (a) increases in the number of competition applicants and (b) reductions in ratio of winners to applicants. The implications are clear. If we want to increase the chances that meritorious applicants will be rewarded and unmeritorious applicants will not, then we must either limit the size of competitions or offer more prizes.

Before discussing these two practical implications, we must acknowledge that not all competition donors or organizers are interested in reducing the errors of exclusion or the errors of inclusion, simply because of the purposes their competitions serve. Consider, for example, an organizer of a professional sport competition. It is safe to speculate that the business plans of these organizations do not list the welfare of competitors as their primary goal. The primary goal of professional sport competitions is to extract money from the wallets of fans. Fans enjoy competitions for their entertainment, drama, struggle, suffering, and spectacle—sometimes even for their corruption. When fans get what they want, they come back, and pay more; otherwise, they spend their time and money elsewhere. So the desires of fans, rather than the desires of competitors, must be attended. Are fans tormented by the human costs of competition? Usually not. So there is no strong business case to worry about the welfare of competitors. Winners are paid handsomely, losers are forgotten, and their personal tragedies can often be parlayed into greater ticket sales. In a move of surprising candor, the World Wrestling Federation recently rebranded itself as World Wrestling Entertainment, Inc. As long as the fans continue to pay for their entertainment—including the entertainment of booing cheaters, crooked judges, and bad referees—who cares if the competitions are not rich in procedural or distributive justice?

It is also worthwhile to acknowledge that many competition donors and organizers place far higher importance on minimizing injustices of inclusion errors than on minimizing injustices of exclusion errors. Consider, for example, a business owner wanting to hire the best possible employees. The owner is likely to be far more concerned about what will happen to the business if a bad applicant is hired than about what will happen to a good applicant if he is not hired. In order to minimize the chances of hiring a bad applicant, the best strategy is to gather applications from as many good applicants as possible, which is why there is a thriving business in job advertising and recruitment agencies. A popular ideal is to hold a job competition that attracts only the best candidates and then to hire the best of the best. Other than a polite rejection letter, no consideration need be given to the best who lost; they are assumed to be capable of recovering soon and flourishing elsewhere. The strategy is reminiscent of the purse-seine netting methods employed by tuna fishing fleets: Cast a huge net through the ocean of candidates to capture as many as possible; haul in the catch; keep the tuna and throw away the rest. Who cares if dolphins, seals, and other undesirables caught in the net do not survive the toss?

Those who do care about the welfare of their competitors should consider the size of their competitions and the distribution of their rewards. As we have shown, large competitions, by definition, have many competitors and thus a higher chance than do small competitions of having several excellent competitors. But large competitions are also expensive and difficult to manage: they increase burdens of effort and time on the judges and, in their hierarchical variations, place similar burdens on the competitors.

How big should a competition be? There is no fixed answer, but there is an easy way of estimating an answer with a few simplifying assumptions. Assume that a donor or organizer estimates from past experience that 10% of applicants are, if not the best of the best, still good enough to be worthy of reward. If their competition had just one applicant, the chances that she would not be worthy of a reward is 90%. If the competition had two applicants, the chances that neither of them are worthy would be 90% × 90% = 81%, so that chances that at least (perhaps both) of them is worthy would be 100% − 81% = 19%. With three applicants, the chances that none of them would be worthy would be 90 × 90 × 90 = 72.9%, so there is a 100 − 72.9 = 26.1% chance that at least one worthy applicant would be in the bunch. If we continue this little mathematical progression, we find that the chances that at least one worthy applicant will appear in a group of 10 applicants is $1 - 0.9^{10} =$ 65%, the chances that at least one will appear in a group of 20 is $1 - 0.9^{20} = 88\%$, and the chances in a group of 30 is $1 - 0.9^{30} = 96\%$. Therefore, if the competition donor and organizer are comfortable with a 90% chance of a meritorious applicant appearing in the competition, then they should feel comfortable seeking no more than two dozen applicants. If donors or organizers believe that 20% of applicants are worthy, then they can be 90% certain of having one in a competition with only 10 applicants. Experience shows that contests of 10–25 applicants do not place excessive burdens on judges and are small enough to be done with resorting to multiple elimination rounds. There remains the challenge of finding which of the two dozen or so applicants is the best; the constraints noted earlier in this chapter still apply. The challenge is daunting beyond about 25 applicants. So we think of 25 as the upper limit of the size of any competition with fair pretensions.

What of the distribution of rewards? In chapter 5 we discussed rules for eligibility—minimum standards that must be passed for an applicant to be eligible to compete. As we noted, this common and reasonable solution to limiting the number of applicants creates a two-step competition: a test of eligibility, followed by a contest among those who pass the test. Often the test of eligibility is based on the same criteria used to judge merit in the contest. Consider, for example, a scholarship committee convened to allocate a $10,000 scholarship to the best applicant. Suppose the competition attracted only three applicants: two with a D average and the third with a D+ average. It would be reasonable for the scholarship donors, organizers, and judges to declare that none of the applicants show sufficient scholarly merit to deserve the prize; in other words, that none of the applicants passed a test of some minimum average—say, a B. The $10,000 might then be saved for the next competition.

Implicit in almost all contests, and explicit in many contest rules, is the understanding that comparisons of merit will determine the outcome of competitions only when at least one competitor meets some minimum standard to deserve a reward. The judges of Jenny Brown's Victoria Sponge cake (beginning of chapter 1) exemplify this assumption. We suggest the same logic be inverted. If all competitors who fail a minimum standard receive no reward, then all competitors who pass the minimum standard should receive at least some reward. Many contests now have a variation of this rule. Minimum rewards include a certificate, plaque, pin, or T-shirt of recognition, an uplifting speech with thanks to all who competed, a media interview or other public exposure, a résumé on file, and SSHRC's "You qualified for funding but we ran out of money" letter discussed in chapter 6.

We should like to suggest something a little less minimum: more prizes. Winner-take-all merit competitions may sound glamorous and attract risk-takers looking for big payoffs, oblivious to chances of failure. But they are also, as we have noted, exceedingly wasteful of talent. Many professional sports have recognized the waste and tried to minimize it. Hockey players, for example, are paid salaries regardless of whether they win or lose their games. Baseball owners shift players between big league and farm teams, allowing those who slip from grace in the former to play in the latter, practice their game, and pay their rent. The U.S. Open Tennis competition awards money to 50% of players who pass the test to enter the first round and increases the money at each subsequent level of its hierarchical contest. The 2006 base prizes for a winner of a singles event (http://www.frontrowking.com/tennis/us_open_tennis_prize_money.html) were as follows:

Winners $1,200,000
Runners-up $600,000
Semifinalists $280,000
Quarter finalists $140,000
Round of sixteen $72,000
Third round $42,000
Second round $26,500
First round $16,500

The money given to first-round winners probably pays for their trip to Flushing Meadows, New York, where the competition is held. Other expenses can be paid with money earned from subsequent wins; profits likely begin to accrue to semi-finalists. Assuming all winners beyond the first round merit some prize, it seems perfectly sensible to give them one, in part so that they can develop their skill for next year's competition.

Offering more prizes to more people may not be feasible in some competitions. It is not feasible, for example, to award astronaut applicants differing numbers of hours in space according to their relative merit. On the other hand, multiple prizes do seem feasible in many competitions where they are currently not given and, we believe, should be given serious consideration.

A simple example comes to mind. Scholarship competitions typically offer a small set of large rewards to applicants with the predictable academic pedigrees: perfect grade averages, courageous leadership skills, trophy-attracting athletic prowess, heart-melting volunteer work, etc. Perhaps the top three applicants are each given $30,000. The next 20 applicants, who likely vary from the winners by less than the breadth of a hair, get nothing. Why not give the beautiful losers more? A finalist certificate to add to a résumé would be a cheap minimum. More tangible would be a chunk of money, at least enough to pay for the time and effort they spent to apply and for their application fees. Ideally, extra money chunks would come from the deep pockets of donors. But if the pockets are empty and the money is fixed, it is quite reasonable to lower the prizes for the winners and distribute what is left to the rest. For example, rather than spending $90,000 on three applicants judged best, give each of them $20,000, give the next best 10 $2,000 each, and give $1,000 to each of the next 10 after them. Or refine the rule to offer a smoother relation between the ranking of applicants in a competition and the amount they win. The rule can be made flexible to allow for some years when a competition has many meritorious applicants and some years when it has only a few.

Scaled rewards like these would, of course, make the big prizes somewhat smaller. But the reduction would be more than offset by the recognition given to those who were judged almost as good as the best. When given a choice between small chances of large rewards and larger chances of smaller rewards, biological rationality—surviving as many competitions as possible—clearly prescribes the latter (Thorngate & Tavakoli, 2005). And there is evidence that this is what prospective applicants prefer. Recently, Wang, Thorngate, and Tashk (2005) asked undergraduate students in Canada and in Iran to pretend they were judges in a scholarship competition and then showed them the grade-point averages (GPAs) of 10 applicants and asked them to allocate any proportion of either $10,000 or $100,000 to each of the 10. On average, the proportion of money allocated to each of the 10 applicants followed a pattern quite similar to that of the U.S. Open tennis prizes. The rank order of money allocations was perfectly correlated with the rank ordering of GPAs. And the more the applicants' GPAs diverged, the more divergent were their allocations. Example: if the top three applicants had GPAs of 98, 87, and 86%, then they would be allocated about $8,000, $1,200, and $800, respectively. If the top three had GPAs 98, 97, and 86%, then they would respectively be allocated perhaps $4,500, $4,000, and $1,500. (Iranians, incidentally, were more inclined than were Canadians to allocate a large proportion of the scholarship money to the winner, regardless of Gold-Silver-Bronze GPA spreads.) Heartwarmingly, participants gave all of the 10 applicants something; even the applicant with the lowest GPA was given a few hundred dollars—presumably just for applying.

The results of this study suggest that few students asked to play the role of scholarship judge adopt a "winner-takes-all" rule for mapping merit into money— the rule most often adopted in official scholarship competitions. Instead, the students adopt a kinder "money should parallel merit" rule, giving the finalists at least something for their effort for applying. A similar rule is sometimes discussed among academics who, having passed a Ph.D. test designed to qualify them for research, wish that funding organizations would give smaller grants to a higher proportion of applicants rather than the current trend of giving larger grants to a small proportion. In the spirit of cooperation and fairness, we think it is worthwhile for competition donors and organizers to poll applicants about their views on preferred mappings of merit to money and, if possible, to adapt the mappings according to applicants' wishes (see Thorngate & Wang, 2004).

In addition to limiting the size of competitions and to spreading the prizes more widely, we believe it is worthwhile for donors and organizers to provide more information to applicants about their chances of success. Applicants are normally anxious about the state of their application, and their anxiety is fueled in the absence of information. Airlines rightfully acquire bad reputations for keeping passengers ignorant about causes of flight delays, attempted solutions, and realistic delay times. Competitions can acquire equally bad reputations for the same sin. There is no good reason for this. Applicants appreciate as much information as possible about the state of their applications and the expected date they will be notified of results. We believe they would also appreciate information about the number of applicants in the competition and some summary information about them. Consider the following two acknowledgement letters.

> Thank you for applying for the chief engineering position in our company. When we have made a decision, we will notify the successful applicant.

> Thank you for applying for the chief engineering position in our company. We received 135 applications for this position. Thirty-seven percent of the applicants have a master's degree in engineering; 12% have a Ph.D. Their years of engineering experience range from 1 to 34. We will do our best to make our decision among the applicants by 12 July and will inform all applicants of the results of our decision by 17 July. If you have any questions or do not hear from us by 17 July, please write us at …

The second letter is more considerate and is more likely to bring meritorious applicants who do not get the chief engineer's job back to the same organization to seek other positions.

Information need not be given only to applicants; it is considerate to give information to prospective applicants as well. We encourage organizers to gather and provide statistical information about recent competitions to prospective applicants. This would assist prospective applicants to make more informed decisions about applying. Many competitions are advertised with announcements about the prizes and little else. Other information, such as the number of applicants in previous competitions, the estimated amount of time needed to apply, and the statistical chances of winning, is rarely revealed. The result is similar to gambling advertisements that emphasize the size of the big prize ("Imagine what you could do with $5 million! It could be yours, but only if you buy a $10 ticket") and no mention of the chances of winning—or losing ("Buy your ticket now for a 99.99999% chance of losing your $10!"). Consider two versions of a hypothetical poetry competition announcement, the first rather typical, the second more revealing.

> Application forms are now available for the $100,000 Renfrew prize in poetry. Deadline: 21 April.

> Application forms are now available for the $100,000 Renfrew prize in poetry. Our 19-page application form should take about 7 hours to complete, not counting time for duplication of all poems submitted for adjudication and time for procuring six reference letters. Last year 232 people applied for the prize, which was awarded in a split decision of the three judges to Mary Jones for her collected works of 13 published volumes. The runner-up, who was not funded, was Michael Smith, who had applied unsuccessfully three years running with his seven-volume collection of blank verse. Deadline: 21 April.

We suspect that the first announcement would attract more applicants than the second. Organizers of such a competition might thus be reluctant to reveal the additional information, perhaps confessing privately that the full truth would drive many good poets away. Their reluctance could serve as a litmus test of competition flaws and limitations. Whatever secrets organizers wish to keep are likely to point to the weak links in competition process.

We dare say, as well, that prospective applicants and their sponsors could do themselves a favor by considering the results of the simulations presented in the earlier sections of this chapter. We think it is sobering but important to realize the role that chance plays in selecting winners among the top competitors, especially in large competitions. An understanding of the mathematical inevitability of this role might prevent parents from uttering silly pronouncements to their children about being whatever they want to be or from assuming that, if hard work made a difference at the beginning of a journey to the top, then more hard work would make a difference when the top was near. The understanding might also give solace to those who almost won and to those who would in ignorance condemn them for not bringing a trophy home.

9

The Evolution and Future of Competitions

Kim Baudains so badly wanted her son to win the Channel Islands annual Jersey junior gymkhana she allegedly fed drugged mints to ponies of competing children. Four of the mounts tested positive for a drug that made them sluggish and unrideable. Said one parent of her child's pony: "It was bizzare. It would jump in lessons, but in any competition it was tired." Three families whose kids competed against Josh Baudains, 12, are considering legal action. ("A Good Mother Will Fix Everything," 2007, p. 58)

*M*any competitions are repeated, including yearly competitions for sports trophies, arts awards, Nobel Prizes, university programs and scholarships; quarterly competitions for sales targets or limited journal space; monthly, weekly, or daily competitions for employment; and occasional competitions for political office. Most of these competitions reveal their winners, often to inspire and to guide the next generation of contestants who wish to model the winning performance. And model they do. People have a natural tendency to mimic or copy the behaviors of others that produce rewards or prevent punishments (see, for example, Bandura, 1986). When people try to mimic a winning performance, they will show less variation among their own performances than when they do not try. To the extent that people are successful in their mimicry, they will all behave more or less the same.

The decrease in variety that mimicry delivers also brings the judges in repeated contests the same difficulty judges face in the finals of hierarchical competitions, as noted in the previous chapter: when contestants become increasingly similar, their relative merit becomes increasingly difficult to assess. Hoping to overcome this difficulty, judges frequently rely on a short-term strategy that produces disastrous long-term consequences. It is the strategy of escalating or proliferating merit criteria, captured in the provocative 1959 film, *They Shoot Horses, Don't They?* and known to competitors as *raising the bar*.

To illustrate the escalation of merit criteria, consider what is likely to happen when a scholarship competition is born. Suppose a rich philanthropist establishes a new, national scholarship competition for promising university graduates that will help pay their expenses in the graduate school of their choice. Suppose as well that the endowment given for the scholarship program provides enough money for 10 $30,000 scholarships each year—a generous amount by current standards. And suppose that in its inaugural year, the scholarship organization establishes that these scholarships will be awarded on the basis of undergraduate grade-point average (GPA). The application form is one page long.

In its inaugural year, relatively few students are likely to apply for the 10 scholarships simply because it takes a few years for word to get around that they exist. So let us assume that 50 students apply for the 10 scholarships in Year 1, and that their GPAs range from 2.84 to 3.85 on the American 4-point scale range (A= 4, B = 3, etc.). The judges will then have a relatively simple task: rank order the 50 GPAs from highest to lowest, draw a line just below the 10th ranked applicant, and send the money to those above the line. Let us say that the 10th person has a GPA of 3.10.

Any publicity about the competition and its outcome is likely to cause a buzz. "Did you hear that only 50 people applied?" "Sally got a $30,000 scholarship with only a 3.1 GPA!" In light of such reports, it is almost certain that more students will apply for one of the scholarships in Year 2. So let us assume that 200 students apply for the 10 new scholarships available in Year 2. Now their GPAs range from 2.77 to 3.96. The 10th-highest has a GPA of 3.74. The losers with a GPA between 3.10 and 3.73 are likely to argue that it is unfair to give at least one student in Year 1 a scholarship with a 3.10 average and not to extend the courtesy to Year 2 applicants. But the winners are likely to rejoice that it is still possible to get a $30,000 scholarship with noticeably less than a 4.0 average—much easier than older, national competitions that attract thousands of applicants with GPAs of 3.9 and above. More publicity ensues.

- Year 3. Ten new $30,000 scholarships are offered. Increasing publicity about the lucrative scholarships, relatively easy to obtain, now prompts 1,000 students to apply. Of these, 27 have 4.00 averages. What should the judges do? Because there is no way to distinguish the best 10 of these 27 on the basis of grades, the judges must scramble for additional merit criteria. Some judges might note that 21 of these 27 perfect GPAs have accrued to applicants from diploma mills or other colleges of ill repute. Other judges might note that 17 of the applicants have a home address in wealthy neighborhoods but the remaining 10 have home addresses in slums. Still others might note that 15 of the 27 applicants are women or that the philanthropist has taken an interest in recent immigrants and that 7 of the 27 are recent immigrants. In all such cases, the judges will be looking for one of more new criteria to distinguish about 10 of the 27 students with 4.0 GPAs. Whatever they choose is almost certain to become a new policy, new rules of the game.
- Year 4. The scholarship committee announces that it has decided to specialize in recent immigrants with high grades. Six hundred immigrant students apply, including 300 who stretch the meaning of recent to 23 years, and 117 from diploma mills. The diploma mills, looking to satisfy

paying customers and pad their success story statistics, inform their professors that they should consider giving higher grades in their courses. It works. In Year 4, 54 of the applicants have a GPA of 4.0. Again the judges scramble. One of them notes that 47 of these 54 are males from wealthy neighborhoods and that many of those with GPAs in the 3.9 range are single mothers. Another new policy ensues.

- Year 5. The application form is now two pages long. The 10 new scholarships are now offered only to female immigrants who have been in the country less than 5 years and who have a degree from a brick-and-mortar college or university. Realizing that diploma mill graduates are out of the game, 457 newly inspired students apply. Three of these have a 4.0 GPA, four have a GPA of 3.98, and 13 have a GPA of 3.97. The judges scramble once more to determine which of the 13 should get the remaining three scholarships. One judge notes that nine of them graduated in film studies, one in math, and two in biochemistry. Another judge remarks that in her day it was much harder to get As in science courses than in arts courses, that it was probably still true, and that the three from science should therefore receive the remaining three scholarships. Another judge laments that no reference letters are available to assess what professors think of the applicants. Scholarship policies are further amended in preparation for Year 6. A third notes that many recent immigrants are from another English-speaking country and probably have an unfair advantage over those from countries speaking another language.

- Year 6. This year's 10 scholarships are offered to the best female recent immigrants who do not speak English as a first language and are graduating from a non–diploma mill college or university—preference given to those graduating in science. Two hundred and seven students meeting these criteria apply. One of them of them has a GPA of 4.0 from a small university in West Virginia and two short, guarded reference letters. One of them has a GPA of 3.7 from MIT, just below the 10th-ranked score, but has two long and glowing reference letters and three publications. After much debate, the latter is chosen. Scholarship policies are again amended.

- Year 20. The application form now runs 17 pages. Ten scholarships are offered to the best female, single-parent immigrants from Africa whose native language is not English, who graduated from a public university with at least 25,000 students, who show dire financial need, who have previously received at least one athletic scholarship, and who have at least three glowing reference letters from full professors and a minimum of five publications as first author in recognized AIDS-related journals. Fifty-three students apply, all of whom have GPAs of 3.9 or above. Thirty-one of them have 4.0 GPAs. Policies are amended. And one judge, a former winner from Year 1, who parlayed his 3.2 GPA-based $30,000 scholarship into a prestigious academic job and a formidable track record, smugly remarks that he would never win the same competition now.

Several phenomena about the evolution of this scholarship competition are worth discussion. First, it is not far-fetched. Athletic competitions that once could be won with a summer of modest preparation now require 15 years of intense training with the assistance of expensive equipment, coaches, psychologists, and travel budgets. In times past, anyone with a pair of scissors, a comb, a chair, and a pair of steady hands could become a barber. Now barbers require all these plus massage equipment, soothing music, a catchy title, styling experience, and educational and health certification. Temporary child care was once the domain of relatives and babysitters. Now it is the domain of licensed day care operators with 4 years' relevant education, health inspections, criminal checks, and massive amounts of liability insurance. Academic jobs could once be had with a Ph.D. and two good reference letters. Now a Ph.D., excellent reference letters, postdoctoral experience, grant funding in hand, and a minimum of 10 publications are the norm. Political office could once be attempted with a $100 sign budget, a few town meetings, and a point of view. Now it requires coaches, speech writers, image consultants, policy advisors, spin doctors, and millions of dollars. Like the one-way street of evolution, we cannot think of any competition that has become less complex or arduous over time.

Second, repeated competitions coevolve according to the interlocking desires of judges and contestants. Judges want to select the best contestants according to their criteria of merit. When too few contestants meet their merit criteria, they can either seek more contestants (usually done either by increasing publicity, increasing the size of the prize) or they can lower their eligibility or merit standards. When too many contestants meet their criteria, they can either seek fewer contestants (almost always done by adding eligibility requirements) or they can raise their merit standards. At the same time, contestants want to win. So whatever they believe were the winning standards of the last competition they will try to meet in the current competition. As a result, more of them are likely to meet last year's standards, increasing the chances that too many will be indistinguishably meritorious, increasing the role of chance or caprice in selecting winners and causing the judges to add more criteria to "break the ties." The coevolutionary consequences are clear: Competitions with too few contestants die out, whereas competitions with too many contestants invariably accumulate either more eligibility criteria or more merit criteria to judge as they evolve.

Third, as the criteria of a competition escalate, so too do entry costs. This year's contestants are likely to require more merit than last year's contestants, and next year's contestants are likely to require more still. Meeting the escalating criteria of eligibility and merit takes time, motivation, and effort. It usually takes money as well. Consider entry costs for job competitions. Remember the stale adage that people will have better jobs with more education (noted in our epigram at the beginning of this chapter)? It was probably true when only 20% of high school graduates entered university and 10% finished, offering the university graduates a huge competitive advantage over the high school graduates. But as high school students and their parents witnessed the success of university graduates, an increasing proportion of students entered university, investing years of effort and lots of money. The result? Perhaps 40% of high school graduates now acquire a university degree, only to discover that, because so many have one, the degree no longer offers much of a competitive advantage. What to do? More of the same. Master's degrees gave temporary competitive advantage over bachelor's degrees. Doctoral degrees gave temporary advantage over master's degrees. Universities proliferated. Student debts skyrocketed. And the average age of graduating students stretched into the late 20s—up from about 18 for their grandparents—just for a chance to be competitive in the job market. Figure skaters used to dream of the day when someone might do a quad (see "Figure Skater's Website," n.d.). Now they practice even more years in fear that if they do not do a quad, a medal will never touch their hands. The term *treadmill* comes to mind. So too does the image of obsessive gamblers, doubling down in hopes of staying in the game.

Fourth, as criteria escalate, current winners are more likely to have more merit than the previous winners (think of what performances led to Olympic medals over the past 100 years). In addition, and perhaps more important, many current losers are likely to have more merit than previous winners. This year's best student in a competition for a single scholarship might have a GPA of 3.8. Five years from now, it is likely that 47 students in the same competition would have GPAs greater than 3.8, leaving 46 of them to ponder the unfairness of escalating standards and asking why previous winners should be held to lower standards than themselves. It does not seem fair and is especially galling when the previous winners were judged by fewer criteria and spent far less time preparing for the competition. In many established organizations, new hires must pass far more rigorous employment standards than their bosses did when they were hired 20 years ago. Indeed, the bosses probably could not pass current hiring standards they themselves have set. Yet the bosses are likely making far more money than the new hires and are far less likely to be fired. There is, it would seem, blatant inequity in this. Bosses often invoke words such as *experience* and *responsibility* to justify their salary advantage. Curiously, words such as *efficient* and *productive*—assumed to be a manifestation of experience and responsibility—are rarely invoked. No wonder a high proportion of junior staff complain about their senior bosses.

Fifth, as judges add eligibility or merit criteria to make ever smaller distinctions among the best contestants, the criteria they add from one competition to the next tend to become more arbitrary and arguably unfair. No set of reasonable or fair merit criteria for a competition is infinite, or even large. As a rough rule, any fair competition probably has no more than six reasonable or fair merit criteria. Beyond these, additional criteria become less defensible and more absurd and often change the purposes of the competition. Consider, for example, what criteria should be used in judging the winners of a competition for bus driver jobs. Driving skill and safety, a good work ethic, frustration tolerance, and politeness seem to be sensible criteria, though the means of assessing these criteria might be open to debate. But when the jobs are scarce and applicants plentiful, many more applicants are likely to meet these reasonable criteria than there are jobs to be filled. What is a judge to do? One response is to jack up the minimum levels of the current criteria that are needed to be considered; no experience thus gives way to a minimum of 2 years, which might later give way to a minimum of 10 years. Another response is to add criteria. What's left? Possibilities include prior knowledge of city streets and bus routes, minimum acceptable starting salary, height, gender, ethnicity, handedness, age, number of languages spoken, possession of a university degree, and scores on a management potential test. Such criteria seem more remotely related to getting the job done than do those in the original set. Yet the temptation to add such criteria increases as the number of competitors indistinguishably qualified on the reasonable criteria overflows. Indeed, it is still common in many civil service competitions to specify a long list of criteria for a job, most of dubious relevance, in order to ensure that only one applicant is eligible—normally the current temporary employee or the applicant previously favored by the boss. A fictional but illustrative job ad illustrating this practice might look like this.

> Minimum Qualifications: A Ph.D. in early childhood cognitive deficits; thorough knowledge of literature on Phatorous disease and handedness; at least 2 years experience using eyeblink research techniques for prefrontal lobe higher-order skills assessment; at least 4 years experience using the PMP, RFDMS (2003 revision), and IBSMQ tests; fluent trilingualism (English, French, and Mandarin). Must pass all necessary security checks and be willing to relocate in Almonte, Ontario. Preference will be given to citizens. We are an equal opportunity employer.

Such an ad, carefully worded, would almost certainly reduce the number of applicants to one. Is it fair? Of course not. But when fair criteria of merit are exhausted, what criteria remain (Thorngate, 1988a)?

Finally, as contests escalate and competition among the contestants increases, so too does the temptation to cheat. Consider, for example, cheating in the Olympics or the Tour de France. Thanks to escalating standards (raising the bar), serious Olympic contenders must now be trained, coached, practiced, motivated, and preened almost from infancy to perform at the limits of their genes and endurance. The difference between gold medalists and fourth-place finishers is now almost always less than 1% of the winning performance—a slice so small that chance largely determines the winner. How can an athlete playing by the rules bend chance in her direction? Bend the rules or violate them. Cheating has a long and colorful history in the Olympics, most recently leading to a cat-and-mouse game between new drugs to enhance performance and new drug-testing methods to detect the new drugs. But we should not single out the Olympics. As Callahan (2004) documents, teachers complain about noticeable increases in the amount and sophistication of student cheating. An increasing percentage of résumés contain exaggerations or lies. And those who cheat seem decreasingly inclined to feel remorse. Cheating, as many argue, is just part of the game.

COMPETITIONS AND REVOLUTIONS

Judgments of merit are invoked to decide who is rewarded and who is not. By way of terminology review, when judges reward someone with sufficient merit, the judges have made a *correct inclusion* (also know as a *hit, detection, positive*). When judges do not reward someone with insufficient merit, they have made a *correct exclusion* (also called a *correct rejection*). Yet, because judgments of merit are fallible, errors of judgment will be made. The errors come in two flavors. It is possible for judges to reward someone without sufficient merit. This is called an *error of inclusion* (also know as an *alpha error, error of commission, false positive, false alarm*). It is also possible for judges not to reward someone with sufficient merit. This is called an *error of exclusion* (or *beta error, error of omission, false negative, miss*). The four possible outcomes of a judgment are shown in Table 9.1.

As noted in the previous chapter, people vary widely in the values they have about the four possible outcomes shown in Table 9.1, especially in their values about the two types of errors. Many people are more worried about errors of inclusion than about errors of exclusion. Hiring the wrong person is costly. Giving a scholarship to someone who subsequently drops out or fails is embarrassing. Awarding a gold medal to someone who cheated is scandalous. Accepting a bad person into the family can be tragic. People with these concerns tend to be cautious in their assessments of merit, seeking more evidence and assurances that contestants they judge are worthy of reward before including them among the rewarded. People with these concerns exemplify political conservatives. Not surprisingly, many of these people are those who own the resources being contested.

In contrast, other people tend to be more concerned about errors of exclusion than about errors of inclusion. These are the people who worry about not hiring the best person, about denying scholarships to talented people, about withholding a gold medal from a winner, about excluding good people from the family. People with these concerns are political liberals. Not surprisingly, many of these people are the contestants themselves. Students, for example, tend to be exceedingly concerned about getting a lower mark than they deserve and less concerned about getting a higher mark than they deserve. In our collective teaching experience, we have encountered hundreds of students who argue that we graded them too low. We are still waiting for the first student who exclaims, "Professor, I must report that your addition of my exam marks was incorrect. You gave me a total of 97%, but I checked your math; the total is really 64%. Please change my A+ to a C," [the letter grade for 64% in Canada].

In a perfect world, judges would never make a mistake, so no errors of inclusion or exclusion would occur. Table 9.2 shows the outcome for a hypothetical competition in which 100 people apply for a reward, 50 of whom really merit it and 50 of whom do not. But the world is imperfect, so, as we have noted repeatedly in this book, errors of inclusion and exclusion will be made. A typical result is shown in Table 9.3.

Conservative judges who want to avoid any possibility of making a dreaded error of inclusion can do so simply by including no one; that is, by judging all

TABLE 9.1   Judgments and Misjudgments of Merit

		Reality: Contestant has sufficient merit?	
		Yes	No
Judgment: Applicant rewarded?	Yes	Correct inclusion	Error of inclusion
	No	Error of exclusion	Correct exclusion

TABLE 9.2   A Contest Outcome in a Perfect World

		Reality: Sufficient merit?		
		Yes	No	Total =
Judgment: Applicant rewarded?	Yes	50	0	50
	No	0	50	50
	Total =	50	50	100

TABLE 9.3   Typical Judgments in an Imperfect World

		Reality: Sufficient merit?		
		Yes	No	Total =
Judgment: Applicant rewarded?	Yes	35	15	50
	No	15	35	50
	Total =	50	50	100

TABLE 9.4   An Extreme Conservative's Judgments in an Imperfect World

		Reality: Sufficient merit?		
		Yes	No	Total =
Judgment: Applicant rewarded?	Yes	0	0	50
	No	50	50	50
	Total =	50	50	100

TABLE 9.5   An Extreme Liberal's Judgments in an Imperfect World

		Reality: Sufficient merit?		
		Yes	No	Total =
Judgment: Applicant rewarded?	Yes	50	50	100
	No	0	0	0
	Total =	50	50	100

people to have insufficient merit and giving no rewards (see Table 9.4). Similarly, liberal judges with a conscience who will not allow errors of exclusion can guarantee that these errors will never be made simply by judging all people to be meritorious (see Table 9.5), though they may not have sufficient rewards to give to all. Conservatives are stingy and frequently uncaring in withholding their rewards. Liberals are generous and frequently wasteful in distributing their rewards.

The examples shown in Table 9.2 to Table 9.5 assume that the numbers of people with and without sufficient merit for a reward are equal. It also assumes that there are enough rewards for every person with merit (defining a test rather than a contest) and perhaps for every person without merit as well. These assumptions are

TABLE 9.6   Infallible Judgments and Insufficient Resources

		Reality: Sufficient merit?		
		Yes	No	Total =
Judgment: Applicant rewarded?	Yes	15	0	15
	No	10	75	85
	Total =	25	75	100

TABLE 9.7   Moderately Fallible Judgments and Insufficient Resources

		Reality: Sufficient merit?		
		Yes	No	Total =
Judgment: Applicant rewarded?	Yes	10	5	15
	No	15	70	85
	Total =	25	75	100

TABLE 9.8   Extremely Fallible Judgments and Insufficient Resources

		Reality: Sufficient merit?		
		Yes	No	Total =
Judgment: Applicant rewarded?	Yes	5	10	15
	No	20	65	85
	Total =	25	75	100

rarely realistic. So let us consider what is probably a more realistic case: 100 people enter a competition; 25 of them definitely merit a reward, and 75 of them do not; but there are only enough rewards to give to 15 people. Table 9.6 shows the certain outcome with infallible judgments of merit; Table 9.7 and Table 9.8 show typical outcomes with increasingly fallible judgments of merit.

All three tables show the same harsh reality: even when judgments are infallible, if there are more meritorious people than rewards, some of the meritorious people will not be rewarded. Insufficient rewards guarantee errors of exclusion and whatever injustice is implied by these errors. Table 9.7 and Table 9.8 illustrate what happens to errors with increasing judgment fallibility. The only people to benefit from increasing judgment fallibility are those without sufficient merit; in Table 9.7, 5 of these 85 people would receive a reward they did not deserve, and in Table 9.8, 10 of them would. When the number of rewards does not match the number of meritorious contestants, increasing fallibility has no benefit for the meritorious; it only results in more of them being unrewarded.

Suppose you are one of the 20 of 25 meritorious people in Table 9.8 who did not receive a reward. How are you likely to interpret your fate and the fairness of the competition? There are several possibilities. You might console yourself that 19 other meritorious people suffered the same fate. You might envy the five meritorious people who got what they deserved. You might fall into depression and withdraw from future competitions. Or you might cry "foul!" at the judges who not only gave twice as many undeserving as deserving people (10 versus 5) rewards but also failed to reward half of the deserving people who remained (10 of 20).

But are you one of the 25 meritorious contestants? Or are you one of the 65 insufficiently meritorious contestants who got what they deserved: nothing? Feelings of fairness and justice depend a lot on self-perception. Whether you truly have merit or not is less important than whether you believe you have merit or not. Few people believe they have no merit, and their number seems to be in rapid decline. Ask 100 people how good they are at driving and almost none will confess, "Much worse than average." Ask 100 yuppie parents to estimate the IQ of their children and almost none will admit, "Far lower than average." In such cases, competition between truly meritorious contestants and 80 truly unmeritorious contestants outlined in Table 9.6, Table 9.7, and Table 9.8 would look more like the delusional "90 meritorious, 10 not" competition shown in Table 9.9, Table 9.10, and Table 9.11.

If, as illustrated in Table 9.9, Table 9.10, and Table 9.11, 90 of 100 people believe they merit a reward, the resulting competition slides toward chaos. When judgments are infallible (Table 9.9), at least the 75 people who believe they are meritorious but see that no reward can console them by noting that all of the 10 unmeritorious people are suffering the same fate. They may not be consoled, however, by noting that the vast majority of meritorious people do not receive a reward. With moderate amounts of fallibility (Table 9.10), the 80 people who feel aggrieved by no reward are sure to grumble that half of the self-proclaimed, unmeritorious people got one. And with greater amounts of fallibility (Table 9.11), the 85 who believe they were deprived of their rightful reward are likely to complain that all the self-proclaimed unmeritorious people were rewarded.

TABLE 9.9   Infallible Judgments and Insufficient Resources

		Belief: Sufficient merit?		
		Yes	No	Total =
Judgment: Applicant rewarded?	Yes	15	0	15
	No	75	10	85
	Total =	90	10	100

TABLE 9.10   Moderately Fallible Judgments and Insufficient Resources

		Belief: Sufficient merit?		
		Yes	No	Total =
Judgment: Applicant rewarded?	Yes	10	5	15
	No	80	5	85
	Total =	90	10	100

TABLE 9.11   Extremely Fallible Judgments and Insufficient Resources

| | | Belief: Sufficient merit? | | |
		Yes	No	Total =
Judgment: Applicant rewarded?	Yes	5	10	15
	No	85	0	85
	Total =	90	10	100

They may do more than complain. The revolution of rising expectations brings with it a pernicious sense of entitlement. Young people who are repeatedly told by their parents and teachers that they are creative geniuses, God's gift to humanity, who can be whatever they want to be and are capable of winning any contest they enter are likely to approach competitions with an inflated assessment of their own merit. When they fail in more competitions than their self-assessment would imply, they are likely to attribute the result to the incompetence, bias, or corruption of judges or to cracks in the competition and are likely to become dolorous, cynical, angry, or depressed. They are also more likely to appeal the judges' decisions or otherwise pressure judges to make decisions more in line with their inflated expectations. Some teachers, for example, facing pressure to give students the grades their parents believe they merit, quit (S. Freedman, 2007). More of them concede. The result is grade inflation.

If pressure does not produce restorative justice, contestants suffering perceived injustices of exclusion errors can escalate to an extreme: revolution. We are willing to speculate that a large majority of first-generation revolutionaries are genuinely meritorious people who have been unjustly excluded from rewards. We also speculate that the second generation includes a high proportion of those who are genuinely unmeritorious but would like a reward and see a new opportunity riding the coattails of the first generation. Those who are talented but rejected are likely to be good at articulating their case against the injustices that affect them. The case will almost certainly be ignored by those who have previously benefited from a competition's rewards, deserved or otherwise. When merit is relatively rare, even fallible judgments produce a higher proportion of truly meritorious people among those rewarded (e.g., 10/15 = 67% in Table 9.7) than the proportion of truly meritorious people among those who have not been rewarded (e.g., 15/85 = 18% in Table 9.7). Why should the privileged denounce a judgment of their own merit and revoke the rewards that have followed? The argument is more likely to be heard by those who genuinely lack merit but who share the deprivation of their articulate leaders. The leaders may not wish to speak for the masses and may even despise them. But it may not matter. If the rhetoric gives hope of future rewards, those with merit deficits are as likely to believe it as those with merit to burn.

THE COMPETITION FOR ATTENTION

One of the most observable and interesting manifestations of the ideas presented above comes from daily competitions for attention (Thorngate, 1988b, 1997;

Thorngate & Plouffe, 1987). Attention is the stuff we all pay to produce and consume information. But attention takes time and we can spend it on only one activity at a time. Alas, unlike money, time is a finite and nonrenewable resource. Most people born today can expect to have about 80 years of attention to spend—about 701,280 hours, 233,760 of them sleeping. Each hour spent is an hour of life gone forever. The remaining hours of attention do not sit in a bank gathering interest. On the contrary, interest gathers attention—as discussed below.

Many people—and all authors like us—spend a lot of their time producing information, almost always in hopes that someone will spend time consuming it. A clever species, we humans have invented dozens of ways to produce information and store and distribute it—everything from language to writing to libraries to film to the Internet. Lyman and Varian (2003) list some recent consequences. In 2003, the world produced about 25,000 newspapers, as well as 80,000 magazine titles, 38,000 scientific journals, and 950,000 new books. In the same year, people took about 75 billion photographs, produced 10,500 films and 90,000 music CDs, and exchanged 4 trillion e-mail messages, across 32 million domain names registered on the Internet. Sullivan (2006) estimates that, just to find all this stuff, people worldwide consulted search engines on the Internet about 213 million times each day.

In short, while attention needed to consume information remains finite, information production continues to expand. It expands in length (history), in breadth (topics), and in depth (detail). Each element of this expanding volume is someone's plea for attention. So each film, CD, television program, magazine article, scientific report, speech, etc., is a competitor for an attentional prize. The number of competitors is increasing exponentially; the prize is not.

How does the increasing competition for limited attention influence the evolution of information? Philosophers of rational persuasion would be quick to argue how it should affect the evolution. Civilization has now accumulated so much scientific truth and artistic beauty that people born today can spend all 467,520 hours of their waking life consuming this truth and beauty and still have lots of it left over for their next life. This is what people should do. Social scientists might argue that the abundance of information and dearth of attention forces each of us to specialize, resulting in an exponential rise in specialization. Our heads can be envisioned as little blobs in a three-dimensional universe of information, floating along the coordinates of history, topic, and detail. As this universe expands, our trajectories of specialization lead us to drift farther and farther from each other, like hot air balloons drifting apart in a cold air race. Little by little, we lose track of each other. The overlap of the information we share becomes smaller and smaller, and with its contraction the set of shared meanings necessary for human communication. No wonder university professors, specialists all, no longer have much at all in common with their local colleagues and migrate in desperation to tiny conferences around the world hoping to find a few people who will pay attention to their work.

In the world of information, every consumer is a judge. What criteria do these consumers use to judge the merit of information? At least three possibilities come to mind. One is truth or credibility. Judges might decide to pay their attention only to credible information and to ignore the rest. Alas, information must at least be sampled before its credibility can be judged. Without skills to make a judgment of truth from a small sample, judges would face the absurd task of paying attention to information in order to determine whether the information were sufficiently credible to pay attention to. It takes time (attention) to learn the skills needed to judge the truth of information. Five hundred years ago, these skills were taught to adolescents (grammar, logic, and rhetoric = the Trivium); later they were taught to university students in liberal arts programs. Those were the old days, long gone. Now most people rely on opinions of others for their credibility judgments, a reliance that has stimulated competitions for the role of trusted source, with entrants ranging from scientists and journalists to film stars and politicians.

The second criterion for judging whether to pay attention to information is importance. Just because information is credible does not mean it is important. Credible and important information, such as the effects of pollution on climate change, coexists with incredible and important information, such as Iraqi weapons of mass destruction. Both coexist with credible but trivial information (during meals, whenever your elbow bends your mouth flies open) and incredible but trivial information (Martha Splonzi has a crush on Fred Schmutz). Given the glut of credible information, it might be reasonable for prospective information consumers to decide where to spend their limited attention by first chucking all incredible information and then turfing the trivial from the credible information that remains. But importance, for better or worse, is hard to define, and measures of importance vary widely among people, cultures, and time. The topics taught in school are a good indicant of what parents, teachers, and others consider to be true and important information. Consider how these topics changed in the past 50 years. Spelling, grammar, arithmetic, history, geography, and religion are out. Putative creativity and self-esteem–building topics are in. University majors in philosophy, history, physics, mathematics, art, and literature languish under declining enrollments, while majors in business, management, engineering, programming, film-making, medicine, law, child studies, and criminology burst at their seams. We doubt that students are making their selections according to the credibility of the knowledge generated by these disciplines. Their preferences seem instead to reflect the importance (called *relevance* in "Hippy" days) they place on the information they pay attention to. These assessments of importance sadly coincide with the great and dangerous political shift in the conception of university. The old conception: a safe haven from the real world and a place to challenge it. The new conception: an expensive resort to prepare for the real world and a place to embrace it.

Credibility and importance are not the only criteria people use for deciding which information they will pay attention to and which they will ignore. At least one more is common: interest. Interesting information arouses the senses, quickens the pulse, and stimulates a host of other emotional responses that attract attention like iron filings to a magnet or children to a puppy. Not surprisingly, only a small proportion of credible and important information is also interesting. Consider scientific journal articles—all, no doubt, rich in credibility and importance. Consider how many people read the articles. Consider how many people enjoy reading the articles, attracted to them like hockey fans to a Stanley Cup playoff. Consider how many people live in Antarctica.

Advertisers, novelists, film editors, journalists, promoters, and similar souls know a lot about interest. Scientists do not, which likely accounts for why people are more likely to pay attention to advertisements, novels, films, newspapers, and the like than to reference sections of articles in the *Journal of Cognitive Development*. Truth, as someone once remarked, is an acquired taste—like opera. Importance, as someone else once remarked, is a matter of taste, for which there is no accounting. Yet the assessment of both credibility and importance require an investment of attention. Interest does not. It attracts attention, by definition. So given the choice between information that is credible and important but boring (think the periodic chart of the elements) or information that is incredible and trivial but interesting (think the sex life of movie stars), which might we predict most people would attend to? Hint: look at the covers of the magazines at your local magazine rack or compare the number of TV broadcast hours per day devoted to genetic research conference presentations versus Hollywood gossip.

In brief, when information is abundant and competes for attention in short supply, interest trumps credibility and importance. As information producers learn this, they seek to improve their competitive advantage by trying to make their information more interesting. Quirky anecdotes, human interest stories, good visuals, test-yourself quizzes, fancy graphs and animations are all used, as are dozens of other interest-grabbing techniques. Evidence for the market in such tricks of the interest trade can be seen in the menu items of PowerPoint, most of which try to capture attention with flashy visuals. Or consider the mad rush of universities to hire public relations specialists who produce ever-so-fascinating text bites of research for public consumption. All point to the triumph of style over substance, package over product, sizzle over steak.

The competition for attention is especially acute in the political arena, where politicians and senior bureaucrats serve as judges who give or withhold rewards and privileges to various constituencies. Attention is not sufficient for political consent—persuasion is also needed. But attention is certainly necessary. So representatives of competing interests are keen to follow any whiff of indication about successful efforts to attract the attention of political leaders. If company X hires a lobbyist who manages to book lunches with 17 senators, we can expect that other companies would hire lobbyists for the same purpose. If president A confesses to reading newspaper B, and if the editor of newspaper B likes to report opinion polls on the front page, then we can expect several interest groups would conduct a poll and send a press release of selected results to the editor. If a study shows that 78% of senior bureaucrats watch the evening news on TV, we can expect that interest groups would rush to vie for 30 seconds of evening news. The experienced groups would know that news does not appear on TV without good visuals.

What are good visuals? People cheering, people suffering, babies, animals, and, of course, things blowing up. Hijackings, kidnappings, and suicide bombings rank at the top of disasters that "interrupt our regular programming" and thus attract the scarce resource of attention that may lead to a chance at more desirable scarce resources: land, wealth, status, and such. So it should not be surprising that hijackings, kidnappings, assassinations, suicide bombings, and such have become the attention grabbers of choice among disenfranchised groups around the world.

They may be repugnant, but at least they stand a chance of putting a cause on someone's political agenda—and they sometimes rid the perpetrators of a few putative enemies. Most early adopters of such horrible tactics had no success with gentler forms of attention getting or persuasion and acted out of desperation. They had nothing left, so they had nothing left to lose. More recent adopters seem to use the tactics to avoid wasting time in normal bargaining or negotiation, which they do not see on TV to be leading anyone to satisfactory political solutions—ironically, in part, because successful bargaining and negotiation offer no good visuals.

Where does it end? Interest has two curious properties. First, interest is aroused by novelty. Our brain is hardwired to focus our attention on whatever is different or unexpected. A woman wearing a chador in the United States will attract attention because she is novel. A woman not wearing a chador in Iran will also attract attention because she is novel. Second, whatever attracts our attention for the first time will lose its attraction with repetition. We habituate. Interesting advertisements, tunes, films, books, and such lose their punch, and can even become noxious, when repeated hundreds of times. And when arousal subsides, we look to new stimuli for a new jolt of interest.

There is, in short, a dialectical relationship between novelty and repetition, arousal and habituation, in regulating attention. Combine this relationship with the rush of losers to imitate winners in competitions for attention and something quite fascinating occurs. A competitor produces something novel. If the competitor's product attracts attention that leads to other rewards, other competitors imitate it. When they imitate it, the product loses its novelty. And when it loses its novelty, attention wanes. The waxing and waning of attention is thus unique among limited resources we know, favoring new over improved, odd over even, mutation over adaptation. This is exactly the trajectory of something known as *fashion*. And it leads us to find much merit in Jacques Barzun's (2001) thesis that the most underrated force of historical change is boredom.

PRACTICAL IMPLICATIONS

In this chapter we have tried to illustrate how repeated competitions evolve. Four trends are likely in their evolution. First, a competition will likely draw more competitors. This will make the task of judging them more tedious and, if rewards do not multiply, will increase errors of exclusion and the resentment these errors engender. Second, competitors will likely be more homogeneous in their indicants of merit. This will increase the difficulty that judges face in distinguishing their merit, leading the judges to adopt increasingly arbitrary or gratuitous criteria to winnow the winners from the rest. Third, as competitors and criteria multiply, the competitors will invest increasing time and effort for a declining chance at receiving a reward. This will waste their time and squander their talents. Fourth, an increasing number of current losers will have more and better indicants of merit than those of previous winners, prompting invidious comparisons between cohorts and adding insult to injury.

None of these four trends suggest that merit-based competitions become kinder or fairer as they evolve. Perhaps the best that anyone can hope for is that increases in procedural fairness will retard the decline in distributional fairness that evolution brings. But we have shown that even this hope is ephemeral. If the rewards of a competition do not increase to match an increase in its size, then even a procedurally perfect judgment process will not stem the tide of those justifiably angered by what they—if not the judges—perceive as injustices of distributional errors.

What to do? An obvious suggestion is to find more wealth for more prizes as the number of competitors rises—in essence, to convert a contest into a test (see chapter 1). Thus, if 20 of the 200 applicants for last year's salesperson of the year competition received a free vacation, then no fewer 40 of this year's 400 applicants should receive the same. Judges being equal, the solution would keep the proportion of exclusion errors and inclusion errors constant from year to year, which may in turn keep the proportion of complaints constant as well.

Finding more wealth for more rewards for more competitors is certainly preferable to making do with less wealth for fewer rewards for more competitors. But the strategy is often naïve and probably inapplicable to many competitions. The earth once gave us the illusion of ever-expanding material wealth as it we explored and exploited its frontiers, but there are no more frontiers. The world's supply of social status may be expanding but not as rapidly as the world's supply of people. Businesses and medical schools, for example, usually do not have the luxury of doubling the number of positions offered whenever the number of good applicants does the same. It makes no sense to offer 1.5 first-place trophies to a hockey league that expands by 50%. If one competition expands its wealth while similar competitions do not, the former would likely be flooded with competitors, perhaps past its limit of wealth. Acquiring more wealth to provide rewards for expanding competitions (for example, competitions for military contracts) usually leads to pilfering wealth from other competitions (for example, education). So there is no net reduction in exclusion errors, only a shuffling of them according to political priorities. In short, while wealth is a good thing, it is probably wise not to count on it alone to rescue a competition in distress.

If wealth cannot be expanded, it can still be spread. When a competition becomes too big, too old, or too jaded, there is merit in subdividing it. A single scholarship competition for the best overall student that expands from 10 to 1,000 applicants is likely a good candidate for subdivision into 10–20 smaller competitions—one for the best mathematics student, one for the best history student, etc. (the biological analogue is called *speciation*). If a history student competition eventually attracted 100 or more applicants, it could then be subdivided as well: a competition for the best student in U.S. history, the best in Canadian history, etc. The divided reward would, of course, not be as big as the one preceding it. But the chances of someone winning would be greater, and judges would face fewer challenges of apple–orange (or math–history) comparisons and of fatigue. Alas, there is at least one major drawback to solving problems of evolution by splitting a competition: the proliferation of judges needed to adjudicate them all. But if judges can be found, the solution is worth a try.

Competitions seem to reach their peak of fairness on about their third iteration. By then most prospective competitors have learned of the competition, most of the knots have been untangled from competition publicity and procedures, most of the defensible merit criteria are being used, and routines have been established that make the adjudication process relatively predictable and efficient. Somewhere between the fourth to eighth competition iteration, toxins begin to take their toll. The adjudication process ceases to be interesting or fun. Judges become cranky or bored. Concern for errors of exclusion wanes as organizers fight the fires of embarrassment about errors of inclusion, cheating, or corruption. Meritorious competitors who do not receive what they believe they deserve grow increasingly suspicious and misanthropic about other competitors, judges, and organizers, and they begin to complain. At this point, the competition begins to go off, like week-old leftovers.

Organizers wishing to delay, if not prevent, the onset of this creeping competition rot might wish to consider how to reduce the repetition that allows the onset to occur. One way is to set a predetermined lifetime for their competition, announcing before its first iteration that it will cease to exist after three or four iterations to make way for one or more new competitions. Each new competition should have a new topic or theme—a thrice-held violin competition, for example, might cede to three viola competitions, which would cede to three cello competitions. The change would encourage new competitors with new forms of merit. Old forms could be repeated; cellos, for example, could cede to violins in a three-instrument cycle. Farmers know the strategy as rotating crops; realtors know it as time shares. In the world of merit-based competitions, the strategy rewards patience with fairness and reminds us of the ultimate solution to all social problems: take turns being oppressed.

Organizers, of course, are not the only actors in a competition who should look for solutions to problems created by evolution. We think, as before, that it is important for prospective competitors to learn about the dynamics of contests and their evolution—the stuff of this chapter and previous ones—in order to make educated decisions about which competitions to enter and which to eschew. If given a choice, for example, it is generally better for inexperienced competitors to enter a new competition than an established one—for the same reason that minnows stay close to the shore to avoid being eaten by the big fish in deep water. It is also worthwhile for competitors to know the history of a competition in order to view its evolutionary trends and judge from these how the next round should be approached or whether it should be entered. As noted in our previous chapter, the more information competitors can gather about a competition—its rules, judges, previous and current competitors, and evolutionary trends—the better.

Which leads us to our final suggestion. If contests are destined to evolve, it is sensible to involve all interested parties in shaping the direction of their evolution. Just as we recommended in chapter 3 that donors, organizers, judges, competitors, and (if present) observers be consulted about merit criteria, we recommend that they also be consulted about everything else that evolution influences, including the size of a competition, its life span, eligibility rules, judge selections, prize distributions, application forms, deadlines, rejection letters, and reactions to complaints. Too often judgments of merit are seen as conflicts between those wanting scarce resources and those deciding who receives them. It is more sagacious to view judgments of merit as a collaboration between all parties, which, if successful, would give a chance for trust and understanding to lubricate sources of friction.

Despite their civilized advantages, merit-based competitions occupy a precarious niche among the various means of distributing limited resources. On one edge of the niche are market competitions—"I want the best grades that money can buy!" On another are lotteries—"Flip a coin to break the tie." On a third are status and privilege. Preventing a merit-based competition from evolving in any of these directions requires the competition itself have sufficient merit to survive. The best chance for survival is to monitor frequently how all interested parties, including the losers, judge the fairness of the competition and to improve the competition according to their judgments and suggestions.

References

A good mother will fix everything. (2007, August 13) *Maclean's Magazine, 120*, 58.

Arkes, H., & Blumer, C. (1985). The psychology of sunk cost. *Organizational Behavior and Human Decision Process, 35*, 124–140.

Arkes, H. R., Shaffer, V. A., & Dawes, R. M. (2006). Comparing holistic and disaggregated ratings in the evaluation of scientific presentations. *Journal of Behavioral Decision Making, 18*, 1–11.

Andrews, R., Biggs, M., & Seidel, M. (Eds). (1996). *The Columbia world of quotations.* New York: Columbia University Press. Retrieved October 10, 2007 from http://www.bartleby.com/66/66/28266.html

Australia Migration (n.d.). Retrieved November 3, 2007 from http://www.immi.gov.au/migration/helptext/terms-conditions/generic-tc.htm

Bales, R. F. (1950). *Interaction process analysis.* Cambridge, MA: Addison-Wesley.

Bales, R. F. (1953). The equilibrium problem in small groups. In T. Parsons, R. F. Bales, & E. A. Shils (Eds.), *Working papers in the theory of action* (pp. 111–161). Glencoe, IL: Free Press.

Bandura, A. (1986). *Social foundations of thought and action.* Englewood Cliffs, NJ: Prentice-Hall.

Barclay, L., & York, K. (2003). Clear logic and fuzzy guidance: A policy capturing study of merit raise decisions. *Public Personnel Management, 32*(2), 287–299.

Baron, R. S. (2005). So right it's wrong: Groupthink and the ubiquitous nature of polarized group decision making. In M. P. Zanna (Ed.), *Advances in experimental social psychology* (Vol. 37, pp. 219–253). San Diego, CA: Elsevier Academic Press.

Bartlett, F. C. (1932). *Remembering: An experimental and social study.* Cambridge: Cambridge University Press.

Barzun, J. (2001). *From dawn to decadence: 500 Years of Western cultural life, 1500 to the present.* New York: Harper Collins.

Being an also-ran can be lonely. (2007, July 23). *Maclean's Magazine, 120*(28), 50.

Belleville Request (2005). Retrieved September 17, 2006 from http://www.gamblingresearch.org/contentdetail.sz?cid=3052

Berger, J., Cohen, P., & Zelditch, M. (1972). Status characteristics and social interaction. *American Sociological Review, 37*(3), 241–255.

Berger, J., & Zelditch, M., Jr. (Eds.). (1985). *Status, rewards and influence: How expectations organize behavior.* San Francisco: Jossey-Bass.

Biernat, M. (2005). *Standards and expectancies: Contrast and assimilation in judgments of self and others.* New York: Psychology Press.

Bizstats (2007). *Free business statistics and financial ratios.* Retrieved March 6, 2007 from http://www.bizstats.com/reports/industry-sales-firm-summary.asp

Bloom, R. F., & Brundage, E. G. (1947). Predictions of success in elementary school for enlisted personnel. In D. B. Stuit (Ed.), *Personnel research and test development in the naval bureau of personnel* (pp. 233–261). Princeton, NJ: Princeton University Press.

Bruine de Bruin, W. (2005). Save the last dance for me: Unwanted serial position effects in jury evaluations. *Acta Psychologica, 118*, 245–260.

Callahan, D. (2004). *The cheating culture: Why more Americans are doing wrong to get ahead.* Orlando, FL: Harcourt.

Carroll, B., & Thorngate, W. (1991). *The Social Sciences and Humanities Research Council: A case study of adjudicated contests.* Unpublished manuscript.

Chaplin, W. F., John, O. P., & Goldberg, L. R. (1988). Conceptions of states and traits: Dimensional attributes with ideals as prototypes. *Journal of Personality and Social Psychology, 54*(4), 541–557.

Cialdini, R. B. (1984). *Influence*. New York: Morrow.

Cohen, S., & Willis, T. A. (1985). Stress, social support and the buffering hypothesis. *Psychological Bulletin, 98*, 310–357.

Correlation (n.d.). Retrieved May 24, 2007 from http://en.wikipedia.org/wiki/Correlation

Cortina, J., Goldstein, N., Payne, S., Davidson, H. K., & Gilliland, S. (2000). The incremental validity of interview scores over and above cognitive ability and conscientiousness scores. *Personnel Psychology, 53*, 325–351.

Cronbach, L. J. (1954). Report on a psychometric mission to clinicia. *Psychometrika, 19*(4), 263–270.

Cyberinfrastructure (2007). Retrieved August 2, 2007 from http://www.nsf.gov/funding/pgm_summ.jsp?pims_id=13553&org=BCS&from=fund

Dawes, R. M. (1969). "Interaction effects" in the presence of asymmetrical transfer. *Psychological Bulletin, 71*, 55–57.

Dawes, R. M. (1979). The robust beauty of improper linear models. *American Psychologist, 34*, 571–582.

Dawes, R. M. (1994). Affirmative action programs: Discontinuities between thoughts about individuals and thoughts about groups. In L. Heath, R. S. Tindale, J. Edwards, E. Posavac, F. B. Bryant, E. Henderson-King, et al. (Eds.), *Social psychological applications to social issues, III: Applications of heuristics and biases to social issues* (pp. 223–239). New York: Plenum Press.

Dawes, R. M., & Corrigan, B. (1974). Linear models in decision-making. *Psychological Bulletin, 81*, 95–106.

Dawes, R. M., & Eagle, J. (1976). Multivariate selection of students in a racist society: A systematically unfair approach. In M. Zeleny (Ed.), *Multiple criteria decision making, Kyoto 1975* (pp. 97–110). New York: Springer-Verlag.

Dawes, R. M., Faust, D., & Meehl, P. E. (1989). Clinical versus actuarial judgment. *Science, 243*, 1668–1674.

Deutsch, M., & Coleman, P. (Eds.). (2006). *Handbook of conflict resolution: Theory and practice*. San Francisco, CA: Jossey-Bass.

DiPrete, T., & Eirich, G. (2006). Cumulative advantage as a mechanism for inequality: A review of theoretical and empirical developments. *Annual Review of Sociology, 32*, 271–297.

Einhorn, H. J. (1972). Expert measurement and mechanical combination. *Organizational Behavior and Human Performance, 7*, 86–106.

Elliott, J. (2006). Jane Elliott's blue eyes brown eyes exercise. Retrieved September 21, 2007 from http://www.janeelliott.com

Elster, J. (1992). *Local justice*. New York: Russell Sage Foundation.

Evaluation (2006). Retrieved September 21, 2006 from http://www.sshrc.ca/web/apply/program_descriptions/standard_e.asp#5

Federation (n.d.). Retrieved July 7, 2007 from http://www.thefederationonline.org/

Festinger, L. (1954). A theory of social comparison processes. *Human Relations, 17*, 117–140.

Figure Skater's Website (n.d.) *Basic reference*. Retrieved November 6, 2007 from http://www.sk8stuff.com/m_basic.htm

Fisek, H., Berger, J., & Norman, R. Z. (2005). Status cues and the formation of expectations. *Social Science Research, 34*, 80–102.

Foddy, M., & Dawes, R. D. (2007). Ingroup trust in a sequential dilemma. In A. Biel, D. Eek, T. Garling, & M. Gustafson (Eds.), *New issues and paradigms in research on social dilemmas* (57–71). New York: Springer Verlag.

Foddy, M., & Riches, P. (2000). The impact of task cues and categorical cues on social influence: Fluency and ethnic accent as cues to competence in task groups. *Advances in Group Processes, 17*, 103–130.

Foddy, M., & Smithson, M. (1989). Fuzzy sets and double standards: Modelling the process of ability inference. In J. Berger, M. Zelditch, & B. Anderson (Eds.), *Sociological theories in progress 3,* 73–99. Newbury Park, CA: Sage.

Foddy, M., & Smithson, M. (1999). Can gender inequalities be eliminated? *Social Psychology Quarterly, 62,* 307–324.

Foddy, M., Yamagishi, T., & Platow, M. J. (2007). *Stereotypes and expectations in group-based trust.* Unpublished manuscript.

Foschi, M. (2000). Double standards for competence: Theory and research. *Annual Review of Sociology, 26,* 21–42.

Foschi, M., & Foddy, M. (1988). Standards, performances, and the formation of self-other expectations. In M. Webster, Jr. & M. Foschi (Eds.), *Status generalization: New theory and research* (pp. 248–260, 501–503). Stanford, CA: Stanford University Press.

Francis, W. (1982). Legislative committee systems, optimal committee size, and the costs of decision making. The Journal of Politics, 44(3), 822–837.

Frank, R., & Cook, P. (1995). *The winner-take-all society.* New York: Penguin.

Freedman, J., & Fraser, S. (1966). Compliance without pressure: The foot-in-the-door technique. *Journal of Personality and Social Psychology, 4,* 195–203.

Freedman, S. (2007, August 1). A teacher grows disillusioned after a "fail" becomes a "pass" [Electronic version]. *The New York Times.* Retrieved from (http://www.nytimes. com/2007/08/01/education/01education.html?ex=1186891200&en=c7a364bf9b738d b0&ei=5070)

Frohlich, N. (2007). A very short history of distributive justice. *Social Justice Research, 20*(2), 250–262.

Gabel, M., & Shipan, C. (2000). *Optimal design for collective medical decision making: A social choice approach to expert consensus panels.* Unpublished manuscript. Retrieved January 28, 2008, from http://www.uh.edu/~rbmorton/GabelPaper.PDF

Gambling Research (2007). *Welcome.* Retrieved October 7, 2007 from http://www.gambling research.org/welcome.sz

Global Health (2006). Retrieved October 23, 2006 from http://www.cihr-irsc.gc.ca/e/30095. html

Goldberg, L. (1969). The effectiveness of clinicians'judgments: The diagnosis of organic brain damage from the Bender-Gestalt test. *Journal of Consulting Psychology, 23,* 25–33.

Grants Committee (2007). Retrieved May 25, 2006 from http://www.cihr-irsc.gc.ca/e/4656. html

Gresham (2007). Gresham 's Law. Retrieved May 29,2006 from http://cn.wikipedia.org/ wiki/Gresham's_Law

Grothmann, R. (2006). Euler math toolbox. Retrieved September 4, 2006 from http://math srv.ku-eichstaett.de/MGF/homes/grothmann/euler/

Grove, W. M., Meehl, P. E. (1996). Comparative efficiency of informal (subjective, impressionistic) and formal (mechanical, algorithmic) prediction procedures: The clinical-statistical controversy. *Psychology, Public Policy, and Law, 2*(2), 293–323.

Guinness World Records (n.d.) FAQ 9: *Who holds the most Guinness world records?* Retrieved July 20, 2008 from http://www.guinnessworldrecords.com/member/faqs.aspx

Hartigan, J., & Wigdor, A. (1989). *Fairness in employment testing: Validity generalization, minority issues, and the General Aptitude Test Battery.* Washington, DC: National Academy Press.

Hastie, R. (Ed.). (1993). *Inside the juror.* Cambridge: Cambridge University Press.

Hastie, R., & Dawes, R. (2001). *Rational choice in an uncertain world.* Thousand Oaks, CA: Sage.

Hastie, R., Penrod, S., & Pennington, N. (2002). *Inside the jury.* Union, NJ: The Lawbook Exchange.

Hayes, S. C. (1983). When more is less: Quantity and quality in the evaluation of academic vitae. *American Psychologist, 38,* 1398–1400.

Helson, H. (1964). *Adaptation level theory.* New York: Harper & Row.

Hines, P. A. (1974). *How adults perceive children: The effects of behavior tracking and expected deviance on teachers' impressions of a child.* Unpublished doctoral dissertation, University of Oregon, Eugene, Oregon.

Hodge, R. W., Siegel, P. M., & Rossi, P. H. (1964). Occupational prestige in the United States, 1925–1963. *American Journal of Sociology, 70,* 286–302.

Hoffman, P., Slovic, P., & Rorer, L. (1968). An analysis of variance model for the assessment of configural cue utilization in clinical judgment. *Psychological Bulletin, 69*(5), 338–349.

IDRC (n.d.) Retrieved July 19, 2007 from http://www.idrc.ca/en/ev-92467-201-1-DO_TOPIC.html

Instant Rec (n.d.). Retrieved August 8, 2007 from http://www.instantrecommendation letterkit.com/

International Cooperation (2005). Retrieved July 8, 2006 from http://www.nserc.gc.ca/intnew.htm#int_joint_venture

Iranian Consulate in Ottawa (n.d.). Visa application form. Retrieved July 20, 2007 from http://www.salamiran.org/Consulate/forms/829_visa.pdf

Janis, I. (1972). *Victims of groupthink.* Boston: Houghton Mifflin.

Kahne, J. (1996). The politics of self-esteem. *American Educational Research Journal, 33*(2), 3–22.

Kalkhoff, W., & Barnum, C. (2000). The effects of status-organizing and social identity process on patterns of social influence. *Social Psychology Quarterly, 63,* 95–115.

Karotkin, D., & Paroush, J. (2003). Optimum committee size: Quality-versus-quantity dilemma. *Social Choice and Welfare, 20*(3), 429–441.

Keller, F., & Schoenfeld, W. (1950). *Principles of psychology.* New York: Appleton-Century-Crofts.

Kroll, L., & Fass, M. (Eds.). (2006). *The world's billionaires.* Retrieved September 19, 2007 from http://www.forbes.com/2006/03/07/06billionaires_worlds-richest-people_land.html

Larrick, R. (2007). Debiasing. In D. Koehler & N. Harvey (Eds.), *Blackwell handbook of judgment and decision making* (pp. 316–337). Oxford: Blackwell Publishing Ltd.

Lerner, J., & Tetlock, P. E. (1999). Accounting for the effects of accountability. *Psychological Bulletin, 125,* 255–275.

Lerner, J., & Tetlock, P. E. (2003). The impact of accountability on cognitive bias: Bridging individual, interpersonal, and institutional approaches to judgment and choice. In S. Schneider & J. Shanteau (Eds.), *Emerging perspectives in judgment and decision-making* (pp. 431–457). New York: Cambridge University Press.

Levins, R. (1968). *Evolution in changing environments.* Princeton, NJ: Princeton University Press.

Lind, A., & Tyler, T. (1988). *The social psychology of procedural justice.* New York: Springer.

Lyman, P., & Varian, H. (2003). *How much information?* Retrieved August 20, 2007, from http://www.sims.berkeley.edu/how-much-info-2003.

Maclean's magazine (2007). *Being also-ran can be lonely. 120*(28), 23 July, p. 50.

Manners, G. (1975). Another look at group size, group problem solving, and member consensus. *The Academy of Management Journal, 18*(4), 715–724.

Mansfield, H. (2001, April 6). Grade inflation: It's time to face the facts. *Chronicle of Higher Education, 47*(30), B24.

Meehl, P. E. (1954). *Clinical versus statistical prediction: A theoretical analysis and a review of the evidence.* Minneapolis, MN: University of Minnesota Press.

Meehl, P. E. (1986). Causes and effects of my disturbing little book. *Journal of Personality and Assessment, 50*(3), 370–375.

Merton, R. (1968a). *Social theory and social structure.* Glencoe, IL: Free Press.

Merton, R. (1968b). The Matthew effect in science. *Science, 159*(3810), 56–63.

Messick, D., & McClelland, C. (1983). Social traps and temporal traps. *Personality and Social Psychology Bulletin, 9*(1), 105–110.

Miller, G. (1956). The magical number seven, plus or minus two: Some limits on our capacity for processing information. *The Psychological Review, 63,* 81–97.

Nisbett, R., & Wilson, T. (1977). Telling more than we can know: Verbal reports on mental processes. *Psychological Review, 84*(3), 231–259.

Norris, P. (2004). *Electoral engineering: Voting rules and political behavior.* Cambridge: Cambridge University Press.

Orbell, J. M., van de Kragt, A. J. C., & Dawes, R. M. (1988). Explaining discussion-induced cooperation. *Journal of Personality and Social Psychology, 54,* 811–819.

Osborne, W. (1994). *You sound like a ladies orchestra: A case history of sexism against Abbie Conant in the Munich Philharmonic.* Retrieved August 27, 2007, from http://www.osborne-conant.org/ladies.htm

Oskamp, S. (1965). Overconfidence in case study judgments. *Journal of Consulting Psychology, 29,* 261–265.

Paese, P., & Gilin, D. (2000). When an adversary is caught telling the truth. *Personality and Social Psychology Bulletin, 26,* 75–90.

Pearson, R. W., Ross, M., & Dawes, R. M. (1992). Personal recall and the limits of retrospective questions in surveys. In J. M. Tanur (Ed.), *Questions about questions: Inquiries into the cognitive bases of surveys* (pp. 65–94). New York: Russell Sage Foundation.

Peer Review (2007). Retrieved November 14, 2007 from http://www.cihr-irsc.gc.ca/e/820.html

Phillips, J., Klein, G., & Sieck, W. (2007). Expertise in judgment and decision making: A case for training intuitive decision skills. In D. Koehler & N. Harvey (Eds.), *Blackwell handbook of judgment and decision making.* Oxford: Blackwell Publishing Ltd.

Platt, J. (1973). Social traps. *American Psychologist, 28,* 641–665.

Posthuma, R. (2003). Procedural due process and procedural justice in the workplace: A comparison and analysis. *Public Personnel Management, 32*(2), 181–195.

Price, D. (1963). *Little science, big science.* New York: Columbia University Press.

Program Descriptions (2006). Retrieved September 21, 2006 from http://www.sshrc.ca/web/apply/program_descriptions/standard_e.asp#5

Project Grants (2006). Retrieved July 7, 2006 from http://www.nserc.gc.ca/professors_e.asp?nav=profnav&lbi=b1

Real, L. (1980). Fitness, uncertainty, and the role of diversification in evolution and behavior. *American Naturalist, 115*(5), 623–638.

Robert, H. M. III, Evans, W., Honemann, D., Balch, T., & Robert, S. C. (2000). *Robert's rules of order: Newly revised (10th edition).* Cambridge, MA: Perseus Publishing.

Rosenthal, R., & Jacobson, L. (1992). *Pygmalion in the classroom, expanded edition.* New York: Irvington.

Sawyer, J. (1966). Measurement and prediction, clinical and statistical. *Psychological Bulletin, 66*(3), 178–200.

Schneider, A. (2000, June 30). Why you can't trust letters of recommendation. *Chronicle of Higher Education, 46* (43), A14–16.

Schooler, J., & Engstler-Schooler, T. (1990) Verbal overshadowing of visual memories: Some things are better left unsaid. *Cognitive Psychology, 22*(1), 36–71.

Sahadi, J. (2004, December 9). *Top 5 Resume lies.* Retrieved April 23, 2006 from http://money.cnn.com/2004/11/22/pf/resume_lies/

Shanteau, J., Weiss, D. J., Thomas, R., & Pounds, J. (2002). Performance-based assessment of expertise: How to decide if someone is an expert or not. *European Journal of Operational Research, 136*(2), 253–263.

Space Politics (n.d.). Retrieved 7 July 2007 from http://www.spacepolitics.com/

Stumpf, S., & London, M. (1981). Management promotions: Individual and organizational factors influencing the decision process. *The Academy of Management Review, 6*(4), 539–549.

Sullivan, D. (2006). *Searchers per day*. Retrieved August 20, 2007, from http://searchenginewatch.com/showPage.html?page=2156461

Tajfel, H. (1970). Experiments in intergroup discrimination. *Scientific American, 223*, 96–102.

Tajfel, H. (1981). *Human groups and social categories*. Cambridge: Cambridge University Press.

Tajfel, H. (1982). Social psychology of intergroup relations. *Annual Review of Psychology, 33*, 1–39.

Tajfel, H., & Turner, J. C. (1986). The social identity theory of inter-group behavior. In S. Worchel & L. W. Austin (Eds.), *Psychology of intergroup relations* (pp. 7–24). Chicago: Nelson-Hall.

Terracciano, A., et al. (2005, October 7). National character does not reflect mean personality levels in 49 countries. *Science, 310*, 96–100.

Tetlock, P. (2005). *Expert political judgment: How good is it? How can we know?* Princeton, NJ: Princeton University Press.

Thorngate, W. (1980). Efficient decision heuristics. *Behavioral Science, 25*, 219–225.

Thorngate, W. (1988a). On the evolution of adjudicated contests and the principle of invidious selection. *Journal of Behavioral Decision Making, 1*, 5–16.

Thorngate, W. (1988b). On paying attention. In W. Baker, L. Mos, H. Rappard, & H. Stam (Eds.), *Recent trends in theoretical psychology* (pp. 247–264). New York: Springer-Verlag.

Thorngate, W. (1990). The economy of attention and the development of psychology. *Canadian Psychology, 21*, 62–70.

Thorngate, W. (1997). More than we can know: The attentional economics of Internet use. In S. Kiesler (Ed.), *Culture of the Internet* (pp. 296–302). Mawah, NJ: Lawrence Erlbaum.

Thorngate, W., & Carroll, B. (1987). Why the best person rarely wins: Some embarrassing facts about contests. *Simulation and Games, 18*, 299–320.

Thorngate, W., & Carroll, B. (1991). Tests versus contests: A theory of adjudication. In W. Baker, M. Hyland, R. van Hezewijk, & S. Terwee (Eds.), *Recent trends in theoretical psychology* (Vol. 2, pp. 431–438). New York: Springer-Verlag.

Thorngate, W., Faregh, N., & Young, M. (2002). *Mining the archives: Analyses of CIHR research grant adjudications*. Retrieved September 1, 2007 from http://www.carleton.ca/~warrent/reports/mining_the_archives.pdf

Thorngate, W., & Hotta, M. (1995). Life and luck: Survival of the fattest. *Simulation and Gaming, 26*(1), 5–16.

Thorngate, W., & Maki, J. (1974a). *Information seeking in multi-cue judgement tasks* (Tech. Rep. 74-3). Social Psychology Labs, University of Alberta, Edmonton, Alberta.

Thorngate, W., & Maki, J. (1974b). *Information seeking in preferential choice tasks* (Tech. Rep. 74-4). Social Psychology Labs, University of Alberta, Edmonton, Alberta.

Thorngate, W., & Maki, J. (1976). *Decision heuristics and the choice of political candidates* (Tech. Rep. 76-1). Social Psychology Labs, University of Alberta, Edmonton, Alberta.

Thorngate, W., & Plouffe, L. (1987). The consumption of psychological knowledge. In H. Stam, T. Rogers, & K. Gergen (Eds.), *Metapsychology: The analysis of psychological theory* (pp. 61–92). New York: Hemisphere.

Thorngate, W., & Tavakoli, M. (2005). In the long run: Biological versus economic rationality. *Simulation & Gaming, 36*(1), 9–26.

Thorngate, W., & Wang, Z. (2004). *From merit to money: Five methods of funding allocation*. Canadian Institutes for Health Research, Ottawa, Ontario.

Thorngate, W., Wang, Z., & Tashk, A. (2005). *Cultural differences in the distribution of limited resources*. Unpublished manuscript.

Thorngate, W., Wang, Z., & Tavakoli, M. (2004). *Improving the CIHR grant proposal assessment rating scale*. Canadian Institutes for Health Research, Ottawa, Ontario.

Treiman, D. J. (1977). *Occupational prestige in comparative perspective*. New York: Academic Press.

Tversky, A., & Kahneman, D. (1974). Judgment under uncertainty: Heuristics and biases. *Science, 185*, 1124–1131.

Tyler, T. (1994). Psychological models of the justice motive: Antecedents of distributive and procedural justice. *Journal of Personality and Social Psychology, 67*(5), 850–863.

Tyler, T. (1996). The relationship of the outcome and procedural fairness: How does knowing the outcome influence judgments about the procedure? *Social Justice Research, 9*(4), 311–325.

Uhlmann, E., & Cohen, G. (2005). Constructed criteria: Redefining merit to justify discrimination. *Psychological Science, 16*(6), 474–480.

Wainer, H. (1976). Estimating coefficients in linear models: It don't make no nevermind. *Psychological Bulletin, 83*, 213–217.

Wainer, H. (1978). On the sensitivity of regression and regressors. *Psychological Bulletin, 85*, 267–273.

Weick, K., & Gilfillan, D. (1971). Fate of arbitrary traditions in a laboratory microculture. *Journal of Personality and Social Psychology, 17*, 179–191.

Weiss, D., & Shanteau, J. (2003). Empirical assessment of expertise. *Human Factors, 45*, 104–114.

Wells, G. L. (2005, April). Eyewitness identification evidence: Science and reform. *The Champion*, 12–21.

Yamagishi, T., & Foddy, M. (in press). Group-based trust: Social exchange bases of trust in group contexts. In K. Cook & R. Hardin (Eds.), *Trust and society*. New York: Russell Sage Foundation.

Appendix A: Euler Program for Simulating Contests

Euler is freeware and is available at http://mathsrv.ku-eichstaett.de/MGF/homes/grothman/euler/euler.html.

Comments on code below begin with ##.

Code can be typed in using Euler's built-in editor (press F9 while in Euler).

To use the function, load it into Euler (press "interpret" button in the built-in editor), then type the word *contest*.

```
function contest()
nc=input("number of contestants");
am=input("Average merit");
sdm=input("Standard Deviation of merit");
nw=input("number of winners");
err=input("Standard Deviation of judgment error = "); ## try a
number from 0 to 30

total=0; ## set counter to zero
for i=1 to 5000; ## run 5000 contests
 truescore=am+sdm*normal(1,nc); ## create a true-merit score
for each of nc contestants
 {a,rnkt}=sort(truescore); ## rnkt = contestant #s ranked from
low to high true score
 error= err*normal(1,nc); ## calculate the amount of error in
judgments of nc contestants
 performance=truescore+error; ## now calculate performance
score = true+error
 {a,rnkp}=sort(performance); ##rnkp = contestant #s ranked
from low to high; ignore "a"
 ht=rnkt(1,nc-nw+1:nc); ## determine which contestants ranked
highest truescore
 hp=rnkp(1,nc-nw+1:nc); ## determine which contestants ranked
highest performance
 sp=sum(sum(ht==hp')'); ## count how many of these are the
same people
 total=total+sp; ## keep track of totals
 end
 "Average percent of highest truescore winners ="
 return total/(50*nw) ## show the average overlap in %
 endfunction;
```

Appendix B: Euler Program for Simulating Effects of Bias

```
function biased()
am=input("Average merit");
sdm=input("standard deviation of merit");
nc=input("number of contestants with no bias");
nb=input("number of contestants with bias");
ab=input("amount of bias"); ## try 0 to 30
err=input("standard deviation of judgment error = "); ## try a
number from 0 to 30
nw=input("number of winners");
nt=nc+nb; ## sum the number of contestants and biased
contestants

total=0; ## set counter to zero
for contest=1 to 5000; ## run 5000 contests
 truescore=am+sdm*normal(1,nc); ## create a group with true-
merit score for each of nc contestants
 biasscore=ab+am+sdm*normal(1,nb); ##create another group with
bias in score
 allscores=[truescore biasscore]; ## make a vector of all
contestants (first nc are true;final nb add the bias)
 error= err*normal(1,nt); ## calculate the amount of error in
judgments of nc contestants
 performance=allscores+error; ## now calculate performance
score = true+bias+error
 {a,rnkp}=sort(performance); ##rnkp = contestant #s ranked
from lowest to highest; ignore "a"
 x=rnkp(nt-nw+1:nt); ## get the contestant #s of the nw winners
 sp=sum(nc<x); ## count how many winners are from biased group
 total=total+sp; ## keep track of totals
end
"Average percent of winners expected from biased group if bias
is 0"
100*(nb/nt)
"Average percent of winners from biased group ="
return total/(50*nw) ## show the average overlap in %
endfunction;
```

Subject Index

Author Index